INDIA - SECURITY SCOPE 2006

INDIA- SECURITY SCOPE 2006
The New Great Game

Brigadier Rahul K. Bhonsle (Retired)

PUBLICATIONS

KALPAZ PUBLICATION

Delhi-110052

India- Security Scope 2006: The New Great Game

Rs. 720

ISBN : 81-7835-512-4

Published in 2006 in India by
Kalpaz Publications,
C-30, Stayawati Nagar, Delhi-110052
Email: kalpaz@hotmail.com

Laser Type: Setting by: Mega Graphics, Delhi
Printed at: Salasar Imaging System, Delhi

Contents

Contents

Foreword

"It (India) is emerging as a potentially very stabilizing and positive force in international politics which is why we are spending a lot of time in that relationship."

Condolezza Rice, US Secretary of State.

Fundamentally the point of this book is that we as ordinary citizens of this great country of ours, India have to take our security situation seriously, as a large number of our countrymen are dying every day, week, month and year, because those amongst us who have the capacity to think and act on behalf of others have gone into an inertia of self absorption. The crumbling edifice of security configuration in India replicates the weakened infra structure in other sectors be it water, electricity, health and education. Ironically each of these constructs is dependent on the other, thus poverty feeds lack of education which leads to unemployment which results in criminality and gangsters in turn forming dependencies based on kinship. Parochialism slowly replaces all other forms of control in an organization. Thus leaders control the power structure through an informal kinship network with the help of friends and relatives, depending on criminals and gangs rather than the government organization which is deliberately undermined by castigating it as elitist. The existing bureaucracy structure is made subservient, suppliant and genuflective through a series of demotivating measures as punishment postings, public admonitions, investigations, pumped up corruption charges, motivated complaints and so on and the state is run by these neo feudal satraps through their underlings who have scant regard for authority.

The economic infra structure is placed in the hands of the land mafia and the criminal-contractor nexus thus roads and buildings remain undeveloped, land is parceled out after heavy extortions, businessmen and professionals are subverted by kidnappings and threats. The maze of bureaucracy seeks alibis for not acting, for not bursting out of their ego bubbles in moving sideways, upwards and down stream, to go halfway to coordinate, integrate and activate their peers, subordinates and superiors alike. They have all perhaps taken one major policy decision, not to take any decision at all. Leaving the comfort of their bungalows, ambys, Page 3 parties, clubs and golf courses is anathema to these self serving elites whose children study in business schools abroad on government or managed scholarships. Security is as much a problem of values and ethics as a structural and organization one. Values and ethics have no place in this set up.

The most grievous harm is caused to security of the people or human security, women and children are the first victims of this conflict as they have the least capability to defend themselves in a situation of hurt, which is hardly recognized in the slew of administrative half measures undertaken to perpetrate the status quo. There is thus a need for the, "Indian security establishment which includes the political apex, the military, the para military and the local police", as per noted security analyst, Mr C Udaybhaskar, "to acquire greater political and military acumen".[1]

The book is organized in roughly three parts. In the first part we will be discussing the issues of internal concern, the various forms of militancy and revolutions within the country from Kashmir to Tripura. In Part 2 we will be covering the regional issues of security significance, mainly Nepal, Bangladesh, Pakistan and Sri Lanka as they affect Indian society while Part 3 covers the international scene along with core issues as policy and politics as well as building capability of our armed forces. With this summation we hope to cover the wide range of security themes that will affect our security in 2006.

This book is a hurt expression of a soldier turned public intellectual and may be some day after gathering enough experience on how to tackle the system for results in the field of security governance, a public activist who is pained by the lack of concern and apathy in bringing about change in the lives of the multitudes who are held ransom by systems which cannot enthuse people empowered to make the difference to reach the grass roots and not merely scratch the surface. This book is thus meant to offend for as Salman Rushdie has said, "What is Freedom of expression? Without the freedom to offend, it ceases to exist." In this the role of the public intellectual will be to again as per Rushdie, "simply point out things. Its up to the people to chose whether to do it or not"[2], but those operating in the domain of public interest have no such choice of only pointing out things they have to act and ensure that others who are supposed to, also do so. It is how deep the impact is made and felt lies the test of effectiveness of the system and system drivers.

Notes

1. Uday Bhaskar, C. "Idea of Bangladesh " *The Indian Express.* 16 December 2005, Lucknow, p. 8.

2. Rushdie, Salman. *Sunday Times of India.* Life. 4 December 2005, Lucknow, p. 1.

May 2006, New Delhi

Rahul K Bhonsle

1

India and The New Great Game

"India is a rising global power. Within the first quarter of this century, it is likely to be numbered among the World's five largest economies --- India will also be a natural partner to the United States as we confront what will be the central security challenge of the coming generation....terrorism, the proliferation of chemical, biological and nuclear technologies, international crime and narcotics, HIV/AIDS, climate change --- our interests converge on all these issues."

Nicholas Burns, US Under Secretary of State

Globalization has entailed emergence of problems at the global level and international scale. These include diverse socio-political-ecological and economic issues such as terrorism, climate change, health crisis, economic imbalances, employment generation, dysfunctional governance and so on.[1] These challenges are replicated at the national level. Inasmuch as India is concerned these represent a great opportunity. This nation of over 100 Crore people is set to reap centuries of heritaged greatness which was denied to it for the past two to three centuries due to stagnation in the agricultural age and its inability to adjust to the industrial one. However the information age has provided new opportunities for our great civilization, the Indian intelligentsia, not merely the software geek in Hyderabad but also the financial wizard in Mumbai, the biotech genius in Bangalore or the diamond merchant in Surat, Indians are driving themselves to glory in all spheres, be it Mittal in turning around sick steel mills in Eastern Europe or Billimoria selling Cobra beer in Britain or Subir Raha of Oil and Natural Gas Commission buying oil fields in Syria. India's Information Technology exports alone are slated to touch an all time high of $ 60 billion by 2010 up three times in just about five years from 2005.[2] However while individuals are sparkling, India as a nation still remains an unrealized dream of our modern fore fathers,

Nehru and Tagore, poets, dreamers and nation builders. The New Great Game wherein India can leverage its strengths of population, intellectual capital, hunger for resources, capital absorption capability provides us an era of opportunity. Are we able to and capable of seizing this opportunity is the question which we seek to address ourselves today.

India's strength in the new millennium is strangely its population, its 500 million working age populace by 2025, if educated and in good health will prove to be its greatest boon as per Finance Minister Mr. P. Chidambaram particularly so as youth are more enterprising, risk taking and out going.[3] The intellectual capital being built up in the country is the second driver as per the Finance Minister. This will place India in the big league in the information and the knowledge age both in the quantity of youth operating at the business processing echelon of computerized clerical work and the more dynamic and value added knowledge management level. India has 2.5 million graduates coming out of college every year with approximately 250,000 engineers. This represents 28 per cent of the available global work force as opposed to 11 percent of China.[4] This further exemplifies the intrinsic strengths of the country. Indian opportunities are also highlighted by the low cost of compensation of production workers in the manufacturing sector which is below $ 1 per hour as opposed to developed nations as USA above $ 20 and the European Union above $ 25.[5]

However for sustained growth, India will have to ensure energy and environmental security, prevent ecological degradation thereby securing against disasters and human tragedies, education of the under privileged as much as those studying in the IITs. To mould the 500 million working age population into productivity rather than a human Malthusian bomb is the growth challenge. A number of India's neighbours as Pakistan and Bangladesh have realized that uncontrolled youth weaned away into madarsas end up as human bombs in jehadi factories. If India does not ensure fruitful employment for its multitudes, jehadis of multiple hues will similarly engulf the country.

As more and more nations line up with foreign direct investment (FDI) into India, whether it is pension and hedge funds or hard nosed Japanese financial samurais, FDI is an essential requirement for our development, however that cannot be restricted to the Golden Western and Eastern Ghat corridors of Gujarat, Maharashtra, Bangalore or Hyderabad-Chennai or the Northern slab of Haryana and Delhi but has to extend in all directions if we want to avoid the growth divide and attendant social turbulence with mass movement of labour to economically viable areas. The need is therefore to develop the political and social environment with effective regulations and law and order which will raise the confidence of the investors in functioning of the system in India to promote holistic growth.

While the internal environment of the country has to be stabilized in many parts, the immediate regional environment represented by the South Asian Association of Regional Cooperation (SAARC) sphere and beyond is also in a state of turbulence. India is surrounded by a number of dysfunctional states; Nepal, Myanmar, Bangladesh, Sri Lanka and Pakistan are all in various stages of somnolence of governance.

Rationalization of relations with these states is essential if India has to progress beyond the narrow confines of its periphery. This failing status and growth of Islamic fundamentalism in the region has raised the stakes for involvement of global powers in the region, the United States of America, European Union, Russia, Japan and China. This will necessitate cooperative engagement of these powers with a view to leverage their innate capabilities to influence India's astringent neighbours positively.

Foreign policy of the nation has to be based on long term strategic interests. Long term considered benefits entail holistic empowerment of the people involving measures which can bring about prosperity and peace while issues such as culture, ethnicity and religion are important; these cannot be considered as primary constituents on which foreign policy of modern nations is based. National power is no longer based purely on the land and population dyad; in the era of globalization these factors are losing their primary relevance. China has perhaps realized the essence of national interests and has thus set about relegating issues such as Taiwan to the background while driving the engine of economic growth through a pragmatic engagement of western countries including the United States of America. India's foreign policy appears to be taking a similar trajectory of basing its diplomatic efforts on long term interests of economic prosperity of the people. Thus strategies which can enhance energy, trade and economic growth dominate engagement of nations today. Energy is gaining primacy, with alternative sources being considered, such as oil, gas, nuclear, wind and other non conventional sources. Countries providing these additives have gained prominence in our scheme of things. Middle East and Central Asia is the playground of diplomats and political leaders alike, with ministers as Mani Shankar Aiyar gaining eminence at times at loggerheads with the foreign office mandarins in South Block. That the honourable Minister himself has been a diplomat may have facilitated in providing the necessary impetus. Since in the oil and gas energy chain transportation is equally important, reconciliation with Pakistan is in the offing, with its support for what it has termed as the Pro-Poor Gas Pipeline from Iran to India recently.[6] No doubt this is also based on its own self interest as Pakistan is attempting to develop an energy hub for gas and oil flows from Central Asia and Iran to India and South East Asia through the Gwadar port. Rebuilding Afghanistan is another step which is aimed at gaining leverage in the new great game for the oil in the Middle East and Central Asia.

Getting Pakistan out of the Kashmir Box will perhaps be the biggest diplomatic accomplishment in 2006 if we are able to achieve it. Pakistan should be engaged on diverse issues as oil sourcing, trade, water and so on by redirecting its focus on concerns which are core to its development such as water being a lower riparian state rather than Kashmir. Pakistan's military-bureaucratic structure will not allow water to emerge as the key issue as it would imply surrender of power to politicians which they would be loathe to.

Pakistan also needs to focus on economic development of the margins in Balochistan, the Northern Areas and so on diverting attention of the people from religious to economic issues. In economy, India will be its most significant partner, is Pakistan game to granting the most favoured nation status to its Eastern neighbour in 2006? As the flow of goods and information crosses the three points of Kaman post in Uri, Wagah in Amritsar and Munna Bao in Gujarat, the solution to the vexed Kashmir issue will emerge.

With China, again trade should dominate rather than the boundary issue which is part of the problem of Sino-Indian estrangement. The opening of the Nathu La in Sikkim expected in April 2006 provides new hope in this direction. Once goods flow, the borders will be settled as time flies. Chinese dominance of World trade is now a reality, it even surpassed the USA in IT goods exports to include telecom, computers, mobile phones and digital equipment at \$ 180 billion in 2004 as opposed to \$ 149 billion of the USA, while its trade in technology to include exports and imports is \$ 329 billion in 2004, to India's \$ 17.2 billion software exports the same year.[7] China is thus not just a growth engine; it is the growth accelerator and barometer of transformation in the global trade order. A strategic partnership with China in all spheres is the necessity and relations with it cannot be held hostage to the border dispute. China has perhaps recognized this need and is drawing us into a strategic partnership in the energy sector based on a common Himalayan heritage to share the World's oil resources. Thus the Indo China joint venture, Himalaya Energy (Syria) Ltd a 50:50 partnership between Oil and Natural Gas Corporation of India and China National Petroleum Corporation, acquired stake in the Al Furat oilfields in Syria recently.[8] Such partnerships with Pakistan are also in the offing with a review of the maritime protocol underway, which will enable shipping from both sides to pick up cargo of third party countries. This will cut down the transshipment time by half and improve the trade between India and Pakistan.[9]

Then we have to look East to gain from the rising ascendancy of the East Asian states and not only the ASEAN countries but Japan and South Korea, Australia and New

Zealand which provide us ample opportunities for economic engagement. A place in the envisaged Asian Union should be another of our prime foreign policy objective for 2006 for this will provide us excellent opportunities for development of our North Eastern states. India qualifies on the Mongoloid, "chinky eyes" criteria, put across by an East Asian diplomat in a light hearted manner recently. An Asian Union going beyond the ASEAN plus 3 and India will prove to be an influential power block in World affairs equaling the European Union and in times to come even challenging the United States.

India is on the path to economic rejuvenation and upliftment of its masses from centuries of poverty and destitution. The determination to emerge from the ashes of the industrial age is writ all over the country's panorama as English speaking youth seek job opportunities in urban areas of the country. The rural-urban divide is also being gradually overcome with enlightened policies. A reduction in the suicide of farmers in Andhra Pradesh has been a major achievement of 2005; we should be able to carry forward this effort to check this menace once and for all. This was achieved by the following measures :

(a) Provision of large scale agricultural credit.

(b) Executing irrigation projects.

(c) Providing farmers with free power and pump sets.

(d) Ensuring good prices for farm produce.

(e) New technology introduced for rice cultivation that reduces water consumption by more than half.

(f) A good monsoon.[10]

All this progress made at home in reducing the socio-political, economic and cultural divides is however marred by a permissive internal security and law and order environment in the country, the result of poor, ineffective and corrupt governance. Andhra Pradesh mentioned above is a salient example of this dichotomy. This is resulting in large scale domestic safety problems in many parts of the country lowering our growth trajectory to just beyond the Hindu rate in many states as Uttar Pradesh, Bihar, Kashmir,

Manipur, Assam and many others. The most perceptive observer and old war horse of Punjab, KPS Gill has on an internal security index of ten points given two points to the country in 2005.[11] Nothing can highlight the need to improve our local security more than this dismal assessment of the state of affairs of the nation. We will continue to depend on security forces with hydra headed capabilities to manage our internal environment and should in the coming years endeavour to reform our local governance and law and order management to a magnitude as to make it independent of extra state or regional assistance.

Security based polity is the need of the year ahead both in national and international spheres. The Year 2006, regrettably began on a note of disquiet, as the cease fire in Nepal was called off by the Maoists, an Inspector General rank officer was killed in Manipur and a railway bridge blown up in Balochistan.[12] Does it spell doom or distress? Can we rise from the vestiges of such violence to end the Year on a note of optimism? The aim of this venture is thus to carry out a reality check of the security issues facing India in the broad environment outlined above and prognosticate their dimensions in 2006 with suggestions for attaining positive outcomes.

References

1. Schwab, Klaus. Newsweek December 2005 – February 2006, p. 13.
2. The Economist Report. The Economist. 17 December 2005, p. 53.
3. Dialogue between Mr P Chidambaram and Bill Gates covered in Economic Times. Economic Times. 9 December 2005, New Delhi. p. 24.
4. The Economist Report. The Economist. 17 December 2005, p. 54.
5. The Economist Report. The Economist. 17 December 2005, p. 54.
6. Times of India Report. "It's a deal". The Sunday Times of India. 18 December 2005, Lucknow. p. 1.
7. The Economist Report. The Economist. 17 December 2005, pp. 53-54.
8. Dutta, Sanjay. "Indo-China oil". 21 December 2005, Lucknow. p. 11.

9. Economic Times Report. "Indo-Pakistan". The Economic Times, 19 December 2005, New Delhi, p. 21.
10. Interview in The Economic Times. The Economic Times. 1 November 2005, New Delhi. p. 15.
11. Gill, KPS. "Containing Ideological Violence." The Pioneer. 24 December 2005, Lucknow. p. 6.
12. Sunday Times of India Report. The Sunday Times of India. 1 January 2006, Lucknow. p. 7 and 9.

2
Kashmir - Imbroglio

"Khushal Kashmir"

New Slogan by Kashmir Chief Minister Azad Kashmir will continue to be an internal and regional policy nightmare for India in 2006. While a number of measures have been undertaken over the past one and a half decade or so, the political and social neglect of the state in the times of yore has necessitated the need for more time to arrive at sustained peace in this vital border state for India. The keen involvement of Pakistan in the affairs of Kashmir over the years has been a thorn in Indian efforts to arrive at a peaceable solution. There are no indications that this has been reduced or will be reduced. Pakistan has inextricably linked itself with the politics of Kashmir by fostering the anti India sentiment in a miniscule section of the population which has been retained as much through the threat of terrorism as the hope of independence or autonomy. Indian ability to persuade Pakistan to abandon its confrontational involvement in Kashmir affairs has been limited by the option of international pressures and a defensive battle to physically eliminate terrorism. While it has been successful in doing both to a large extent, the tipping point of Pakistan abandoning terror has not been reached so far. Whether it will reach it in 2006 is difficult to say. Suffice to say in 2006, the hapless state will continue to suffer the rigours of bloodshed.

Politically and economically however there are some hopes of stability as the state under the new leadership of Ghulam Nabi Azad a sage politician and deft coagulator with many years of experience, sets about his task of reconciliation amongst the political parties of the state with full vigour. Kashmir is no doubt a political minefield, but Azad is well set to lay a safe path through it. He has already sought the goodwill of the main opposition party in the state, National Conference and appeased a sulking Mufti by offering a seat at the Centre to him or his daughter. Keeping all men happy in a tricky situation is Azad's forte and he is fully exploiting his talent in the Valley at least in the initial days. Azad has come up with innovative slogans as, "Khushal Kashmir" (Happy Kashmir) and also promised to reply with an eye for an eye replacing Mufti's one point policy of, "goli nahin boli".[1]

(Talks not bullets) While this may bring about political stability, whether this will translate into peace and tranquility on the ground in the year ahead is not so clear, for the challenges are far too many and not restricted to mere elimination of terrorists or their leaders. The terror structure in the Valley has assumed a hydra headed dimension of which we will see more in the paragraphs to come.

The military – terrorist stand off is likely to continue in the Valley however with greater advantage to the military as is seen from recent reports of reduction in violent incidents and favourable ratio of SF:terrorists killed in encounters. A total riddance of incidents is not practicable as infiltration is likely to continue as it lacks grass roots check at the Line of Control by Pakistani troops. The terrorist movement within Pakistan continues to grow with financial support, arms, ammunition and of course eternal cannon fodder available in the large volume of unemployed and uneducated youth who can be easily swayed by the idea of jihadi fundamentalism studying in madarsas.

The people in Kashmir undoubtedly want peace and normalcy. They have had some influence on the terrorists who have not harmed one million tourists who came to the Valley in 2005. There have also been large crowds at the meetings of Mehbooba Mufti and Omar Abdullah the youth leadership representing along with Mirwaiz Farooq the future of the Valley. Growth of employment opportunities from agrarian to Information Technology and other fields has seen that Azadi (independence) does not remain the sole objective of the youth.[2] This mood of peace is likely to grow in the year ahead as the people get used to lack of daily bloodshed, sounds of gun fire and grenades, the jingle of cash registers and interact with groups from all over the country as well as the World. This mood unfortunately is not brought about without the security shackles and will not be sustained without the presence of the khaki in the streets of Srinagar. Pakistan more than anybody else holds the key. It can well turn off the tap of terrorism what ever Musharraf may chose to say or believe. Thus the Kashmiri situation has to be tackled on multiple fronts. The Indo-Pakistani dialogue, political dialogue with various groups in Kashmir, the intra political dialogue within Kashmir, the containment of terrorism by security forces and control of public antagonism for counter terror measures.

Political Space in Kashmir

The political space in Kashmir is denoted by the multiplicity of divides such as at the regional level there is the India – Pakistan divide, at the international level the Pakistan – Kashmir split, at the national level the Kashmir – Delhi while within the state, Jammu – Kashmir, Jammu – Kashmir – Ladakh and Ladakh – Kargil and within Kashmir there is the Kashmir – Kashmir separation such as National Conference vs PDP, National Conference and PDP vs Hurriyat, Kashmir versus Pakistan Occupied Kashmir and finally Kashmiri Pandits vs the unknown factor of resistance to their return. Need for sagacity in political leadership at all these multiple levels alone can ensure that the segregation is bridged. The political space in Kashmir is made up of main stream Kashmiri political parties – National Conference, Progressive Democratic Party (PDP), Panther's Party, the Mainstream National Parties – Congress, BJP, and the Pak Aligned Parties – Hurriyat Conference (moderate) and Hurriyat Conference (Geelani), JKLF, People's League. On the Pakistani side it is the mainstream political and military leadership of Pakistan, mainstream political leadership in POK –Sikander Hayat Khan, Sardar Abdul Qayyum Khan, Prof Mohd Abdul Razzaq Khan and the terrorist aligned political organizations, the United Jehad Council by Syed Salahuddin and the Jamaat ud Dawa which controls the Lashkar-Led-Taiyyaba.

We must also understand the politics of militancy in Kashmir, led by the two factions of the Hurriyat on one side, the Progressive Democratic Party of Mufti Mohammad Sayeed and the Congress, the National Conference, the Bhartiiya Janata Party which has a significant presence in Jammu region and a clutch of smaller parties such as the Panthers Party and the Communist Party of India (M). The survival of the two Hurriyats depends on their anti India stand. They derive their power on being anti India and of the hawkish Geelani element on being pro Pakistan. These elements being deviants are very vocal and get maximum ear of the masses as all such assemblages generally get in the modern media rich environment.

Success of the anti militancy operations depends on how we can veer these antagonists towards a pro India stand, this in turn will depend on their ability to derive power from such a position. If they can do so then they will become pro India. This will require that the people accept the pro India image of their leaders. Thus how people react to such a turnaround will determine the motivation of these leaders to adopt a pro India stance. What will come first, the chicken or the egg is the most important facet in this game? Ideally the inflection point will have to be adopted simultaneously through a web of actions and activities supported by information operations. The ideal situation would come about when Kashmiri Pandits return to the Valley. Regrettably this is not seen to be forthcoming in 2006.

Peace Proposals on the Table

Various peace proposals being discussed currently are outlined as follows:-

Demilitarization. President Musharaff of Pakistan has proposed demilitarization and self rule to resolve the Kashmir issue. This was also proposed during the Organization of Islamic Conference. Self rule is an issue of concern for the parties who are relatively unclear of what that means. Is it return to the pre 1953 position or democratic governance based on elections.[3] Troop reduction is a long standing ploy used by the Pakistani military for it provides it a significant advantage of saving on troops and ease to infiltrate terrorists across the line of control. In addition internationally it benefits by demonstrating reduction in the level of deployment on ground. Musharraf has been proclaiming on CNN that this was a main factor for, 'providing relief to the Kashmiri people.'[4]

United States of Kashmir – The Political Idea for the Year in Kashmir. The United States of Kashmir is said to be the idea of Mirwaiz Umar Farooq, which implies a federal structure for five regions of Kashmir, the Valley, Jammu, Ladakh, Pakistan Occupied Kashmir and the Northern Areas. A united assembly is to be established for all these areas with Pakistan and India having full control over it after demilitarization of the region.[5] The proposal has it is believed found favour with the United States and is reported to have been discussed with Indian leaders during the visit of the Congressional delegation to India in November 2005 led by the so called anti India Congressman, Dan Burton. The proposal is however fraught with vehement Indian opposition as India believes that the areas falling within its geographical jurisdiction do enjoy the fruits of federalism and no further changes are required. The intervention by outside powers as the USA is also anathema for India and hence the proposal is not likely to find any favour at New Delhi. This may however be the trial balloon which may generate hot debates and even recrimination in the year ahead, 2006.

Widening the Political Space

India has been attempting to widen the political space by engaging maximum parties and leaders from the State as well as in Pakistan. With this in mind Intra Heart to Heart Talks were organised by J and K Leaders and intellectuals in Jammu University. Farooq Abdullah an erstwhile Chief Minister and doyen of the National Conference, participating in the talks condemned cross border terrorism as the main cause for distress in the Valley. He also proposed that the Line of Control (LOC) should be the permanent border, while Pakistan Occupied Kashmir (POK) leaders opposed it.[6] An invitation by the Pakistan Government to mainstream political leaders in the Valley and not only the Hurriyat was put forth by a visiting delegation of political leaders and intellectuals from the POK. President of the National Awami Party, Prof Mohmmad Abdul Razak Khan Khalique raised this call on the side lines of the Intra Heart to Heart Talks. Prof Khalique called for widening the representative character of the Hurriyat which at present is restricted to only some parts of Kashmir and not inclusive of Ladakh and Jammu regions. This is said to be the second time the representative nature of the Hurriyat has been questioned by POK leaders. Earlier, Mr Sikander Hayat Khan the Prime Minister of POK had questioned this while participating in a debate in the POK assembly in June 2005 after the Hurriyat delegation had boarded the Srinagar – Muzzafarabad peace bus. "The decision of Kashmiris of both sides including the non-Muslims will be welcomed but implementing a decision of one faction or an area cannot be accepted", Sikander Hayat Khan is quoted by Muzafarabad dailies. Government of India had allowed the so called Prime Minister of POK Sikander Hayat Khan and former President of POK, Sardar Abdul Qayyum Khan to participate in the second session of the Intra Heart to Heart Talks in New Delhi on 20 September 2005.[7]

Close on the heels of Mirwaiz Umer Farooq's meeting with President Musharraf on 17 September 2005, an offer was reportedly given for Musharraf – Mufti meet as well as meeting with Mufti's daughter Mehbooba and Omar Abdullah. This was initially scuttled in April when it was proposed alongwith the Srinagar – Muzaffarabad bus.[8] This will be the first contact of mainstream Kashmiri politicians with Pakistani establishment and will provide credibility to these parties in Pakistani eyes and also assumed acceptance of elections held in Kashmir. However the litmus test will come when the leaders of Jammu and Ladakh region, Baltistan – Skardu and Gilgit also join in such meetings.

While parleys with militant organizations have been proposed from time to time, writers as Radha Vij feels that diplomatic dialogue is a calculated political tool which must be used with political and cultural sensitivity and not flippantly or with loose connotations. Dialogue is generally used amongst governments of states with bureaucratic structures employing enlightened rationality and consensus oriented power distribution or power structures with a distributed rather than a concentrated autocratic authority formation as that of the LTTE, perhaps that is the reason why the talks with the LTTE have not succeeded so far. The first stage in such cases could perhaps be to foster evenly distributed power formations in militant organizations so that a consensus building approach towards negotiations can be evolved to arrive at realistic solutions. Terrorist groups have disparate logic and concentrated religious idolatory power configuration. Having dialogue with such organizations is a difficult proposition.[9] In the case of Kashmir the militant groups have been very adroitly placed at the mercy of the Pakistani leadership and any group or leader attempting to negotiate is either physically or politically marginalized in the popular struggle, thus creating impossible hurdles in the same. However a strategy which can achieve direct dialogue between the Kashmiri political parties and the militants will ensure success and peace for it will break the umbilical links of terrorists with Pakistan. The process will also contribute to decline of militancy and as the revolutionary fervour declines, more and more people will join the political process.[10]

Politics of the Valley

Kashmir has been over the centuries the home of the moderate and mystic strain of Islam, Sufism. However some observers as the Professor of comparative religion in Kashmir University, H Naseem Rafiabadi and the National Conference leader Omar Abdullah have brought out the Sufiana school of Islam is being gradually eroded as a part of a prevalent phenomenon in the World.[11] This has been achieved by induction of followers of the Deobandi school who represent the radical Islam from Bihar, Uttar Pradesh and West Bengal funded by money from Pakistan and Middle East countries. Since migration is free the induction of such elements in recent years has been substantial. Orphans, poor and the victims of insurgency are easy prey for propaganda and money incentives. Apart from the psychological aspect any person who opposes the Deobandis is systematically eliminated as per an Inspector General of the Kashmir Police. Head priest of Hazratbal mosque, Imam Bashir Ahmad Farooqi, however provides some hope as he says, "You can't deny that fear is playing a part in all this. But Sufism runs in the veins of our people. It can be suppressed for some time, but won't be killed".[12] Systematic measures have to be however undertaken to reduce the threat and apart from encouraging Sufism, the following tangible actions need to be considered:-

(a) Effective checks on migration of Deobandis. This should not be a problem given that they cannot settle down permanently in Kashmir and hiding a Deobandi from West Bengal is very difficult in the Valley or even in Jammu. Hounding these out may not be the answer but stringent curbs should be imposed.

(b) The vulnerable elements of society who can fall prey to the minions of Deobandis, the victims of insurgency particularly those affected by state police measures, the widows, the orphans should be provided aid and relief. In this, the Scheme launched by the Prime Minister in 2005, Naunihalon Ka Naya Savera, for care of orphans is a welcome measure.

(c) Orphans are likely to be next contentious political issue in Kashmir. In typical antagonistic policies, the Hurriyat Conference is reported to have expressed anger over mass shifting of orphans from Kashmir to locations in India, terming this as a, "conspiracy".[13] Sadly nothing can be far from the truth, as the Hurriyat needs to come out of its blind animosity which is harming the interest of the Kashmiri people in the short as well as long run. Opposing the move of orphans without providing adequate provisions for their care within the Valley is blatant politicizing of issues with a totally indifferent attitude for their safety and security.

The Year 2005 saw a gradual decline in the support to Hurriyat hawk's Geelani faction. The Peoples Conference and National Front left his camp. Dr Ghulam Mohammed Hubbi leading one of the factions of Peoples Conference said that decisions were forced on the constituents. Also complaints of Geelani propagating his own party, Tehreek-e-Hurriyat-e-Kashmir at the cost of the entire forum were also received. Nayeem Khan has also deserted the conglomerate so has Agha Syed Hasan Shia clergyman from Anjuman-e-Sharie. Nayeem Khan also similarly protested that Geelani failed to promote coalition culture. As Geelani refused to change his attitude the remaining leaders are supposed to have left the Hurriyat Geelani faction. Analysts feel that this is in line with Islamabad's policy of supporting the doves in the Kashmiri Hurriyat during the year 2005.[14] Sadly no progress was made in return of the Kashmiri Pandits to the Valley. This is not only a security but also a political and economic issue. Here again the rhetoric of anti India, anti Hindu ideology fostered by Pakistan will have to be lowered to achieve any substantial gains.

Challenges before Azad

Ghulam Nabi Azad, the new Congress Chief Minister in Kashmir has managed to bridge the divide amongst all parties in Kashmir with a coalition with the PDP and also a reconciliation with the main opposition the National Conference.[15] Azad's political skills are well known in the Congress, he has now decided to use it for coalition of political parties in Kashmir. While these are just the early days, the true test will be when he is able to integrate the state security grid to successfully combat and then contain the terrorism in the state and coalesce with separatist leaders and bring them around to reconciliation with what is good for the people of Kashmir. He should activate the Unified command which has been dormant over the years for that alone will enable posing a united front to the militants. Running the coalition successfully and enlarging the base of the Congress party overcoming the challenge of regional parties as the National Conference and the Progressive Democratic Party, persuade the separatists to join the mainstream are other challenges. Buffering the Centre against the ire of the Kashmiri separatists who see him as the puppet of the Delhi regime particularly when the same party is ruling at the Centre and the State is another aspect so would be alleviation of grievances of Hindu Pandits.

Terrorism in Kashmir-The Varied Dimensions

Militant Strategies

Dukhtaran-e-Millat activist Asiya Andrabi raided several restaurants, cyber cafes and targeted boys and girls sitting in cabins using these facilities in September 2005. She was arrested under the Public Safety Act. Impact of the assault by Ms Andrabi has been that the government banned setting up cabins in cyber cafes and restaurants. Syed Ali Shah Geelani, leader of the Tehreek-e-Hurriyat accused government of abetting cultural imperialism by India and planned to launch a protest on 23 September 2005.[16] Such fatwas are to be seen in the light of the social revolution taking place in Kashmir wherein the new and the old are clashing. The old represented by the likes of Geelani and their foot, "soldiers" Andrabi are attempting to ensure that liberal society does not come forward through such draconic measures. On the other hand Geelani's of this World seek such issues to foster their agenda of self survival.

Terrorists were also seen to be subverting the police by asking them to join their ranks by 22 September 2005 or face dire consequences. Harkat-ul-Mujahideen spokesman, Abdullah Ansar is reported to have issued this warning through the local news agency asking them to join either the Al Badr, Lashkar, Jaish or Hizbul.[17] The employment of suicide squads in Kashmir is said to have commenced after the Kargil operations of 1999 when terrorists decided to upgrade their tactics to cause greater casualties to spread fear through violence as the movement was losing its impetus after the Indian success in Kargil.[18]

Terrorists are using high technology for training as well as communications in the Valley. The Army has discovered Compact Discs in Gurez sector with formulae and manuals to assemble Improvised Explosive Devices (IEDs), bombs, rockets, arms training manuals and bomb making techniques. Also sophisticated gadgetry such as modern hand held radio sets and night vision binoculars have been seized.[19] Terrorists are also known to be using satellite telephones for communications which are jamming and monitoring proof, thereby having virtual access from the Valley to all areas of the World.

Indications of commercialization of the terror network in Kashmir is coming forth with the arrest of a bank robber in Srinagar on 30 November 2005 who took the police through his conduit, a lawyer who had permission for unhindered movement with access to even the highest security zone where Kashmir politicians and other high security leaders lived. Mushtaq Ahmad, the robber also indicated that political activists provided with high security hotel rooms in Hotel Dolphin especially for such high risk leaders were part of the network which had helped smuggle in terrorists who killed Education Minister Ghulam Nabi Lone in his residence after they were thwarted from entering Mohammed Yusuf Tarigami's house. They were also using Maruti Gypsy provided with security testimonials for entry into high security areas and was used for ferrying fidayeen attackers. These attackers had carried out reconnaissance of the area on 08 October, planned but postponed it on 10 October and finally launched it on 18 October 2005. Sofi and Bukhari alleged to be activists of the Youth National Conference and Youth Congress had been operating this network for one and half years.[20]

J and K Government has evolved a policy of surrender without incentives to militants across the LOC to facilitate their return. These are youth who had gone across for training but want to return home and join the mainstream. This was stated by the J & K junior Home Minister, Abdul Rehman Veeri in the state legislature. The motion was proposed by the local CPI leader, Yusuf Tarigami. Tarigami stated that these youth were misguided and were confused and need to be brought home. The NC and the PDP supported the move with their representatives Ali Sagar and Sartaj Madni respectively stating their approval. Informally the proposal was discussed with the Central Government but no formal offer has been taken up.

'A' 12 feet high fencing zigzags around the line of control in two tiers with an eight feet gap in middle filled with coils of razor sharp concertina wire. It can be electrified and surveillance is carried out by thermal imagers with ground sensors having multiple alarms. Terrorists have scaled the fence by using insulated suits in some cases as also by blasting through it.[21] However by and large the fence has been effective. Snowfall is perhaps the greatest destroyer of the fence and it requires almost 25 per cent repairs after every winter. Army troops are also known to carry out regular anti penetration drills to prevent scaling of the fence. The fence by itself cannot be regarded as an effective anti infiltration measure unless it is supported by physical surveillance by troops deployed at selected points to ensure that it is not being ascended by ingenuous means of which the militants have no dearth. The thermal imager is said to be the most effective check on infiltration even greater than the fence, perhaps as it very clearly denotes movement of human forms in any given area.

In 2005 as per a report published on 15 December, 65 infiltration attempts have been foiled and 165 terrorists killed on the LOC. Security forces claim that with over nine high profile strikes by the terrorists in the Valley in the three months from September – December 2005 the infiltration has increased.[22] 500 infiltrations were reported in 2004 as per the Chief Minister which had gone down to 192 in 2005 by end August.[23] The modus operandii of the Pakistani Army and terrorist groups to infiltrate into the Valley is novel. They have been infiltrating even in large numbers. Reports published in the Times of India indicate on 7 and 8 September 2005, a group of Lashkar-e-Taiba militants sneaked into the Valley with the help of Pakistan Army through Uri sector. 50 terrorists of Al Badr, LeT, Jaish-e-Mohammad and Hizbul Mujaheedin crossed over to India. 60 LeT terrorists assembled at Kherati Bagh in POK and about the same number at Changniya. These were shifted to Sharif camp in Nakote to facilitate entry into the Valley. 2 Baluch is reported to be actively involved in surveillance of the border with a view to induct terrorists based on the intensity of movement of Indian troops on the LOC. This has been noticed at Yaduri area near Handwara when terrorists were not able to cross over due to presence of Indian troops.[24]

Human Rights in Kashmir

Jammu and Kashmir Government has dismissed eight and placed under suspension nine policemen besides appointing 87 magisterial enquiries in last three years as per the report in the state assembly on 27 September 2005. 68 BSF personnel and 131 soldiers have been punished since 1990. BSF received 206 complaints till date and awarded punishment including dismissal and rigorous imprisonment up to 10 years in civil jail in 68 cases, including one officer of the rank of Deputy Inspector General, Commandant and Deputy commandant, three assistant commandants and many other ranks. Police have undertaken 17 cases for investigation in two years ending July 2004. Three Special Police Officers out of 21,763 Special Police Officers were disengaged, six constables, an Assistant Superintendent of Police and Deputy Superintendent of Police were dismissed and the rest placed under suspension. 22 civilians were killed in custody in last three years and 15 persons disappeared, magisterial probes were ordered in 87 cases, of 115 complaints received by the State Government, 100 proved untrue, 11 proved and charge sheet filed. Army received 1385 complaints till date and found 1311 false, 42 under investigation, 32 stand substantiated. Punishment has been awarded to 131 personnel as per the erstwhile Chief Minister Mufti Mohd Sayeed.[25] As per procedures Police will accompany the Security Forces in all operations in order to ensure that civil liberties of the people are held up as per a statement by Mufti Sayeed in State Assembly on 27 September 2005. Opposition flayed the State Government for neglecting human rights. SHRC received 1551 complaints none of its recommendations has been honoured as per the Opposition in the State Assembly.[26]

Fortunately cases of mistaken killing during the year were few. One such occurred in Kulgam, Anantnag on 25 September when 25 year old Tariq Ahmed was killed while another youth Shabir Ahmed was seriously injured when troops of the Rashtriya Rifles laid an ambush. This led to strident protests in the area and necessitated apology from senior military commanders.[27] A general apology in such situations should be immediately forthcoming and once truth has been established, then a specific public explanation to the victim's family is called for. This should form a part of the counter terrorist operations procedures at all levels.

There are an estimated 3000 orphaned children in Kashmir who need immediate care, shelter and protection. In a novel proposal Rs. 17.5 Crore have been earmarked for the special needs of 350 orphaned children under the Naunihalon Ka Naya Savera scheme financed from the Prime Minister's National Relief fund. The scheme is designed to ensure survival, protection and development of affected children extending care, food, nutrition, health services, shelter, education and rehabilitation. Rs. 5 lakhs is being kept in fixed deposit and the income from the same will support the child.[28]

Human rights implementation is a major issue in counter terrorist operations particularly in areas as the Kashmir Valley where terrorists are known to employ various ploys to draw in security forces to commit violations for propaganda effect. State Human Rights Commission (SHRC) Kashmir has issued recommendations in 2112 of the 3187 cases received but was not aware of the implementation of these recommendations. Justice Retd A M Mir, SHRC Chairman feels that the Commission lacks the bite due to poor support by State authorities as also teeth to execute warrants against police officials as it is dependent on the same force for implementation of warrants. Kashmir has better human rights implementation than peripheral areas of Doda, Kupwara, Poonch, and so on as assessed by the SHRC Chairman.

It is also felt that the Army and Central Police Organization Forces do not cooperate on the plea that they are not within the purview of the SHRC. The Chairman feels that, "they fail to understand that J & K state has got its own constitution and the state legislature has not ratified the particular central law that offers them immunity." However some cases taken up by the Commission with the Defence and Home ministry has led to court martial proceedings.[29] It needs to be emphasized to the central security forces that by subjecting themselves to scrutiny by the Human Rights Commission be it of the State and the Centre they will improve their own credibility in the eyes of the people, which is important given the need for winning the hearts and minds battle. As also once forces operate on a common platform of values, it will automatically overcome the propaganda derived by Pakistan of large scale human rights violations by Indian security forces in Kashmir, an issue which it has been constantly harping on in international forums.

Kashmir-Impact of Earthquake on Security

On 8 October 2005, earthquake struck Kashmir at 0920 AM. Apparently there is no impact on terrorist activities in the Valley and in the Jammu region as indicated by the following:-

(a) Continued recovery of arms and ammunition.

(b) Obstruction by terrorists of relief activities carried out by security forces.

(c) Attacks on locals who are working in concert with security forces.

(d) 100 kg of RDX was recovered from a truck carrying sheep. Truck drivers were asked to deliver consignment of four ghee cans to Ghulam Mohammad Rather in Qazigund in J & K.

(e) On 10 October 2005, 10 members of two families were killed in Rajauri district by terrorists reportedly of Hizbul Mujaheedin.[30] This attack is reported by Pir Panjal Regiment of Hizbul Mujaheedin led by self styled deputy divisional commander, Sangat Pathan alias Abu Hamza on village Rajnagar, Budhal Tehsil in Rajouri. The attackers slit throats of Munshi Ram and two sons, brother and a nephew followed by raid on Mora Gaber where Kartar Singh and three sons were killed.[31]

Terrorists are also reported to have taken advantage of the Army's diversion in relief work and rebuilding collapsed bunkers to infiltrate in maximum numbers before the on-set of winters. Eight militants were killed on 11 October in the Nowgam sector of Kupwara district with recovery of 5 AK 56 and 2 assault rifles. Eight militants have been killed on 9 October a day after the earth quake in Gulmarg sector. The fence along with thermal imagers and detection sensors had brought down infiltration by 80 per cent but in the long term if the fence is damaged, then infiltration goes up.[32]

700 militants are reported to have died in the earth quake including a few top commanders and controllers of Lashkar-e-Toiba and Hizbul Mujaheedin in POK. This was based on intercepts received at the Kilo Force Headquarters in Kashmir. Control stations of Lashkar and Hizbul are said to have been destroyed opposite Kupwara sector. Lashkar message intercepted said that it had lost 200 men in a POK camp. 15 messages were intercepted on damage to infra structure and communications.[33]

In the immediate aftermath of the earthquake, United Jehad Council leader Syed Salahuddin is reported to have called for a cease fire. News reports indicated that Lashkar-e-Taiba spokesman said, "Many of our members have been killed. They are in scores while several others are still trapped under the rubble." 50 terrorist training camps all over Pakistan were affected, 29 camps located in Pakistan occupied Kashmir, 15 or more in North West Frontier Province, 7 in Punjab and three in Northern Areas of Gilgit-Baltistan. Manshera Forest in North West Frontier Province is a major location for terrorist training camps with several madarsas which however appears to have been outside the quake zone. Camps in Kotli, Nikial, Bagh, Muzaffarabad were hit by the quake but since these have only make shift structures, the damage is not likely to be heavy. Major infiltration bid launched on 09 October 2005 was foiled. There could be others which could have been successful. Some losses in terrorist cadres are expected but the leadership was still safe and hence could rejuvenate the cadres very effectively. The Aid flow is also said to have an impact in that it could lead to diversion of resources for terrorist purposes.[34]

A report in the Pioneer of 11 October has brought out the following facets –

(a) 85 terrorist camps operated by Pakistan's Inter Services Intelligence (ISI) along the line of control had not been closed despite evidence provided by the Indian government.

(b) Terrorist camps in Chakothi, Muzaffarabad, Kahuta and Bagh totally obliterated being within 10 km of epicenter of earthquake.

(c) Camps in Kotli and Nikial were damaged, camps in Palani, Palak and Kund and Samani, Dudhnial and Fagosh hosting Jaish-e-Mohammad (JEM), LET, Hizb-ul-Mujaheedin (HUM), Al Badr, Harkat-ul-Mujaheedin and Al Barq also suffered heavy defacement.

(d) LeTs Muzaffarabad office was completely damaged.

(e) Harkat's training centre at Balkote and Batrasi, JEM's camp at Attuck, Al Badr's at Oghi, Lashker's at Mansera and recruitment camp of HUM at Jungle Mangal had been damaged to a great extent.

(f) Balkote host for large number of terrorist training camps has suffered huge losses.[35]

Operation Imdad - Indian Armed Forces Quake Relief in Valley

The Indian Armed Forces particularly the army and the air force were uniquely placed in providing relief to the quake hit Valley. Their locations in the heart of the quake affected areas, discipline, reach, resilience and capabilities implied that the Armed Forces would be at the forefront in the relief work. Army presence of troops in Uri and Tangdhar at the epicenter of the quake helped. These troops were asked to patrol into the interiors. The Indian Air force was the only Air Force in the World which had the required number of helicopters in place to provide immediate relief. It was a three phased operation as follows:-

(a) Reach help earliest.

(b) Communicate the help needed.

(c) Follow it up by sending the requisite assistance.

Thus 470 tons of supplies for the quake affected people was air lifted. In the first three days, the IAF rescued 477 people by undertaking 378 flying sorties 90 of which were by helicopters. Army dispatched more than 300 tons of rations to the remote areas. 2100 tents were sent to Uri and 1150 tents to Tangdhar. The civilian establishment had dispatched 1,75,000 blankets and 2500 tents. Six villages were adopted by the Army and the IAF in addition to the 6 villages adopted by the National Hydro Power Corporation. The Government had to adopt innovative strategies to force the people to raise shelters in a short time before the winters by providing a Rs. 5000 reward for completing their temporary sheds. This brought about quick response from the people who were initially awaiting other agencies to do the work. This is classically known as the dependency syndrome wherein the phenomenal response by NGOs and aid agencies leads to total reliance on the aid provider and survivors await aid agencies to rehabilitate them rather than help themselves. The situation at one stage had so badly deteriorated that aid agencies had to get workers from

Srinagar as the people in the affected areas preferred to just look on. The reward scheme however accelerated the pace of rehabilitation.[36]

Main tasks carried out by the Army also included evacuation by helicopter from remote areas where army helipads proved very useful. Makeshift medical camps were put up by the Army after the hospitals in Uri, Tangdhar and Kupwara were damaged. Electricity was partially restored in Uri and Tangdhar by Army electrical engineers. Communications of the Army were restored in six hours, civil communications in 18 hours and mobile communications in 24 hours by army signalers. The Uri-Kamalkot road was opened. Tented accommodation was provided to displaced personnel at Tangdhar and Uri. In the first 48 hours itself 2500 troops were deployed, in addition to eight teams of engineers in Uri, Tangdhar, Baramulla, Kupwara and Poonch. Kupwara civil hospital was established in a row of tents for medical help. A Kruppman bridge was launched in Akhnur. Civil administration was also provided with 25 tons of medicines, 95 tons of rations, and more than 3000 tents. Help was provided to Bharat Sanchar Nigam Ltd to revive exchange in Uri. 21 teams were deployed for relief efforts and civil patients treated in Military Hospitals in hundreds. 15 generators were rushed to Srinagar to help NGOs run community kitchens. The Indian Air Force dropped 5000 food packages along with 2340 sleeping bags, 500 mattresses, blankets and cooking utensils in addition to 200 tons of relief material in nine sorties of IL 76 and 40 sorties of AN 32.[37]

Upto 11 October 2005 within three days of the quake the following was achieved –

(d) 201 tonnes rations supplied, 13000 food packets distributed.

(e) 2050 tents given at Uri and 950 at Tangdhar.

(f) 20 tonnes of medical equipment to affected areas.

(g) 3000 blankets each to Uri and Tangdhar.

(h) 26 medical teams send to interiors.[38]

Thus Imdad proved to be the biggest hearts and minds operation launched by the Armed Forces in Jammu and

Kashmir. Hopefully this changes the perception of the Army as a force for the good, particularly after the brutal killings by terrorists in Rajauri.[39]

Terrorist Outfits Do Relief Work In POK

The situation on the Pakistani side of the line of control was exactly the opposite. In the wake of the quake it is said that the Pakistan Army fearful of an Indian attack taking advantage of the calamity rushed its reserves to man battle positions, abandoning the people to their hapless fate. A sad commentary indeed of a so called professional army. The vacuum was filled up by terrorists with walkie talkies and AK 47s busy providing relief in Muzaffarabad. Jamaat ud-Dawa the political matrix of the banned Lashkar-e-Taiba was at the forefront of the relief effort. Hafiz Muhammad Said is the founder of the organization. The group launched relief even before the government reached the spot. Medical and Surgical Camps were organized under the Jamaat ud-Dawa banner and it provided ambulance, rescue, temporary villages and even burial service.[40]

Perceptive observers as Wilson John have stated that the failure of the state apparatus has given space to the jehadi groups to come closer to the people by organizing relief in Pakistan Occupied Kashmir during the great tragedy and its aftermath. Wilson states that Jamaat-ud-Dawa, (JuD) emerged as the alternative source of relief and rehabilitation as a civilian and non governmental organization committed to the welfare of the people of Kashmir. It set up several mobile dispensaries, mobilized teams of doctors from various countries and provided immediate relief like tents, food and medicines even to the farthest areas. It is stated that it also bought a mobile field surgical and medical centre, worth Rs 1.6 Crore recently.[41] Of greater significance is the linkages it has established with the political parties and political leaders in Pakistan including some important constituents of the Muttahida Majlis-e-Amal (MMA) the six party coalition in Islamabad. Linkages are also reported between Hafiz Saeed and Yasin Malik, the Chief of Jammu and Kashmir Liberation Front meeting on 6 and 7 November as reported in the Pakistan media.[42] The emergence of the JuD as the principal player in the Kashmir scene will have very ominous implications for the militancy in Kashmir in the year ahead. We are likely to see an increase in the levels of recruitment of jehadis in POK in the immediate as well as the long term. These would be infiltrated in Kashmir most likely in summer after training in winters in Pakistan or POK. Support of the Pakistani political leadership would imply that the Army will provide all the help needed to induct these new found liberators. Of greater import is the coalition of leadership between the two radicals in the Kashmir struggle, Malik and Saeed.

In the wake of the earthquake, it was expected that terrorists in Kashmir were on the down side but it proved otherwise as two terrorists killed a Jammu and Kashmir Minister, Ghulam Nabi Lone on 18 October 2005 in the high security Tulsi Bagh area. It was also reported that more than 100 militants had sneaked into the Srinagar city as per IGP Kashmir, K Rajendra up to 21 November 2005. 21 militants were killed trying to infiltrate in three to four attempts during the same period.[43] What is the percentage that are not checked or are successful remains unclear? On 10 October 2005, Additional Secretary (Cabinet Secretariat) R Banerji, had sent a classified letter saying that senior political leaders will be targeted in Kashmir. The attack on Lone thus had sufficient notice. On 9 October 2005 it was evident that there would be no let up in LeT operations despite the casualties during the quake. A fortnight before from 16 to 28 September Banerji had given detailed information of directions to terrorists for suicide attacks and claimed 100 kgs of RDX had been moved by terrorists from the Baramulla route. In June 2005, M Y Tarigami CPM leader's security was increased following request by CPI(M) leader Karat to the Home Minister.[44] Thus the somnolence and indifferent attitude of the police in Kashmir to intelligence inputs needs to be chastised.

Parting Shots

It is always hazardous to claim that terrorists have been decimated or are on the run as the diffused nature of the threat implies that small groups will continue to operate in networks, as they do not have a central command as security forces and are thus not affected even by calamitous events as earthquakes. While 200 terrorists may have been killed they still had considerable potential to launch strikes as that on Lone. The proclamation of heavy losses to terrorists could also have been a part of the information warfare campaign by the Armed forces but should have been launched with security beefed up on the ground as troops too are likely to be lulled into a sense of complacency. A careful weighing of the impact on own troops must be made as they are in receipt of such news due to all pervasiveness of the media much before the official channels are activated. We must learn from past actions of the jehadis as they are predictable and take additional precautions during periods of tension which could generate attacks.

It should be possible to judge the intentions of the jehadis and Pakistan through the daily mayhem of violence on the ground. The jehadis will always react to events, be it celebratory days as the Independence day or mourning days as anniversaries of their compatriots. The jehadis will also react to statements of dominance by the security forces particularly their leaders and change of government or leadership. They welcomed Azad's installation as Chief Minister by a suicide attack, killing a number of innocents and followed this up with an increase in the violence.

Thus 2006 promises to be an year of engagement in Kashmir. Engagement between India and Pakistan, between India and the Hurriyat, Pakistan and the Hurriyat, perhaps Pakistan and even Azad. Within the Valley hectic political activity would have to be undertaken to engage the people actively by the coalition along with the PDP as well as getting the moderate Hurriyat in the political process. Economic engagement of the people at the grass roots is also essential which will demonstrate earnestness of the government and ensure their weaning away from the voice of the terrorist ideologies through gainful employment. Above all the security forces will have to continue to engage the terrorist leadership, the terror perpetrators and the foot soldiers of terrorism in a meaningful manner avoiding the bane of rights violations.

References

1. Rocky, Rakesh. "Healing touch—". The Indian Express, 31 December 2005. Lucknow. p. 2.
2. Chowdhury, Neerja. "J & K Tough Choice for Sonia." Indian Express. 27 September 2005. Lucknow. p. 8.
3. Hussain, Masood. "Hurriyat" . The Economic Times. 16 December 2005. New Delhi. p. 2.

4. Lakshman, Kanchan. "J &K: Troop Withdrawal - Musharraf's Bid to Reopen Terror Routes". *South Asia Intelligence Review. Downloaded* Weekly Assessments and Briefings. Volume 4, No. 13, October 10, 2005.
5. Gupta, Kachan. "What's cooking on J & K". The Sunday Pioneer. 11 December 2005. Lucknow. p. 1.2.
6. Times of India Report. Times of India. 21 September 2005. Lucknow. p. 7.
7. Kandhari, Mohit. "Hurriyat does not represent Kashmir" The Pioneer. 17 Sep 2005. Lucknow. p. 2.
8. Hussain, Masood. "Mufti welcomes Pak invite if true" Economic Times. 19 September 2005. New Delhi. p. 2.
9. Vij, Radha. "Talking with Al Qaeda". The Pioneer. 30 September 2005. Lucknow. p. 6.
10. Naqvi, Saeed. "After the—" The Indian Express. 4 November 2005. Luckow.
11. Soondas, Anand. "Sufism steps—". The Times of India. Lucknow. 6 December 2005. p. 8.
12. Soondas, Anand. "Sufism steps—". The Times of India. Lucknow. 6 December 2005. p. 8.
13. Hussain, Masood. "Hurriyat"—. The Economic Times. 16 December 2005. New Delhi. p. 2.
14. Hussain, Masood. "Geelani's flock is cracking gradually" Economic Times. 23 September 2005. New Delhi. p. 2 and Wani, Khursheed. "When Hawks become doves". The Pioneer. 23 September 2005. Lucknow. p. 5.
15. Hussain, Masood. "Opposition Vanishes in J and K" the Economic Times. 13 December 2005. New Delhi. p. 2.
16. Pandit, M Saleem. "Militants ask police to join their ranks" The Times of India, 19 September 2005. Lucknow. p. 7.
17. Pandit, M Saleem. "Militants ask police to join their ranks" The Times of India. 19 September 2005. Lucknow. p. 7.
18. Jaleel, Muzamil. "Ferocious father". The Sunday Express, 18 December. New Delhi. p. 11.
19. Jahangir, A Majid. Militants go hi tech in Valley. Indian Express, 20 September 2005. Lucknow. p. 5.
20. Express News Service. "A Bank Robber's—" The Indian Express, 3 December 2005. Lucknow. p. 1,2.
21. Hussain, Masood. "LOC fence—". The Economic Times, 2 December 2005. New Delhi. p. 2.
22. Singh, Pramod Kumar. "Bloody Winter in Valley—". The Pioneer, 15 December 2005. Lucknow. p. 2.
23. Hussain, Masood. "Cops to Accompany—" The Economic Times. 28 September 2005. New Delhi. p. 2.
24. Pandit, M Saleem. "Pak—" Times of India. 26 September 2005. Lucknow. p. 7.

25. Hussain, Masood. "216 Securitymen—" The Economic Times. September 2005. New Delhi. p. 2.
26. Hussain, Masood. "Cops to Accompany—" The Economic Times. 28 September 2005. New Delhi. p. 2.
27. Indian Express Report. Indian Express. 26 September 2005. Lucknow. p. 6.
28. Sen, Sudhi Ranjan. "Home ministry—" The Indian Express. 2 December 2005. New Delhi. p. 5.
29. Hussain, Masood. "I'm whipping—" Economic Times. 23 September 2005. New Delhi. p. 2.
30. Mishra, Bisheshwar. "Militants—" Times of India. 11 October 2005. Lucknow. p. 9.
31. Indian Express Report. "After Quake—" 11 October 2005. Lucknow. p. 3
32. Datta, Rahul. "Terrorists—" The Pioneer. 12 October 2005. Lucknow. p. 1,4.
33. Jahangir, Majid. "About 700—" The Indian Express. 17 October 2005. Lucknow. p. 5.
34. Bagchi, Indrani. "Terror meets—" Times of India. 11 October 2005. Lucknow. p. 9.
35. Singh, Pramod Kumar. "Quake wipes out—" The Pioneer. 11 October 2005. Lucknow. p. 3.
36. Hussain, Masood. "Reward did the trick—". The Economic Times. 30 November 2005. Lucknow. p. 2.
37. The Week. 23 October 2005. p. 52.
38. Gupta, Shishir. " Air bridges to foot patrols—". The Indian Express. 12 October 2005. Lucknow. p. 1,2.
39. Indian Express Editorial. "A force for the good—" 11 October 2005. Lucknow. p. 8.
40. Carlotta Gall and Arif Jamal. "Camps Gone—". Indian Express. 19 October 2005. Lucknow. p. 1.
41. John,Wilson. "General's Losing Battle". The Pioneer. 7 December 2005. Lucknow. p. 7.
42. John,Wilson. "General's Losing Battle". The Pioneer. 7 December 2005. Lucknow. p. 7.
43. Jaleel, Muzamil. "Terror sneaks—". The Indian Express. 25 November 2005. Lucknow. p. 1.
44. Sen, Sudhi Ranjan. "Week ago—". The Indian Express. 19 October 2005. Lucknow. p. 1,2.

3

Naxalism-Security Monster of 2006

"I believe that peace in our troubled and violent age requires eternal vigil, patience and wisdom. We must all work together to analyze potential sources of conflict to find solutions without recourse to arms. It is this that is the challenge before Governments and humankind as a whole."

Honourable Prime Minister, Manmohan Singh

2006 ominously portends to be the year of the Naxals. The multi dimensional threat of the leftist insurgencies is likely to raise its hydra headed dangers to new levels in terms of level and intensity of violence. The geographical spread of the menace would be evident by the fact that it is affecting 12 major Indian states, Andhra Pradesh, Maharashtra, Madhya Pradesh, Chattisgarh, Uttar Pradesh, Orissa, Bihar, Jharkhand, Karnataka, Tamil Nadu, West Bengal and Kerala. On 13 November, the Maoists launched their biggest attack at Jehanabad in Bihar with operations on a military scale on the jail. On 11 November they attacked a Home Guard training centre at Pachamba in the Giridih district in Jharkhand, looted 183 rifles, two pistols and 2,500 cartridges. On 23 June 2005, 200-armed Maoists raided a Police Station, State Bank of India and the Central Bank of India in the Madhuban area of East Champaran District in Bihar, near the Nepal border.[1] All these are ominous signs for the year ahead. Reports indicate that the Maoists have formed what is curiously called as the Compact Revolutionary Zone (CRZ) which extends from Pashupati in Nepal to Tirupati in Andhra. Their control over this area which virtually slices the country down its midriff enables easy move of arms and personnel for quick retreat in case of pressure in one or other state.[2]

While the impact of naxalism on the state will not prove to be vitally damaging, it will cause mayhem and casualties in many parts hitting the poorest of the poor. The state police forces tasked to deal with this danger are ill prepared with the exception of Andhra Pradesh. It would take almost half a decade or so for other local police to be able to combat the naxalites on their own. In 2006, there is likely to be increased dependence on central police forces maybe even the Rashtriya Rifles if things get worse. Geographical control of the menace could possibly be feasible and it would be restricted to the present expanse which is perhaps the only silver lining.

India is in the throes of internal dissent which has assumed violent dimensions in the past half a decade or so. Starting from the backward region of Telangana in Andhra Pradesh, this movement which assumes its name from a rebellion in West Bengal which lost its momentum many decades back is now engulfing a large portion of Central India, a region most neglected over the years. The Indian Ministry of Home Affairs has indicated that 125 districts in 12 states are affected by naxal violence. Other reports state that approximately 170 of 600 districts are affected by Maoist violence creating a virtual Red corridor of dissonance from Nepal to Andhra Pradesh.[3] On the other hand Mr K P S Gill has assessed that 165 districts are affected by Naxalite violence in 2005.[4] The data of violence in 2004 and the first

Table 1

Year/ State	*Incidents*	
2004	*Number of cases*	*Deaths*
Andhra Pradesh	577	140
Jharkhand	342	117
Bihar	250	128
2005 Upto August		
Andhra Pradesh	412	164
Jharkhand	212	64
Bihar	145	63

eight months of 2005 for Maoist activities in the three major states of Bihar, Jharkhand and Andhra Pradesh is as given below at table 1.

It would be seen that there has been a rise in naxalite violence in Jharkhand with some links seen with Maoists in Nepal with reports of three Nepali extremists caught in the state.[5] The Minister of State for Home Affairs dealing with the subject of internal security related to naxalism, Mr Sriprakash Jaiswal had in a written reply to the Parliament on November 29, 2005, intimated that 1,353 Maoist-related incidents were reported in which 570 civilians and police personnel were killed in 2005 up to October. Andhra Pradesh was the worst affected with 448 incidents, 163 civilians and 15 police personnel killed, Chhattisgarh, Jharkhand, Bihar and Maharashtra with 317, 271, 161 and 76 incidents, respectively, were the other Maoist affected States which had greater violence.[6] In the entire country, in 2004, 1,597 violence cases were registered in which 518 people died. Till August 2005, 1157 incidents and 448 people were killed in Maoist violence. The total for the year upto 21 December 2005 was 678 persons killed against 566 in 2004.[7]

Apart from the state of casualties and geographical spread, the diverse organizations associated with this movement create problems of defeating it. In Uttar Pradesh Akhil Bhartiya Nepali Ekta Samaj (ABNES), an organization of Nepali community has been identified as a facilitator. Maoist connection with National Democratic Front of Bodoland (NDFB) and Kamtapur Liberation Organisation (KLO) has been established with the arrest of Mohan Kiran Vaidya a Nepali Maoist leader in Siliguri district of West Bengal.[8] This will underline the problem of Naxalism in the country which includes the intensity of violence as well as its expanse involving many states. The federal structure of law and order in the country also contributes to networked naxalism. The details of the Naxal menace and prognostication is as per succeeding paragraphs.

Andhra Pradesh

Andhra Pradesh experimented with a cease fire which however was called off during 2005. The people friendly approach generated by the cease fire was squandered as Andhra government did not prepare its monitoring. Allegations and counter allegations dotted the peace parleys. The most significant error was government demand that terrorists surrender weapons which no terrorist group will generally be willing. This led to consolidation of militancy in the state. Andhra Naxals have reportedly strengthened their financial state, thereby enabling them to buy sophisticated weapons and explosives from abroad. Extortion from contractors and tendu leaf cultivators is a major source of income. Contractors in Andhra pay 5 % of their contract amount as taxes. Funds are laundered through front organizations in cities involved in legitimate business. The need to crack down on these front organizations through the department of revenue intelligence is thus essential.[9]

On 12 October 2005, an event of significance occurred which may have a long lasting impact on naxal violence in Andhra Pradesh. A suicide bomber of 20-23 years of age carrying a bag on his back reportedly blew himself up at the Police Commissioner's Task Force office in the high security Begumpet area, 100 meters from the Chief Minister's residence. Three pieces of paper stating, "intikhab", "jihad" and "Mujahid 75" were recovered from the location of violence. Mujahid 75 may establish links with the October 2004 death of a terrorist in police firing in Hyderabad. A home guard, A Satyanarayana was killed in the blast in the Task Force office. Police investigations are on to determine if the violence was related to terrorist organizations supported by the ISI or the naxalites. Preliminary Police misgivings were of involvement of the ISI.[10] The bombings are a worrying trend no doubt.[11] Some inputs from investigations have revealed that the terrorists involved had links with terrorist organizations in Bangladesh and were trained there for well over two to three months.[12]

One of the significant operations by the police forces include the one in the Nallamalla forest area which straddles the five districts of Andhra Pradesh; Mahbubnagar, Kurnool, Prakasham, Guntur and Nalgonda to trap a large number of Maoist leaders including the AP State committee secretary, Burra Chenniah or Madhu or Madhav and State military

Commission Chief, Shakhamuri Appa Rao alias Ravi and three district in charge of the Rayalseema region. Madhav has taken over as the State Committee chief from Ramakrishna who is reported to have been promoted as central committee member. The police however could not spring the trap as the Naxalites escaped taking help of the darkness.[13]

The failed experiment of cease fire does not raise the confidence of a political solution to the Naxalite problem in Andhra in the year ahead. The human rights activists too appear to have gone into the background after failing to reconcile the differences between the state and the deviants. Thus there appears to be no motivation for politicization of the issue. The Naxalites can be seen to have reorganized their resources during the year, the state police too have reinforced themselves with weapons, communications and transport. Intelligence should have been improved, but the abortion of the operations in the Nallamalla forests indicates that there is a hesitation to go for the kill. Stand off is not likely to result in any military solution. All in all with lack of political gyrations, a bloody battle for ascendancy looms large on the horizon in Andhra Pradesh in 2006.

Jharkhand – The Year Ahead

Of Jharkhand's 22 districts, only four, Ranchi, East Singhbhum, Bokaro and Dhanbad have seen some discernible progress and development as per a report by Gautam Siddharth in the Sunday Pioneer. Other districts are well below the marginal development line, in fact Gumla neighboring Ranchi is amongst the least developed. The failed state set of symptoms is seen in many districts as Godda, Sahibganj, Pakud and Dumka which has resulted in Maoists control of the area who compare the development divide between these areas and Ranchi and Jamshedpur to draw in recruits to their cause.[14] Maoists are thus reportedly active in 16 of the 22 Districts of Jharkhand. Garhwa, Palamau, Chatra, Hazaribagh, Giridih, Bokaro, Ranchi, Latehar, Lohardaga, Gumla, Simdega, East Singhbhum, West Singhbhum, Dhanbad, Seraikela-Kharsawan and Koderma can be called as very seriously affected of which Dumka,

Deogarh, Jamtara and Godda are currently 'targeted'.[15] Starting 2001 to 31 January 2005, 652 deaths have occurred in Jharkhand, as compared to 540 in the neighbouring State of Bihar and 509 in the southern State of Andhra Pradesh as per the Ministry of Home Affairs. Communist Party of India-Maoist (CPI – Maoist) is the main political formation which is active. The states forested area provides ideal sanctuary and training camps for the Naxalites, while its common border with almost all the affected states in the Eastern region such as Bihar, Orissa and West Bengal enables transmigration of terrorists of all hues to the state and outside it.

Some violent incidents during the year would indicate the type of threat. One occurred in Baniadih village of Chatra District, 270 kms. from Ranchi which saw the killing of 10 security men in a blast on 8 September 2005. 25 Security men were on long range patrol in five vehicles when the incident occurred. An assistant commandant of the paramilitary forces and a deputy superintendent of police were also injured in the blast.[16] It is also reported that the Maoist Ultras had lured the security personnel by a money bag. While on patrol the personnel saw a container on which was written Money which attracted the security forces and exploded when the personnel tried to open it.[17] This was followed by another incident on 12 September 2005, when 17 civilians were killed by a group of Maoists in Beluwaghati village, Giridh District, by a large group of approximately 200 Maoists. All the victims were members of a Village Defence Committee formed by the State Government to fight Maoists in the villages by mobilizing the villagers. There are reports to indicate that there are confirmed links between Maoists and politicians in the state. A report by the Inspector General of Police (law and order), R.C. Kaithal, alleges that Welfare Minister Ramesh Singh Munda had paid Rupees 15 lakhs to the Maoists for support during the elections in 2005.[18] Such links underline the complexity of resolution of the militancy in the state due to its effective coagulation with political interests.

The Jharkhand police too do not appear to be fully prepared for taking on the terrorists who may run riot particularly in the underdeveloped districts. All this denotes that the year 2006 would be a violent one for the state. Jharkhand has beefed up jail security after attack on the Jehanabad jail in Bihar. The additional security measures undertaken for jail security include solar fencing, jammers against phone transmissions to include mobiles of BSNL, Reliance and Airtel. Solar fencing will give a shock and also raise an alarm bell. Two central jails, Birsa Munda Central Jail, Ranchi and Jay Parakash Narayan Central Jail, Hazaribagh are said to beefed up in the first phase. Overcrowding of jails is another problem which is hard to overcome. For instance in Jharkhand, 17,000 prisoners are housed in the jails against a capacity of 7600.[19]

Chhattisgarh – The Heart of Naxalism

Chattisgarh is the heart of Naxalism with the state sharing borders with six Maoist affected states. Naxalites are reportedly active in eight out of the State's 16 districts: Bastar, Dantewada, Kanker, Surguja, Jashpur, Koriya, Rajnandgaon, and Kawardha.[20]

It falls in what the Maoists' call the 'Dandakaranya Special Zone Committee' (which covers Bastar, Kanker and Dantewada in Chhattisgarh; Chandrapur, Gadchiroli and Bhandara in Maharashtra; Balaghat in Madhya Pradesh and parts of northern Andhra Pradesh). The Maoists are well organized in 18 Guerrilla Squads (*Dalams*), four 'divisional

District-wise Fatalities, 2005

Table 2

District	*Civilians*	*SFs*	*Maoists*	*Total*
Dantewada	35	12	2	49
Bastar	1	0	3	4
Surguja	1	5	1	7
Kanker	0	4	0	4
Rajnandgaon	0	2	0	2
Total	37	23	6	66

committees' – South Bastar (5 *Dalams*), North Bastar (4 *Dalams*), Bhandara-Balaghat (4 *Dalams*) and Gadchiroli (5 *Dalams*). They are reported to be running parallel government and *Jan Adalats* ('People's Courts') to settle both civil and criminal disputes. The district wise fatalities in the first eight months of 2005 in Chattisgarh were as per Table below[21]

Apart from the police action by the government an anti Naxalite movement, known as *Salva Zudoom* (peace initiative), has been launched by Mahendra Karma, a Congress party leader and Leader of Opposition in the Legislative Assembly.[22] With 250 villages of the Bastar region mobilized Maoists killed at least 32 tribals in separate incidents. These activists of the *Salva Zudoom* are also being offered weapons and appointed as special police officers thereby enabling saturation of the area. Similar action is also evident in Jharkhand where village defence committees when formed, faced the ire of the Naxalites.

However the state government in Chattisgarh has undertaken urgent measures to modernize and familiarize its police forces in tune with the requirements of fighting militancy. Chattisgarh is also reported to be establishing a counter naxal training school. As of now, the threat of the naxalites in Chattisgarh continues at a high level.

Bihar – The Naxalite Cauldron

Bihar was the worst affected State in the country due to Naxalite violence in 2004 as per the Union Ministry of Home Affairs. The trend continued in 2005. Maoists were active in 30 out of its 38 districts, with 155 killings between January and November 30, 2004, a rise from 128 in 2003. 93 people, including 22 civilians, 27 Security Force (SF) personnel and 44 Maoists, have died in 2005, till November 20.[23] As far as operational areas are concerned, the CPI-Maoist has a presence in all parts of Bihar, with the primary support base located amongst the lower castes and poor peasantry.[24] The jail break in Jehanabad is the most alarming incident of Maoist violence in Bihar as well as in the country during the year. In terms of sheer scale and audacity, it marked a new phase in the struggle. This operation led to freeing 341 prisoners, abduction of more than 20 activists of the Ranvir Sena and loss of a large quantity of arms and ammunition. It was a synchronized attack on the District Court, Police Lines, District Armoury, the residence of the District Judge, and the S.S. College. There were enough indications of the strike as the Maoists had disconnected electric supply to the city two days earlier and had disconnected telephone services to the Jail and police line area.[25]

Awadesh Singh, a suspected Maoist was arrested by the police who is claimed to have been involved in the 13 November 2005 jail break at Jehanabad. Singh is claimed to be the right hand man of Arvind Kumar alias Deo Kumar a Central Committee member. The elite National Security Guards rushed to the scene, carried out raids at a number of places, such as Sherghati (Gaya), Kurtha (Jehanabad), Govindpur (Nawada), Bhabua, Maaurhi and Paliganj in Patna district but reportedly did not achieve much success.[26]

The problem of naxalism in Bihar is also related to poor state of police administration in the state. Bihar Police has suffered 43 Maoist attacks between January 2003 and November 2005, killing over 150 police personnel and looting of a large quantum of arms and ammunition.[27] This is evident from the The *Crime in India – 2003* report, published by the National Crime Records Bureau. Bihar has a ratio of 1:1,652 in terms of actual police strength to the estimated mid-year population of 2003 as compared to say Andhra Pradesh ratio of 1:1052; Chhattisgarh, 1:1061, Jharkhand (formerly part of Bihar), 1:1333; and Orissa, 1:1072. According to the Bihar Police Association, a majority of about 300 police stations, 92 police picquets and hundreds of police outposts in the Maoist-affected districts are facing severe infrastructure shortages. Creation of a composite organization in the home department of the state government in the form of a counter naxalite wing and a special task force to tackle this menace on a war footing is the need of the hour. Modernization of the police force in terms of weapons and communications is also a priority and hopefully the new state government in Bihar is up to the task in the coming days and months ahead.

The Naxalites buoyed by the success in Jehanabad, have threatened to launch suicide attacks for which they claim to have had some training from the Tamil Tigers as well as coordination with the Nepali Maoists. An Intelligence Bureau report indicated 12 members had vowed to undertake suicide operations for the cause. This however may not be a classic suicide operation as such actions go against leftist ideology, it may be an risky operation involving large number of casualties.[28]

Maoists in West Bengal

Development has raised the likelihood of violence in West Bengal which is an ironical paradox. Fast paced development and associated socio-economic hazards in West Bengal may push more people towards naxalites as per intelligence officials based on a secret note for the professional revolutionaries. They are aiming to hit intelligence network of the police alongside certain high profile targets in the state. They not only aim to target class enemies but also their-protectors and benefactors. Protectors being the police and benefactors are informers or CPI(M) sympathizers. According to the report, the CPI (M) zone and local committee leaders on CPI (M) in Purulia, Midnapore and Bankura districts could be targeted. They are intending to target officers in charge police stations involved in enticing locals to spy on Maoists. Maoist Politburo member Koteshwar Rao or Ramji has reportedly hatched this policy of targeting the intelligence network. He is also suspected to be the master mind behind killing of four CPI – M leaders and officer in charge in Bankura.[29]

Greater Cooch Behar Movement

The Cooch Behar District has strategic significance as it is adjacent to the Siliguri Corridor. Hitosadhani Sabha is said to be the sub national group which had convinced the monarchy to sign the instrument of accession on condition that Cooch Behar be declared as Union Territory and it did not favour union with West Bengal but Assam. Cooch Behar has a population of about 24 lakh, 60 per cent of which are Rajbhansis which also comprises of 35 per cent of the 1.5

Crore population of the six West Bengal districts asked by the GCPA. A large section of the population around 7 lakh is Bihari and Jharkandi tribal who work in the tea gardens. Rajbhansis do not have a separate language but have Bengali as the script and language. Forward Bloc leaders believe that economic deprivation is the main cause. The simmering discontent in the region has been ongoing for a long time with organizations as the Hitosadhini Sabha, Utjas, KPP and KLO showing rising discontent.[30]

The Greater Cooch Behar People's Association (GCBPA) has proposed a separate state of Greater Cooch Behar to comprise of North Bengal stretching from South Dinajpur and extending on to Kokrajhar District of Assam including Jalpaiguri, Siliguri, Cooch Behar, North Dinajpur and South Dinajpur. All these districts have majority of Rajbhanshi-Cooch population. This is said to be in line with the full implementation of the clauses of the agreement of accession between then King Bhup Bahadur and the Union Government. GCBPA Chief, Banshibadan Burman states, "—a separate state is our birthright."[31] Origins of the conflict lay in the 1996 Kamtapur People's Party (KPP) demanding for a separate state. This fielded the Kamtapur Liberation Organization (KLO) that was supported by the ULFA as well as the Directorate General of Forces Intelligence (DGFI). The KLO had initially established camps in Bhutan and later in Bangla Desh where three camps have been intimated to the BDR by the BSF. The Cooch Behar people identify themselves as Rajbansis. This identity and status of the Rajbansis is not easy to reconcile.[32]

GCBPA had carried out a strike on 20 September 2005 in Cooch Behar which resulted in mob violence and the death of five persons including an Additional Superintendent of Police and two constables. Approximately 30,000 people are known to have participated in the agitation. The agitation was a protest prior to the visit of the West Bengal Chief Minister on 24 September 2005. Incident prediction is thus easy and is related to events which are likely to come up. In this case it appears that the police were aware of the likelihood of violence hence Additional Superintendent of police from Kalimpong who was lynched and a large number of policemen were present during the agitation. West Bengal Chief Minister, Buddhadeb Bhatacharjee vehemently denied that Greater Cooch Behar and Gorkhaland will ever be made into states while addressing a rally in Siliguri on 25 September 2005.[33]

Some of the remedial measures suggested are as follows:-

(a) West Bengal government should strengthen the intelligence set up in the area.

(b) Strategy of strong action against the violent groups and elimination of genuine grievances should be adopted.

(c) Dialogue amongst the political parties such as Forward Bloc which has clout in the region.

(d) Avoid political power play.[34]

Arms Supplies to Naxalites

Intelligence reports indicate that the ULFA has been a major source of supply of arms to the CPI (Maoists) from the South East Asian region to groups in the North East. CRPF and internal security agencies have indicated that ULFA has been the source. Naxals are increasingly being equipped with sophisticated weapons as AK 47 bought and also stolen from police. Sophisticated communications are also reported with Andhra Naxals.[35] In addition the LTTE is also reported to be supplying arms to Naxalites with suspicions of a hand of the ubiquitous ISI of Pakistan. LTTE is active in supplying arms and training in IEDs to the People's War Group cadre with the coastal areas of Krishna and Guntur district forming the main conduits of supply in Andhra Pradesh. Land mine blast in Chattisgarh with 24 casualties is said to have the imprint of training by LTTE.

Tackling the Menace of Naxalism in India

Anti naxal operations should be planned in an integrated manner to include the following aspects as per noted security specialist, Mr Prakash Singh :-

(a) Coordination of operations in all states so that we have either peace in all naxal areas or absence of it in all states. No island of peace surrounded by a sea of conflict phenomenon. However this appears too idealistic. This is not only because of the political dynamics but also because of concurrence of law and order between states and the center.

(b) States should coordinate efforts and launch joint operations as undertaken in1971 based on the Operation Steeplechase model.

(c) Intelligence sharing between states will be vital.

(d) States should raise elite forces such as the Greyhounds raised by Andhra.

(e) CPI (Maoists) have two components – Maoist Communist Centre and People's War, each should be treated differently.

(f) Socio – economic issues as unemployment, poverty, and tribal rights to be tackled on priority.[36]

Mr Prakash Singh should be happy that during the year, special efforts were made to achieve synergy between states in tackling the naxalite menace, which are outlined in the paragraphs below:

The Home Ministry has been seeking alibis in ensuring law and order in states citing the federal nature of the Constitution. It has not been able to get states on board for a common anti naxalite strategy. The Joint Task Force between states has also not been activated due to problems of command during joint operations between states. Modernization of police force and local intelligence gathering has also not been concluded.[37] This pathetic approach to deteriorating law and order situation bordering on militancy if not a revolution is inexcusable. In addition the span of Naxalism affecting 12 states also necessitates a unified nation wide approach. The Union Cabinet Secretary Mr B K Chaturvedi thus ordered the Home Secretary Mr V K Duggal to set up a special cell for tracking ultra left extremism. This will be headed by an officer of the rank of special secretary and would have two joint secretaries and many directors replacing the present arrangements of a special secretary in the internal security division of the Ministry of Home Affairs dealing with the subject. While this is an encouraging step, it will take time to be fully activated for coordination of functioning of state police forces across 12 state borders.

A conference of 13 Chief Ministers of Naxal Affected States was held on 19 and 20 September 2005. The aim was to obtain a seal of approval for coordinated operations across the borders. The thrust was on joint action by states as per Home Secretary, V K Duggal. Last meeting of states-centre coordination panel was held in Hyderabad in June 2005 and chief ministers conference on 21 September 2005. During this meeting setting up of joint task forces (JTF) and coordinated action was agreed upon for anti naxal operations in the Compact Revolution Zone (CRZ). Dispute amongst states of command of the JTF had prevented joint action except by states as Andhra and Orissa. Command of the JTF was suggested to be either rotated or given to the senior most officer.[38] This will remove hurdles for forces of one state pursuing terrorist in another estate. States were also to raise India Reserve Battalions and prepare action plans to combat Naxalism by both security and developmental issues in a time bound manner. Nodal officers are to be appointed to deal with Naxal related issues and better coordination amongst states and the Central govt. Each state is required to prepare an action plan, upgrade and strengthen police forces as well as intelligence networks.[39]

Carrying forward the concept, a workable plan of joint task forces was being evolved by the Home Ministry to avoid any operational glitches in the form of an operational code between all states involved in anti naxal operations, mainly Andhra Pradesh, Orissa, Bihar, Jharkhand, Chattisgarh, Maharashtra, West Bengal, UP, MP and Karnataka. From an initial aim of involving all the states, modalities are now being worked out to evolve a joint operations parameter for states at tri junctions like Orissa, Andhra Pradesh and Chattisgarh. The constitution of the JTF will be flexible and will depend on the kind of operation being undertaken and the adjoining border areas that may need cover for the same. Personnel of the anti naxal special task force of the states in question will form a part of the JTF. The JTF will be commanded by the police SP of the district in which the state is operating. However this will entail that when the naxalites cross from one state to another, the command of the JTF will also switch which may create operational glitches and will have to be fine tuned on the ground. Three JTFs may be finally evolved.[40]

Joint operations in the Indian environment have always proved a difficult proposition even when the nation is fighting a virtual war on terrorism. This is due to cultural inhibitions of cooperation, multi tiered structure of state police and para military agencies and lack of an institutional approach to the command structure due to multiplicity of cadres.

The connection of organized crime, terrorism and naxalism was the subject of discussion of a meeting of police of naxalite affected states in Agra in November 2005. Strategies for preventing spread to other unaffected areas were also discussed. An inter state cooperation and information network between the police forces of all states was also discussed keeping in view the trans border movement undertaken by criminals as well as naxalites after an incident. The police officers at the conference had concluded that the best way to control the spread is to cut the umbilical links of terrorists with criminal gangs to break the terror – crime network.[41]

Andhra Pradesh police which have been dealing with the problem of naxalism for many years are said to have a greater ability to combat the menace than say states as Jharkhand as per the Andhra Chief Minister, Y S Rajasekhara Reddy.[42] There is thus a need to systematically build up the capabilities of the police forces in states as Jharkhand, Orissa and Chattisgarh to combat the threat of naxalism by modernizing and retraining them. This will need an effort of more than one to three years for being fully effective, by this norm it is not likely that the naxal threat in these states is going to recede in the coming year, if it is contained it would be a great achievement but that too appears unlikely given the recent incidents of violence in the states.

What is essentially required is to consolidate the intelligence gathering process, create a centralized on line data base on similar model as the Interpol with access to police forces of all states. Incentives based system for modernization of police forces is another essential step required to be taken to ensure that the states which are ensuring modernization as Tripura and Chattisgarh are given added resources and laggards as Bihar are motivated to modernize their forces in tandem. Standardization of training and evaluation which can create uniformity in training and enhance effectiveness of police forces across the country creating peer pressure of efficiency is another suggested measure. Just as the army has uniform standards for assessment of training such as physical training and firing, the police services could very easily evolve the same based on the army model. Thereafter a systematic quantitative assessment model could be worked out and over the years peer pressure will build up to strive for excellence. These centralized assessment teams are well within the constitutional provisions to be undertaken by the Centre as a concomitant function of law and order.

A readiness reporting system for each unit should be prepared and units placed at different levels. Their attainment of a certain level should then dictate their employment. For example in a scale of 5 to 1 with 5 representing the lowest grade and 1 the highest, units as well as different security forces could be graded. Thus an unit which is initially inducted in an area could be given a grade of 5 and gradually upgraded as it gains experience and expertise in conduct of operations to a final level of 1. The employment of the unit in high or low value operations could be based on the grade achieved with Grade 5 being employed in low threat areas while 3 and above in highly sensitive areas. Similarly a gradation between forces could be carried out with the Rashtriya Rifles and the Army units being given grade 1 or 2, para military forces grade 3, central police forces grade 4 and the local armed police grade 5. This will greatly enhance understanding of employment of forces even by the uninitiated.

Grass roots level measures such as good turn out, bearing, physical fitness and so on should be enforced which is well within purview of local police officers as the superintendent of police and the alibi of political interference cannot hold water in this regard.

Some Unconventional Solutions

Cobra Force in Andhra. Nallamalla Black Cobras is a shadowy organization which has been carrying out selective killings in Andhra Pradesh recently. A Dalit activist, Alladi Ravi was killed in Prakasham District in Andhra Pradesh on 18 September 2005. This was the third killing in a month. Nallamulla Black Cobras informed the Sarpanch of Gonugunta Village that they had killed Ravi. Ravi was a member of Anti Casteist organisation, Kula Nimulana Porata Samiti. Wide spread protests were held by human rights organizations in Andhra to include the Andhra Pradesh Civil Liberties Committee and outlawed Writers Association (Virasam). These private armed gangs are alleged to be sponsored by the state government. Narsi Cobra reportedly killed APCLC activist Kanakachary in Mahbubnagar. Nallatarachu or Black Cobra killed Mannam Prasad in Prakashan district on 10 September. The CPI (Maoist) leaders are agitated and threatened to avenge the killings by holding trial and punishing Congress leaders and police officials responsible for the Cobras in Praja Courts.[43] Pseudo gangs is a favourite tactic of the counter insurgents. It appears that Cobras are also a part of this tactic in Andhra however there is no confirmation available at present. A number of human rights organizations from Punjab, Maharashtra, Tamil Nadu and Andhra Pradesh visited the three districts of Mahbubnagar, Karimnagar and Prakasham in Andhra Pradesh to assess the impact of the Cobras and the alleged nexus between the police and the Cobras and concluded that there was an unhealthy affiliation between the two and called for action against the police. The group also alleged that Cobras have threatened to kill 12 prominent human rights activists.[44]

Chattisgarh has raised vigilantes which have been supported by the state. These have had mixed success. They seem to have compounded the problem in causing atrocities on civilians by the Maoists as an act of reprisal.[45]

Proper use of mine protection vehicles and road opening parties to reduce casualties also needs to be considered. Ordnance Factory Board Kolkota was asked to develop a Standard Operating Procedure for use of Mine Protection Vehicles (MPVs) in the short term and carry out technical improvements in conjunction with the CRPF, DRDO and State police. MPVs were supplied under the police modernization programme. States were also asked to raise more India Reserve Battalions and denied additional CRPF. India Reserve Battalions should be raised from youth of the Maoist affected areas.[46]

Concluding Remarks

Naxalism has arisen due to poor governance and apathy of the state implying its elites to get out of the comfort zone and attend to the problems of the masses. The Naxalites have put forth very basic demands such as land distribution to the landless, minimum wages for agriculture labour, fair price for forest produce, and freedom from the vice like grip of money lenders and land lords.[47] Regrettably the state is unable to fulfill these bread and butter demands resulting in the masses taking to violence. Once violence has commenced it is difficult to break the cycle just as it is difficult to wean away a man eater from its human prey. The complexities of human social organization pose even greater challenges in overcoming the violence cycle and bringing peace to the region. 2006 should be a year of containment as far as the Naxalite threat is concerned. In case the state controls the threat to 100 plus districts of the country, reasonable success can be presumed to have been achieved. For this greater coordination not only between the states as far as police operations are concerned but also within states between different agencies are called for. Thus the social forestry, rural development, tribal welfare, roads and buildings, education, health as well as numerous other departments concerned with public welfare in a district need to coordinate relief to the needy in conjunction with the police for a holistic approach for tackling this menace from the grass roots level upwards. The present dispensation of governance on the district administration model is not producing the desired results and hence needs a revamp. A model system can be created in each state as a start point and then followed up in other districts. 2006 can thus be an year of containment and experimentation.

References

1. Nayak, Nihar. "Bihar : The Shape of Things to Come". Institute of Conflict Management. Downloaded from SAIR.org.
2. Singh, Pramod Kumar. "ULFA—," The Pioneer. 23 September 2005. Lucknow. p. 3.
3. Mitra, Chandan. 'Dangerous Liaisons, perilous drift'. Sunday Pioneer. 18 September 2005. Lucknow. p. 12.
4. Gill, KPS. "Containing ideological violence." The Pioneer. 24 December 2005. Lucknow. p. 6.
5. Shukla, Nityanand. "Jharkhand—" The Pioneer. 1 December 2005. Lucknow. p. 5.
6. SAIR. Report. Downloaded from the internet. 10 December 2005.
7. Gill, KPS. "Containing ideological violence." The Pioneer. 24 December 2005. Lucknow. p. 6.
8. Singh, Pramod Kumar. "ULFA—," The Pioneer. 23 September 2005. Lucknow. p. 3.
9. Indian Express Report. 29 September 2005. Lucknow. p. 6.
10. Farooq, Omer. "Stunned—" The Pioneer. 14 October 2005. Lucknow. p. 5.
11. Johnson, T A. "Hyderabad—" Sunday Indian Express. 16 October 2005. p. 4.
12. Pioneer Report. "Police closer—". The Pioneer. 24 December 2005. Lucknow. p. 5.
13. Farooq, Omar. "Top Maoist—". The Pioneer. 14 December 2005. Lucknow. p. 5.
14. Siddharth, Gautam. "In search of a model state". The Sunday Pioneer. 11 December 2005. Lucknow. p. 4.
15. Nayak, Nihar. "Red Spread over Jharkhand." Institute of Conflict Management. Downloaded from SAIR.org.
16. Hindustan Times Report. "10 Security men—" 09 October 2005. Lucknow. p. 16.
17. Shukla, Nityanand. The Pioneer. 9 October 2005. Lucknow. p. 4.
18. Nayak, Nihar. "Red Spread over Jharkhand." Institute of Conflict Management. Downloaded from SAIR.org.
19. Shukla, Nityanand. "Jharkhand Jails—". The Pioneer. 19 December 2005. Lucknow. p. 5.
20. Shukla, Shivanand. "Chattisgarh—" The Pioneer. 26 September 2005. Lucknow. p. 4.
21. Data till August 24, 2005; Source: South Asia Terrorism Portal.

22. Nayak, Nihar. Chattisgarh : Dangers of Vigilantism". Institute of Conflict Management. Downloaded from SAIR.org.
23. Data Source: South Asia Terrorism Portal
24. Nayak, Nihar. "Bihar : The Shape of Things to Come". Institute of Conflict Management. Downloaded form SAIR.org.
25. Nayak, Nihar. "Bihar : The Shape of Things to Come". Institute of Conflict Management. Downloaded form SAIR.org.
26. Times of India Report. The Times of India. 22 November 2005. Lucknow, p. 7.
27. Nayak, Nihar. "Bihar : The Shape of Things to Come". Institute of Conflict Management. Downloaded form SAIR.org.
28. Tewary, Amaranth. "Maoists plan—". The Pioneer. 19 December 2005. Lucknow. p. 5.
29. Saugar, Sengupta. "Maoists Plan to hit cop-comrade camaraderie" The Pioneer. 16 September 2005. Lucknow. p. 4.
30. Sengupta, Saugar. "Sitting—". Sunday Pioneer. 2 October 2005. Lucknow. p. 2.
31. Sengupta, Saugar. "ULFA—" The Pioneer. 26 September 2005. Lucknow. p. 5.
32. Mukherjee, Shikha. "Gayatri Devi—". The Pioneer. 23 September 2005. Lucknow. p. 1,2.
33. Nagchoudhary, Subrata. "No Greater Cooch Behar:Buddha" Indian Express. 26 September 2005. Lucknow. p. 5.
34. The Pioneer Editorial. 24 September 2005. Lucknow. p. 6.
35. Indian Express Report. 29 September 2005. Lucknow. p. 6.
36. Singh, Prakash. "Maoist violence must be dealt with afresh". The Pioneer. 19 September 2005. Lucknow. p. 7.
37. Sen, Sudhir Ranjan. "Home Ministry" The Indian Express. 2 December 2005. Lucknow. p. 5.
38. Sen, Sudhir Ranjan. "On Naxals, Home wants states to act". Indian Express. 19 September 2005. Lucknow. p. 4.
39. Pioneer Report. "States to set up anti – Naxal joint forces" The Pioneer. 20 September 2005. Luckow. p. 1.
40. Jain,Bharti. "Anti Naxal—". Economic Times. 17 October 2005. New Delhi. p. 2.
41. Upadhyay, Vijay. "Police discuss—". The Pioneer. 28 November 2005. Lucknow. p. 5.
42. Interview in The Economic Times. The Economic Times. 1 November 2005. New Delhi. p. 15.
43. Farooq, Omer. "Cobras strike again killing one; Maoists threaten retaliation". The Pioneer. 19 September 2005. Lucknow. p. 5.

44. Farooq, Omer. "Nexus—" The Pioneer. 1 October 2005. Lucknow. p. 5.

45. Nayak, Nihar. Chattisgarh : Dangers of Vigilantism". Institute of Conflict Management. Downloaded from SAIR.org.

46. Singh, Pramod Kumar. "Centre may send Air Force after Naxals". The Pioneer. 26 September 2005. Lucknow. p. 3.

47. Haksar, Nandita. Economic Times Debate. The Economic Times. 8 November 2005. New Delhi. p. 15.

4

North East - Half a Century of Conflict

"Whether it is war in its classical sense, or in its many variations such as internal conflict, insurgent movements or even transnational terrorism, non-military measures are invariably needed to evolve durable solutions. Hence, policy analysts must adopt interdisciplinary approaches and policy planners should develop sophisticated, multi-pronged responses. These must result in improving our security in all its dimensions: economic, social, political and even in terms of food and energy security. Such an approach is even more important as military and police forces grapple with new and unconventional challenges. "

Honourable Prime Minister of India, Mr Manmohan Singh

Since India's Independence in 1947, some 50,000 plus people are reported to have lost their lives in insurgency in the states of the North East.[1] The main issue in the North East is systematic denial of political justice when demands are made in normal course, for instance the Bodo request of recognition of their language since 1959 was denied till they undertook an armed struggle.[2] Another case is the Meghalaya governments, decision to move the Meghalaya Board of School Education to Shillong from Tura in the Garo hills. This led to a violent agitation with police firing killing 9 people and 100 injured in Tura and Williamnagar, headquarters of West and East Garo Hills districts respectively on 30 September 2005. Judicial inquiry under Justice (Retd) of Guwahati High Court Mr T C Das was ordered by the State govt.[3] Thus people have been taking up an armed struggle due to lack of alternative means of empowerment despite democracy having taken roots there. The complexity of the situation can be understood with even AIDS being used as a weapon of marginalization of the security forces. Reports indicate that insurgent groups in the North East have been threatening to use HIV infected women to spread the disease in Jawans posted in Manipur,

Meghalaya, Manipur, Nagaland and Tripura. National Aids Control Organization NACO says the Defence Minister had raised the issue with them a while back. These are supposedly new and less expensive ways to combat security forces in the North East.[4]

The militancy situation in the North Eastern states is extremely complex and we cannot expect quick gains in the year or even years ahead. There is a layered structure of rebellion with the militant, the executive, the legislator, the judiciary, the police man and the soldier seeped to varying degrees in the torrid space of violence in the states which also have a volatile border with Bangladesh and Myanmar. This organizational complexity is supplemented by ethnic convolutions where tribe, clan and ethnic loyalties play on the minds of officials as well as the people functionaries to subvert their loyalties to the state. The only certitude in the year ahead appears to be the fatalistic one, continued strife in varying intensity. We take an overview of the state of militancy in the troubled states of the North East and prognosticate for the year 2006.

Naga Issues - Cease Fire and Peace Parleys

The Naga Cease Fire was put in place in August 1997 between the government and National Socialist Council of Nagaland. Isak Chishi Swu and Thuingaleng Muivah, (NSCN IM), one of the oldest and most powerful of about 30 groups operating in the North east. 45 rounds of peace talks have been held since 1997 to end South Asia's longest standing insurgency that has claimed 25,000 lives since 1947. The last round of talks were held in Bangkok in November 2005. The main demand of the Naga rebels at present is creating of a Greater Nagaland by carving it out of Naga areas of neighbouring states, Assam, Manipur and Arunachal Pradesh. These states have obviously rejected the claims.[5] The Central government's Inter Ministerial Group is headed by the Programme Implementation Minister, Mr Oscar Fernandes, Minister in the Prime Minister's Office, Mr Prithviraj Chauhan and Minister of State for Home, S Regupathy thus representing all the influential segments of governmental functioning. Mr. K

Padmanabhiah an ex Home Secretary is the government interlocutor. The challenge is to meet or veer away the Naga groups from their demand of unification of the Naga inhabited areas which is an unlikely proposition given the resistance both political and armed that would result from other areas of the North East.

National Socialist Council of Nagaland (Isaak-Muivah) has reportedly accepted to reconcile that immediate and complete sovereignty for Nagaland is not realistic and Nagas have to live peacefully with the India, China, Mynamar troika. Naga Hoho Secretary has indicated this to The Sunday Express. However, Naga National Council has usurped the agenda of separatism and said that it would stop nothing short of sovereignty. NSCN is the break away faction of NNC. NNC does not accept the peace talks in progress between the Government of India and the NSCN and has rejected the same. The Naga Mothers Association or NMA President Khesheli Chishi a delegate at the 5th Naga Consultative Meeting held in Bangkok on 6-7 September has also called for a more representative body of Nagas than the NSCN. Naga Students Federation (NSF) President Phushika Awomi, says that differences are bound to arise amongst brothers.

The territorial integration issue and leadership are key topics of contention between various factions of Nagas. There is much confusion on the integration of tribes, many feel that Nagas of Manipur except Tangkhul Nagas are originally Kuki tribes brought under the Naga banner.[6] In the latest proclamations by the NSCN (IM) it has asked for firm commitment on the integration of Naga inhabited areas before the next round of talks. It is willing to even engage the Manipur and the Assam governments to overcome their opposition and achieve an amicable compromise. The Nagolim proposal involves areas which are already volatile, Karbi Anglong, where killings between tribal Karbis and Dimasas has been ongoing in the months of November and December in 2005, North Cachar Hills district, Golaghat, Sibsagar, Dibrugarh, Tinsukhia and Jorhat in Assam, Tamenglong, Senapati, Ukhrul and Chandel in Manipur, Dibang, Lohit, Tirap and Changland districts of Arunachal Pradesh.[7]

R H Raising a senior leader of the NSCN (IM) has reportedly indicated that unless during the tenure of the present 8 year old cease fire ending 31 January 2006, a solution was obtained, they would call off the truce and resume the fight. The people, claimed the leader were getting increasingly restive and do not see any seriousness from the Indian government to work out a tangible solution. Community consultations are reportedly already underway to get the views of all villages and communities. Church leaders as T Ao, however despair failing of the talks as they say that every Naga is hoping for peace talks to succeed.

The Naga negotiators also claim that the government is simultaneously carrying out discussions with the Khaplang group. A newspaper report indicated heavy clashes between militants of the Khaplang group and a 3500 strong Burmese army contingent in Northern Myanmar. A Khaplang spokesman, K Mulatonu stated that there were 7000 militants who were in 50 locations. In addition to the Naga groups, four more Indian militant groups are reported to be active in Myanmar to include, ULFA, PLA, PREPAK and UNLF.[8] Is it a ploy by the Government in conjunction with Myanmar's government to assuage the Isaac-Muivah faction just before talks are scheduled in mid December? One can only wait and watch.

The truce is in favour of the militant groups as they continue to operate in aliases and pseudonyms while the security forces are restricted from undertaking offensive operations. The cadres also continue to carry out their economic activities of extortion, tax collection and so on with aplomb. The Naga militant leaders perhaps know that their demand is not practical and hence not implementable. Their stance could be viewed in any number of ways as follows :-

(a) A strategy of brinkmanship to force the government into an acceptable favorable decision.

(b) Improve their hold within the Naga community.

(c) Continue their game of hide and seek with the law as staying on its periphery is to their advantage.

Ground swell of community opinion is the way to defuse the crisis in Nagaland as also other areas of the North East as the people are tired of the long struggle which has not yielded peace so far. A mute point is whether the NSCN is really honouring the cease fire as it is carrying out operations under different aliases as the strike on 5/8 Gurkha Rifles on 19 September 2005. Cease fire is now extended for a period of six months from 1 August 2005 to January 2006.[9] 9a Cease fire has since been extended till July 2006 for six months. What happens on January 2006 is anybody's guess?"

Manipur

Of all the North Eastern States, Manipur continues to be a cause of concern as the situation there during the year 2005 remained on the boil due to poor political and social handling of the sensitivities of the general populace. Thus the people killed in Manipur rose alarmingly from 218 in 2004 to 314 in 2005 upto 12 December of the year.[10] Other reports indicate that over 50 percent of the 472 insurgency related incidents in the North East have taken place in Manipur though it has only a fraction of the population and area amongst all the states. Al the Valley districts are now said to be affected by the militancy.[11] One of the major incidents was an ambush on 19 September 2005, of 12 soldiers of 5/8 Gorkha Rifles by the banned terrorist group, Kanglei Yawol Kanna Lup (KYKL) in Tamenglong district. It is said that such a major attack had taken place way back in 1999 in Churachandpur district.

In a serious allegation, it is reported that the chief Minister of Manipur Okram Ibobi Singh had paid Rs 15 million to two militant organizations. This allegation is reportedly made by the Chief of the Army Staff to the Union government and leaked to the press.[12] The groups reported to have included KYKL which had carried out a strike against the Army in September 2005. While it is a well known fact that militants are paid off by political parties, it is for the first time that direct accusations have been made by the Army with receipts presented as evidence. The move is likely to create fissures within the government in combating insurgency in the state. The relations were already strained due to allegations of human rights violations and disagreements on removal of the Armed Forces Special Powers Act and do not augur well for peace. While there are efforts to induce the Myanmarese Government to launch operations on militant camps in its areas, simultaneous cease fire agreements are being worked out with a number of terrorist groups in the state. However regrettably the main groups in the region, the UNLF, the PLA, the PREPAK and the KYKL, continue to oppose negotiations for peace, not for any ideological reasons but as it provides them a strand for self growth and survival.

The complexities of the situation in Manipur can be understood better once we envision the involvement of politicians to sponsor terrorist groups split on tribal lines. The KYKL and Revolutionary People's Fund (RPF) are Meiti groups, Okram Ibobi Singh the Chief Minister of Manipur who allegedly paid them money is a Meiti. Now we have the Naga groups led by the NSCN (IM) bidding for Nagolim which includes the hill districts of Manipur which is predominantly Thankul Naga. T Muivah, one of the principal leaders of the NSCN(IM) is a Thankul Naga and has very good support in the area. Undermining the NSCN(IM)'s efforts for greater Nagaland could possibly be one of the principal political designs of Meiti leaders as O Ibobi Singh. In the power game being played out in the North East, ethnic loyalties are thicker than allegiance to Delhi. Thus politicians are quite deft at using militant groups to foster their or the clans aims. This perhaps gives a Meiti versus Naga colour to the whole episode of pay offs. There would thus be many political and militant squabbles in the North East in the year ahead. Perhaps the Army has never understood this game well immersed as it is in physically eliminating the terrorists, oblivious to the double game being played by the political overlords in the North East. We will continue to have many gory stories of death, destruction and engineered conflicts from Manipur as well as Nagaland in 2006.

Tripura

Tripura has been the only success story in the North East. By effectively creating a successful counter insurgency grid and tracking the terrorists relentlessly with the help of good intelligence, militancy has been controlled under the dynamic leadership of the Police Chief, G M Srivastava. An analysis by Ajai Sahni of the Institute of Conflict Management has stated that the number of extremist incidents dropped to 210 in 2004 from 380, civilian deaths reduced from 205 to 70, Security Forces (SF) fatalities from 216 to 105, terrorist deaths rose from 61 in 2003 to 63 in 2004. The positive spiral of reduction of violence continued in 2005 when during the January-July period in 2005 deaths had gone down to 30, 12 civilian, 6 SF personnel and 12 terrorists.[13]

A significant achievement of the year was peaceful holding of elections to the Tripura Tribal Area Autonomous District Council (TTAADC) in March 2005. This success has been achieved with the establishment of a counter insurgency grid of 386 security forces camps dotting the country side, nominating 2,600 Special Police Officers (SPOs), 105 'Special Police Pickets' (SPPs) in addition to the existing 37 police outposts and 55 police stations in 20 police sub-divisions. Provision of arms and ammunition, upgrading of communications and vehicles have all contributed to the unprecedented success which Ajai Sahni has compared to that achieved in Punjab in the 1990's. This has led to a secure environment fostering steady growth of commercial as well as development projects in the state.[14]

All this shows what a determined police force backed by the political leadership can achieve in a short time of two years. However the situation cannot be normal till the time the camps across the Bangla border are not neutralized, for the state engulfed from many sides by Bangladesh continues to be vulnerable and thus the vigil has to be maintained in the tribal and forested areas of the state.

Indo Myanmarese Relations

The Indian Prime Minister had a meeting with his

Myanmarese counter part General Soo Win and emphasized the need for a national reconciliation and movement towards democracy and fundamental human rights at the pace and desire of the people of Myanmar who must find the solution themselves.[15] India and Myanmar have a 1640 km long border which is across some of the most inhospitable terrain in the World and is difficult to patrol much less fence which has never been attempted. This is providing the militant groups in the North East easy access for moving to and fro into Myanmar where they have established bases.[16] In addition a lot of smuggling takes place causing loss to the state. The NSCN Khaplang group is said to be having 50 camps and 7000 guerrilla fighters in Myanmar. A Myanmar Army Brigade had undertaken an offensive in the Sagaing Division in the North in the beginning of December 2005 in which the Khaplang group has claimed that three of its cadres had been lost and a large number of houses and granaries had been burnt with many villagers made refugees.[17] A similar offensive in January 2005 had been launched with some good results. There may be a tacit agreement between the Myanmarese and the Indian government as India has repeatedly brought out the presence of militants on its soil to the Myanmarese government. It is such cooperative engagement across the Wire which can bring about positive change in the area.

References

1. Syed Zarir Hussian. "Myanmar Army". The Pioneer. 16 December 2005. Lucknow. p. 4.
2. Haksar, Nandita. Economic Times Debate. The Economic Times. 8 November 2005. New Delhi. p. 15.
3. Indian Express Report. "Former HC—" Indian Express 9 October 2005. Lucknow. p. 4.
4. Sinha, Kounteya. "NE Rebels threat to forces : AIDS. 26 September 2005. Lucknow. p. 7.
5. Hussain, Syed Zarir. NSCN IM Threat to End Truce. The Sunday Pioneer. 6 November 2005. Lucknow. p. 5.
6. Venkatraman, Kartyk. The Greater Naga Problem. Sunday Express. 25 September 2005. Lucknow. p. 12.
7. Aurora, Bhavna Vij. "Next Naga—". The Indian Express. 7 December 2005. Lucknow. p. 3.

8. Hindi Hindustan Report. Hindustan. 7 December 2005. Lucknow. p. 14.

9. Sen, Sudhir Ranjan. "NSCN(I-M)—". 22 September 2005. Lucknow. p. 5.

10. Gill, KPS. "Containing ideological violence." The Pioneer. 24 December 2005. Lucknow. p. 6.

11. Routray, Bibhu Prasad. "Manipur: Old Script, New Lessons". South Asia Intelligence Review. Weekly Assessments and Briefings Volume 4, No.13, October 10, 2005.

12. Routray, Bibhu Prasad. "Manipur: Fissures Within". South Asia Intelligence Review Weekly Assessments and Briefings Volume 4, No. 23, December 12, 2005.

13. Sahni, Ajai. "Tripura: Counter Insurgency Success. Institute of Conflict Management. Downloaded SAIR.org.

14. Sahni, Ajai. "Tripura: Counter Insurgency Success. Institute of Conflict Management. Downloaded SAIR.org.

15. Pioneer Reprot. The Pioneer. 15 December 2005. Lucknow. p. 2.

16. Syed Zarir Hussian. "Myanmar Army—". The Pioneer. 16 December 2005. Lucknow. p. 4.

17. Syed Zarir Hussian. "Myanmar Army—". The Pioneer. 16 December 2005. Lucknow. p. 4.

5

Assam-A Glimmer of Hope Elections and Beyond in 2006

"Bombs and pistols do not make revolution—. The sword of revolution is sharpened on the whetting stone of ideas"

Shahid Bhagat Singh's Statement before Lahore High Court

The broad expanse of the meandering Brahmaputra flows through Assam, a state of simple hardy plainsmen unaffected by the cruel polity of modern power games even to this day. Engagement with modernity in various spheres, polity, social and economic as also the population implosion from Bangladesh has raised fears amongst the people of Assam of losing their identity. They have thus taken up arms. In this armed struggle 15,000 people have reportedly lost their lives since 1979.[1] Home Ministry officials say that 700-800 ULFA cadres are active in Upper Assam and Garo hills with their leadership safe in Bangladesh.[2] The militancy in Assam was on the ebb after the ULFA had lost its base in the Bhutanese jungles due to successful operations carried out by the Royal Bhutan Army in 2004. There after the leaders are operating from Bangladesh which has elements fostered by agencies as the Pakistani Inter Services Intelligence or ISI, hostile towards India. Illegal immigrations are thus encouraged by Bangladesh. The dyadic relationship between illegal immigration and insecurities in Assam led to the growth of ULFA which ironically does not identify this as an issue due to tacit support to it by Bangladesh. ULFA's silence is explained as a part of greater agenda of battle against Indian hegemony. That it is being used as a ploy of political one up man ship in the region by Bangladesh has perhaps never occurred to the ULFA leaders safely ensconced in that country. Reportedly even the ruling Tarun Gogoi government in Assam has had a deal with the separatist ULFA which has resulted in its rearming and reorganizing.[3] The complex wheel of insurgency has turned full circle.

The security apparatus in Assam as compared to other states in the North East and even in Kashmir is well organized and integrated. Assam has the only functional and evolved unified civil government and security forces headquarters, no doubt the efforts of its past governors as General S K Sinha (Retired). The Unified Headquarters is headed by the Chief Minister with the strategy formulation cell under the Chief Secretary. Operations Group is led by the local Corps Commander and the Para Military Forces, Police and intelligence agencies are intimately involved in the process of security governance of the state.[4] This has facilitated a joint strategy and review of operations from time to time thereby rebuilding peace in the state which has not been possible in other areas in the country. Unified headquarters need to involve the political functionary to be effective and coagulate all agencies involved in combating the militancy. While it is always difficult to get all security forces on board as they are deeply conscious of each individual service's identity, the clear and firm direction from the Chief Minister supported by the Governor of the state can make this possible as seen from the example of Assam.

The state assembly elections in Assam are scheduled in 2006. This has spurred particularly the ruling party the Congress to activate the peace process and thus there have been parleys with the ULFA recently. A People's Consultative Group (PCG) has been formed by the ULFA for talks with the government. The key issue being non acceptance of sovereignty by the ULFA and the Government's insistence of not holding talks beyond the Constitution and avoidance of violence by the ULFA.

Given the keenness of the State Government to conduct elections in the state peacefully, there is hope of an outward peace in Assam in the coming year but for sporadic violence in the areas of Karbi Anglong where active measures need to be taken to ensure that the Karbis and Dimasas do not indulge in fratricidal killings any more. The peace with ULFA will be only an outward posture as it continues to develop and retain its capability for undertaking terrorist attacks with impunity. The Government needs to thus ensure that the talks result in simultaneously defanging militant capability and not merely be an interregnum of rest and reorganization for the terrorists. The Army on the other hand has to ensure that it continues to carry out surveillance and active intelligence operations seeking encounters without recourse to human rights violations, a tall order for any security force but operating procedures exist and can be refreshed.

The conduct of elections may however create major law and order problems. The voters list in Assam is likely to be one of the contentious issues. 1.5 lakh names have been categorized as D or doubtful category in Assam recently as per Chief election Commissioner, Mr B B Tandon. This was done to overcome the possibility of illegal migrants from Bangladesh registering as voters. The Foreigners Tribunal has examined over the years names of suspects and of the 3.5 lakh at present 1.5 lakh voters remained.[5] The role of the Election Commission in Assam will thus be crucial as in the elections in Bihar in 2005. All in all 2006 will be a year of decision in Assam.

Assam Peace Talks

People's Consultative Group (PCG) was formed for preparation of ground work for peace under the guidance of noted Assamese writer, Indira Goswami with the task of, "ensure that the road to peace is smoothened so that ULFA leaders and the Government emissaries could begin direct face-to-face talks at later stage". The group comprises of individuals who are independent and without the past baggage of active involvement in the insurgency in Assam but with sympathy for the struggle of self identity for the people of Assam. These individuals include the following:-

- Mukul Mahanta, a sympathizer of the struggle by ULFA.
- Lachit Bordoloi head of the Manab Adhikar Sangram Samiti (MASS).
- Ajit Bhuyan, editor of vernacular daily *Aji*.

- Dr Brajen Gogoi, a former executive of Tata Tea and ULFA sympathizer.
- Hiranya Saikia, an intermediary courier between ULFA leadership and Indira Goswami.
- Arup Borbora, lawyer and human rights activist.
- Dilip Patgiri associated with the Assam Jatiyatabadi Yuva Chhatra Parishad (AJYCP).
- Dignata Konwar, journalist and general secretary of the defunct front for ULFA, Jatiya Unnayan Parishad.
- Hyder Hussain, Editor, *Pratidin*, a pro-ULFA Assamese newspaper.
- Rebati Phukan, a relative of Paresh Baruah.[6]

Impetus to the talks is said to be provided by the quagmire in which, the, '28th Battalion' of the ULFA , its major force in the region after the 2003 Bhutan operations, found itself after the successful operations by the Army in the Dibru-Saikhowa National Park in Tinsukia district This park covers an area of 756 square kilometers with a primary area of 340 square kilometers and was encircled by the Army. It succeeded in killing Achintya Saikia the leader of the group.[7] Assamese leadership has been constantly known to resort to talks to resolve the difficult issue of militancy. The PCG succeeded in ensuring that Army operations in the Dibru Saikhowa Park were suspended. The forthcoming elections in 2006, will result in further compromises.

The ULFA seems to be under mounting public pressure to adopt a conciliatory stand. It has probably lost public sympathy with killing of some 20 children in the landmine blast on Independence Day parade 2004. Reports also say that after the 2003 Bhutan operations, the ULFA has not been able to regroup and hence is keen for a cease fire. Peace parleys held in 1992 with ULFA had failed as five senior ULFA leaders jumped parole after a single round of talks with the Government thus raising apprehensions of success at present. The difference this time is said to be that the people are yearning for peace. What are the negotiating parameters? Will the ULFA water down its negotiating stand like the NSCN (IM) did. It had initially demanded an homeland outside the Indian state but now wants a integrated Naga tribal area in the North East. Similar moves in August 1997 led to cease fire in Nagaland brokered by members of the civil society between the Government and the NSCN (IM). Mizo National Front and Tripura National Volunteers were also brought to the negotiating table successfully in the 1980's despite their initial stand of fighting for an independent state.[8]

Lachit Bordoloi, a member of the PCG and advisor to the Manav Adhikar Sangram Samiti (MASS) held forth on major expectations from the peace talks in a public rally, in Nalbari, which has contributed a large number of lower rung members of the ULFA cadres. He wanted immediate halt of Army counter insurgency operations in Assam, claiming that the army has been attempting to derail the peace process. While ULFA leaders said that their organization had not launched any operations since 15 August but it was claimed that Army had carried on indiscriminately. The principal facilitator, Ms Indira Goswami, had brought out that the Government should clarify what had happened to several ULFA members who were missing after the operations in Bhutan in December 2003, release ULFA cadres launched in jails and should not object to discussing the sovereignty issue raised by the ULFA as several constitutional experts had said that it could be discussed.[9]

The trigger for accelerating the peace talks is said to have been cornering of the ULFA cadres in Dibru Saikhowa National Park in Eastern Assam by the Army. The operation was launched based on orders from the Home and Defence ministries to crack down on militants. 181 Mountain Brigade under 4 Corps based in Tezpur had launched operations in which 25 ULFA cadres escaped to Myanmar while 15 militants were reportedly killed. However the operations also brought out lack of inter agency coordination as the ULFA had offered to have talks under the guidance of Assamese writer Indira Goswami and formed an 11 member group of public representatives. This was info to the Prime Ministers Office(PMO) which had welcomed this step. Defence minister had also announced that there was no cease fire with ULFA and the operations will go on. But ULFA leadership and the PCG had threatened to pull out. Assam Chief Minister is said to have intervened through the PMO to stop the operations and let the talks continue. Minister of State for Defence from Jorhat Mr B K Handique stepped in writing letters to the Prime Minister Manmohan Singh and Congress President, Sonia Gandhi. On 29 September 2005 Army Headquarters is said to have instructed 4 Corps to stop operations, a day after ULFA's letter to the Prime Minister, that it will be ready for dialogue. It is felt that if ULFA comes for talks many other groups will follow and join the peace process.[10]

The Guwahati High Court also admitted a PIL alleging violation of human rights in the Army operation at Dibru Saikhowa forest. The PCG has claimed that this and the pressure from its constituents has resulted in calling off of the operation by the Army, while the Army said that the reason was accomplishment of the mission. The PIL filed by Lachit Bordoloi of the Manav Adhikar Sangram Samiti (MASS) alleges that the Army had detained and denied food and medicines to approximately 10,000 people in the region.[11]

The ULFA has been using the ploy of talks and cease fire when ever its cadres have faced a difficult situation on the ground. In 1991 the security forces had picked up the ULFA general secretary, Anup Chetia who was given safe passage to bring President Arabinda Rajkhowa and Commander in Chief, Paresh Barua, at present all three remain in Bangladesh.[12] In the instant case two Army battalions had undertaken a painstaking combing drive in dense forests for a month. Contradictory statements by political leaders in Assam and Delhi about ULFA cease fire had confused the uniformed men. Though why should uniformed men get confused with such statements is not understood. The security soldier has to undertake relentless operations until he is stopped from doing so by his superior commander and not affected by any other indications.

The peace parleys will have to followed up successfully over a period during which the government forces should consolidate their goodwill in the region and also ensure that regrouping by the ULFA does not take place by continued surveillance of their training and recruiting areas, surveillance of their supporters and sympathizers. The peace dividend demanded by the people has to be transformed into effective measures on the ground by vigilance on both sides. A much needed rest and recoupment cycle should be put in place. The intelligence network however must be sustained. We must understand that the revolutionary processes are a form of transformation in the society, in the case of Assam the sub elites assimilation in the modern Indian society is the major issue. Once these feel secure in the Indian state and are able to identify with modernisation, the militancy will go away. In addition their desire to form a part of the power structure in the state would also have to be fulfilled. Their assimilation in the existing power structure will also enable resolution of this crisis. Thus there is a need to follow up the peace talks to their logical conclusion.

Karbi Anglong

The continuing violence in the Karbi Anglong district, 320 kms from Guwahati has led to the loss of approximately 100 people till mid December 2005, 2500 homes were set ablaze by the warring armed groups of tribes and more than 50,000 people displaced, disrupting normal life in this tribal region. Some 10,000 children in 39 relief camps set by the government have been without any education since October 2005.[13] Ethnic violence in Karbi Anglong in Central Assam between the Karbis and rival tribals Dimasas is a long term phenomenon. These killings represented the latest phase of differences between the United People's Democratic Solidarity (UPDS) and Dima Halim Daogah (DHD) which commenced on 26 September 2005. DHD is a rebel group fighting for an independent homeland for the Dimasa tribe in Eastern Assam as a part of struggle between the Karbis and Dimasas for control over territory. The clashes reportedly started with the murder of three youths from the Dimasa tribe, allegedly by the UPDS. The DHD subsequently retaliated by carrying out attacks on Karbi villages. On 8 October 2005, ethnic violence once again erupted with five Karbis including a 3 year old girl killed and over 83 houses of Karbis as well as Dimasas torched in Borsingbe village. A group of 20 unidentified armed miscreants are supposed to have swooped in military fatigues on the village at 2 pm. This is said to be in retaliation to the torching of 58 houses of two Dimasa villages at the dawn of 8 October 2005, at Walingdisa, Doldoli near Diphu police station where 14 houses were burnt down, followed by the Kathalbari village where 44 houses were torched. This was claimed to be a Karbi attack.[14]

09 October 2005 night, DHD hacked to death nine Karbi villagers in two villages. 14 more villagers were killed in a fresh wave of violence between the Karbis and Dimasas. In retaliation 80 armed Karbi tribals attacked village Kheroni, 290 kms east of Guwahati. Five Dimasas including three women were killed on 10 October 2005. The mob also put fire to the huts.[15] 12 houses were burnt down in the next cycle of violence on 10 October 2005. 8000 people, majority Karbis are reported to be in make shift camps. Army and para military forces are patrolling remote area to built up the confidence of people.[16]

The militancy in Assam and the curious situation of encounters versus talks in 2005 exemplifies the pressures on the resolution of insurgency in the North East. There is a overlapping mix of state and central government interests, political parties, human rights groups posing as fronts for militant organizations, commercial interests of tea planters, the oil industry and so on which have been over the years using the militancy to further their respective interests. The commitment of the Army and the hard core insurgents is the only constant factor, all other players tend to veer their stand and opinion based on the local situation, and this has bred a cycle of perpetuity wherein the elites in thc state have developed a vested interest in continuance of bloodshed. It is only when this cycle is disrupted and the elites demonstrate some concern for the well being of the lower strata of political, social and economic slice of community that the militancy will be resolved. In India's recent history, it is only in Mizoram and Punjab that such a sacrifice by the elites has been observed for the sake of bringing peace. In the case of Punjab, Beant Singh paid with his life while the flaccid players who survived continue to dwell in the pelf and perfidy of the 1980's.

References

1. Hussain, Syed Zarir. "Weary Assamese—" The Pioneer. 14 October 2005. Lucknow. p. 5.
2. Gupta, Shishir. "ULFA camp surrounded, 14 killed." Indian Express. 19 September 2005. Lucknow. p. 4.
3. Mitra, Chandan. Dangerous Liaisons, perilous drift. Sunday Pioneer. 18 September 2005. Lucknow. p. 12.
4. The Pioneer Report. The Pioneer. 6 October 2005. Lucknow. p. 1.
5. Kashyap, Samudra Gupta. "1.5 lakh—". The Indian Express. 15 December 2005. Lucknow. p. 5.
6. Routray, Bibhu Prasad. "ULFA: Desperate Deception". Institute for Conflict Management. Dowloaded from SAIR.org.
7. Routray, Bibhu Prasad. "ULFA: Desperate Deception". Institute for Conflict Management. Dowloaded from SAIR.org.
8. Hussain, Syed Zarir. "Playing to the Gallery" Sunday Pioneer. 09 October 2005. Lucknow. p. 2.
9. Kashyap, Samudra Gupta. "ULFA talks—" The Indian Express. 7 November 2005. p. 5.

9(a). Cease fire has since been extended till July 2006 for five month.

10. Hussain, Syed Zarir. "Calm after Army ends action against ULFA" The Pioneer. 30 September 2005. p. 2.
11. Kashyap, Samundra Gupta. "Army winds up" The Indian Express. 29 September 2005. Lucknow. p. 5.
12. Gupta, Shishir. "Congress does an Andhra—" The Indian Express. 4 October 2005. Lucknow. p. 1,2.
13. Hussain, Syed Zarir. "Karbi Anglong—". The Pioneer. 10 December 2005. Lucknow. p. 4.
14. Indian Express Report. "Five killed—". Indian Express 9 October 2005. Lucknow. p. 4.
15. Hussain, Syed Zarir. "Army out—" The Pioneer. 11 October 2005. Lucknow. p. 1, 2.
16. Hussain, Syed Zarir. "12 more—" The Pioneer. 12 October 2005. Lucknow. p. 4.

References

6

Nepal-Peace with Dignity or Anarchy

"The country is more important than the King".

King Jigme Singye Wangchuk, BhutanNepal – the Way Ahead - Constitutional to Ceremonial Monarchy

Indian security is likely to be dictated by the happenings in Nepal in the year ahead as India has a vast and latently explosive border with its Northern neighbour proximating the naxalite infested state of Bihar and a criminally volatile Eastern Uttar Pradesh. The linkages with the Compact Revolutionary Zone of the Maoists in India will provide synergy of geographic contiguity to extremists in both the countries. The Seema with Sashastra Suraksha Bal or SSB deployed on the Indo-Nepal border is still finding its feet to thwart hostile bids for crossing by armed gangs, criminals, narcotic and people smugglers. The present efforts of the Indian Government to thrash out an agreement between Maoists and the political parties through politicization of the situation in Nepal has to be supported by veering the King away from his obdurate path of denying the people genuine democracy based on a titular parliamentary system which will bring peace to the region. An editorial in the Economic Times of 29 November 2005 has called for support of the emerging coalition in Nepal which is comprising of Nepali Congress-Communist Party of Nepal (United Marxist-Leninist) bloc and the Maoists. The overwhelming support from all sections of the society has led the Indian government to tacitly back this coalition.[1] Reports of Nepal receiving 18 truck loads of arms and ammunition from China followed by hobnobbing of the Nepalese Army Chief with Pakistani counter parts assuring him of training assistance do not augur well for peace in the region.[2] Apart from the China card played by the Nepal monarchy, the impact of the induction of these arms what ever be the content needs to be taken into account carefully. Ordinary people in Nepal do not know about China's ruthless suppression of dissent in Tibet and Nepal's ruling class has been playing the China card against India, this has resulted in lack of any apprehensions on China in Nepal. The recent call by the US ambassador to ask the Maoists to succumb to the monarchy added another dimension to the issue though the context in which it has been made is still not clear. The Maoists have a very real social and economic grievance, political leaders are weak and monarchy has no control mechanisms in terms of arms and police to control the country side.[3] International efforts to achieve a symbiosis of the Nepalese power troika are necessary and even China should come on board for this cause of bringing peace in the Himalyan region as well as provide much needed succour to the hapless people of this mountainous area. It is the least that the international community can do for Nepal in the year ahead – 2006.

Nepal – The Basic Issues

Nepal is a monarchy over 237 year old. The Narayanhiti Palace has been ruling the country as the only Hindu kingdom. The geography of the country being entirely mountainous and in large parts intractable by motorized transport, reach of the government is limited particularly so when the ruling elite is unenlightened, focused on profligacy be it the monarchy or varied hues of political parties that have been in power over the years. The emergence of an egalitarian state was a political and structural necessity which should have been ushered in through reforms by the monarchy as well as by the political parties. The absence of enlightened parity meant emergence of a struggle for equality as Nepal's people came into contact with the World outside especially India and tasted the fruits of liberation. The main issue in Nepal is thus a central power struggle between the troika, the monarchy, the political parties and the Maoists each an important constituent of the power politics in the mountain kingdom.

In Nepal, the monarchy controls Kathmandu Valley and that appears to be its justification for continuance in power for the central governments control over the West Central,

Far West and Terai areas is limited while in Northern Nepal formal governance has been hardly ever established, state's dominance of the eastern districts is also said to be weakening as per P G Rajamohan, Research Associate, Institute for Conflict Management. What remains is an iron control over a progressively beleaguered Kathmandu Valley. But that control is exercised through the Royal Nepal Army or the RNA whose loyalty has been very assiduously cultivated by the King through pelf and privileges. As per noted Nepal analyst, Ashok K Mehta, the RNA is being upgraded to a strength of 1 lakh with 15 fighting brigades, 48 infantry battalions, two corps headquarters and a unified command. In addition avenues for promotion have been enhanced with 58 brigadiers, two lieutenant generals posts and three retired generals being send as ambassadors. Half the strength of the RNA is in the Kathmandu Valley thus giving the King a safe sanctuary. The loyalty of the RNA as per the Chief, General Pyar Jung Thapa is towards the monarchy, the country and the people.[4] Lt Gen Rukh Mangat Katuwal, the next in line to Rana in May 2006 is also a strong king loyalist. Off late the RNA is getting arms from China, It has contracted two transport aircraft, four helicopters, 36 guns and mortars and large quantities of ammunition as per Mehta. 20,000 hand grenades, 15,000 AK 47 rifles and four million rounds of 7.62 ammunition have been received by the RNA in September 2005.[5]

It is unlikely that with such a loyal military force, the King is likely to give up his throne and may even opt for being a modern day Nero much to the chagrin of the international community. Thus the build up of the RNA recently raises alarms for human security in Nepal. The solution lies in convincing the King and the RNA that salvation lies in an understanding with the political parties and the Maoists, preserving their integrity at the same time accepting the Maoists demand of a ceremonial monarchy. Perhaps China can exercise some influence on the King, if he or the RNA are not amenable to the sage advice of India, Nepali people's long standing friend. Sino-Indian relations with Nepal should be cooperative and not competitive, this may require an understanding with China at the highest level but is the need of the times for peace in Nepal. While Mr Shyam Saran has highlighted this facet during his recent visit to Nepal, what efforts are being undertaken with China are not very clear.[6]

Nepal has seen the collapse in governance due to the following indications over the years:-

(a) Maoists gaining ground steadily in the rural areas beyond the reach of the central administration.

(b) The policy of some external states of bolstering the monarchy has not paid as it has been considerably weakened over the months and years.

(c) Monarchy is digging its own grave so to say as it is preparing fall back plans to move out of the country including furnishing homes outside Nepal and assets to safer hides.

The population had been disillusioned with the democratic dispensations so far as they could not deliver. Monarchy's failure include:-

(a) Stifling harmless political dissent in the mainstream.

(b) Economic deterioration leading to disillusionment with the business and international community.

Political parties have also been wooed by Maoists who are calling for a republican democracy. The Army has an important role to play if the monarchy weakens or collapses and will decide the course adopted.[7] The three pointed power structure in Nepal, monarchy supported by the police and army machinery is in a limbo and the political parties are weak in structure as well as resolve. The Maoists are strongest on the ground representing a strength of approximately 10,000 to 15,000 with about 12,500 deaths since 1996, but have a philosophy of violence which is unacceptable to the World. The challenge is going to be how to get the Maoists give up the armed struggle and work towards a political solution with devolution of power by the monarchy.[8] Amongst the political parties, Citizens Movement for Democratic Peace wants republican democracy. Nepali Congress largest non left party also publicly renounced constitutional monarchy. Only few insignificant parties support Nepali monarchy. Demands of the political parties are that the dissolved 1999 parliament should be restored. Army should be brought under parliamentary control and Article 127 of the Constitution should be abrogated under which the King had acquired sweeping powers. The Army is likely to refuse to serve under parliamentary control. Option of the parliamentary parties and the Maoists joining together for a joint struggle to oust the king is the one likely to perhaps be the easiest to succeed with the least blood shed particularly if the King opts for an honourable exit.[9]

It is elitist cadre, the self obsessed Kathmandu privileged with proprietary interests who are unwilling to part even with the smallest privileges.[10]

The International Dimension

The US Ambassador to Nepal recently commented that parliamentary parties should cooperate with the monarchy to combat the Maoists. This remark appeared to be out of tune with the realities in Nepal due to the following reasons:-

(a) The hold of the Royal Nepal Army on the state apparatus is weak thereby there is no reasonable hope that it will be able to bring the insurgency under check even if supported by the parliamentary parties.

(b) Royal Nepal Army owes allegiance to the King and has remained more of a palace guard rather than a combating army.

(c) The terrain in Nepal is so difficult that even larger deployment of forces and professional armies as say the Indian will find the space to force ratio totally out of synch with their ability to conduct operations against the Maoists and win, the Royal Nepal Army lacks the strength as well as the will to fight such a hard battle which is likely to be protracted.

(d) The King holds only the towns and particularly Kathmandu and its surroundings, while the Maoists hold the villages and the country side.

China on the other hand is following a perilous course

with its own power calculus 18 trucks are reported to have been escorted by Royal Nepal Army via the Kodari Highway from China containing specific arms and ammunition though the Royal Nepal Army spokesperson refused to offer comments. Nepal army will continue to get arms and ammunition from friendly nations said acting spokesman of the Royal Nepalese Army Umesh Bhattarai. The spokesman also claimed that unilateral truce by the Maoists had not been peaceful, it had resulted in killing of 19 people, 4,013 abductions, 51 cases of loot, 14 reports of fighting, bombing and firing and 14 other cases registered and maintained that the strength of the Maoists had decreased due to actions by security forces.[11] Pakistan's interests in Nepal are primarily centred on it being an anti India play of limited significance. Thus if it meets its ends of creating additional hurdles for India, Pakistan will willingly support any party or move. The recent discussions between the Pakistani leadership and Nepali Army Chief, General Pyar Jung Thapa on provision of training assistance needs to be read against this backdrop.[12]

A UN delegation consisting of Special Advisor to the Secretary General Lakhdar Brahimi, senior political advisor to the Secretary General Tamrat Samuel and representative of UN High Commissioner of Human Rights, Ian Martin was in Delhi from 29 August to 1 September 2005. India has been consistently against UN mediation in Nepal. However it has indicated that it should put pressure on the monarch to be flexible in accepting ground realities, facilitate coordination between the anti monarchy forces and support human rights groups and issues. A working group comprising of US, UK, EU and the UN to evolve a policy to restore democracy and initiate a peace process has also been recommended.[13]

Nepal – Politics Beyond Emergency and Cease Fire

On 22 August 2005, the seven party political alliance decided to hold talks with the Maoists while on 29 August 2005 the Emergency imposed by the King on 1 February 2005 was lifted. Asian Centre of Human Rights has estimated that 665 persons were killed, 374 by security forces and the balance by Maoists between 30 April and 12 September.

Large scale abuse of human rights by security forces has also been reported in Nepal by groups such as HimRights, Lifeline, INSEC, CWN, CVICT, Advocacy Forum and Human Rights Monitoring Committee. Press Freedom in Nepal remains restricted. Maoists are also guilty of rights violation. The seven-party alliance includes the Nepali Congress (NC), Nepali Congress - Democratic (NC-D), Communist Party of Nepal - United Maoist Leninist (CPN-UML), Nepal Workers and Peasants Party, People's Front Nepal, Nepal Sadbhavana Party (Anandi) and United Left Front. Between them, these parties include an overwhelming proportion of the political mainstream, and leave out only the Rashtriya Prajatantra Party (RPP), a pro-Palace group, among the country's major political forces. These parties called for a cease fire and creation of a new political alliance in the country to restore peace.

On 3 September 2005, the Maoists in Nepal announced a cease fire for three months which was unilateral. They assured that they will not undertake any offensive activities but retain, "position of active defence and resist if there is any offensive from the side of the Government" Maoists also declared that they would have peace talks with the seven party opposition and not the monarchy. Analysts believe that this a period of military consolidation and recovery by the Maoists while simultaneously expanding the political space. An alliance between the opposition parties and the Maoists is apparently being forged at the cost of the monarchy. Maoists by declaring unilateral truce have demonstrated that they can dictate terms now and hold the initiative.[14] Indian delegation led by Sitaram Yechuri, CPI (M) politburo member visited Nepal from 28 September 2005 onwards and was asked to lend moral support and solidarity to the cause of democracy in Nepal.[15]

The contrary pulls and pressures between the political forces in Nepal appeared to be heading for a solution when the 'strongman' of Nepal politics and prominent leader of the seven-party alliance, Nepal Congress President Girija Prasad Koirala declared an 'open dialogue' with the Maoists to restore peace and to bring the rebels into political mainstream, 'irrespective of the consequences'. The very next day, Maoist 'chairman', Pushpa Kamal Dahal alias next day, Maoist 'chairman', Pushpa Kamal Dahal alias Prachanda, sent out a 'positive signal', stating, "Earlier, we were surprised at the way the political parties had been conspiring, directly or indirectly, with the despotic monarchy. Now, although late, the parties have given (their) commitment to a constituent assembly, absolute democracy and an end to the despotic monarchy." Subsequently, considering the "historic demand of the movement against authoritarianism as well as the request of the seven political parties", Prachanda issued strict directions to all organs of the party, the People's Liberation Army and the new 'People's Government', not to carry out physical attacks on unarmed persons 'even if they are criminals'. Responding to Koirala's statement, Prachanda expressed his readiness to collaborate with all political parties and called on them to constitute an official negotiating team in order to create a "massive people's pressure for a democratic way out". Ruling out the possibilities of resumption of peace talks with the Royal Government, the Maoist political wing leader and politburo member, Baburam Bhattarai, declared further that his party was "not attempting a final military victory right now, but is working for a negotiated political settlement either directly for a democratic republic or for the election to a Constituent Assembly." These announcements became stepping stones to an emerging alliance between the insurgents and the constitutional parties. On the other hand, the Chairman of RPP, Pashupati Shumshere Rana, had called on all democratic forces to evolve a 'national consensus' between political parties and the Monarchy, and urged the formation of an 'all-party government'.

Certain differences, however, do persist within the seven party alliance itself, regarding the approach to the Maoists. Even CPN-UML General Secretary, Madhav Kumar Nepal, urged caution, insisting on a peaceful movement for restoration of democracy during a meeting he stated, "Parties cannot trust them (the Maoists) as they have repeatedly committed mistakes regardless of their commitments expressed earlier." Another senior CPN-UML leader, Jhalnath Khanal added, "There exists (a) 'Pacific Ocean of distrust' between us. The Maoists need to walk

Clearly, the incipient alliance between the Maoists and the political parties is intended to isolate the Monarchy. This certainly weakens the King's present position. The political parties have already conceded the Maoist's major demands for a Constituent Assembly and creation of a Republic and abolition of the Monarchy as a centre of power in Nepal's political system. Analysts have long predicted that the longer King Gyanendra continues to hold on to absolute power, the more he will push the beleaguered political parties into a deal with the Maoists, and this appears to be what is happening now.

The response from the palace has been ominous, with Government spokesperson Tanka Dhakal describing the 'ongoing attempts for an alliance with a terrorist outfit' as 'unfortunate'. In a thinly veiled threat, he added, "If the parties join hands with the Maoists, the Government will be forced to see them from the same viewpoint."[16]

On 2 December 2005, Chairman of the Communist Party of Nepal (Maoist) Prachanda declared extension of the Cease fire for one month based on the demand by various forces within and outside the country as per an emailed statement. This is said to have increased the credibility of the Maoists in the eyes of the Nepali populace as well as the international community. This happened when King Gyanendra returned from a long trip to Bangladesh and Africa, which itself appears propitious for a king who is facing wide spread rebellion at home and approbation abroad. Perhaps Gyanendra was confident of his position at home secured mainly by the Nepali Army and the ruling feudal bureaucracy or did he have a tacit understanding with the political forces now aligned towards the Maoists or secret parleys with any of the parties involved. All these are surmises which should raise hopes of the King coming to grips with the realities of his land locked kingdom. International human rights groups have been propagating a mutual cease fire and steps towards lasting peace to bring to an end, "the grave human rights and international humanitarian law violations by both the Maoists as well as the State" as stated by Louise Arbour, the UN High Commissioner for International Human rights.

Commissioner for International Human rights.

12 Point Agreement Political Parties and Maoists of Nepal

The twelve point agreement between the political parties and the Maoists in Nepal after a month long protracted negotiations with the help of sources in India has heralded a new beginning for the hapless state of Nepal and gives fresh signs of hopes. The issues seem to have been watered down by all sides, with the Maoists now apparently not insisting on a republican state and perhaps accepting a titular monarchy. The main points of the agreement also includes acceptance of elections under an international organization including the United Nations. The full text of the agreement is as given below:–

1. Today, the main desire of most Nepalis is to have democracy, peace, prosperity, social upliftment and an independent and sovereign Nepal. Toward that end, we fully agree that the main obstacle is an autocratic monarchy. Without an end to the autocratic monarchy and establishment of complete democracy we are clear that there will be no peace, progress and prosperity in the country. Therefore, we have reached an agreement that all forces against autocratic monarchy will step up their movement to end the autocratic monarchy and establish complete democracy.

2. The agitating seven political parties are fully committed to the plan to reinstate parliament whose decision will lead to the formation of an all-party government, hold talks with the Maoists and go for an election to a constituent assembly. They identify this as the way to end the present conflict and restore sovereignty to the people. The Communist Party of Nepal (Maoist) has made the commitment to organise a national political convention of democratic forces. The meet should decide on the formation of an interim government and hold elections for a constituent assembly to achieve the agreed goal. The seven political parties and the CPN (Maoist) will engage in dialogue and explore a consensus on procedural matters. It has been agreed that People's power is the only alternative to meet the goals.

3. The country wants a positive solution and a

goals and an end to the armed conflict through the end of autocratic monarchy, elections for the constituent assembly and the establishment of absolute democracy. The CPN (Maoist) expresses its commitment to move ahead in a peaceful new political current through this process. There has been an understanding on keeping the Maoists' armed forces and the Royal Nepali Army under the supervision of the United Nations during the elections of the constituent assembly, conduct elections in free and fair manner, and accept the results of the elections-all these after an end of the autocratic monarchy. We also expect the involvement of reliable international interlocutors in our dialogue process.

4. The CPN (Maoist) makes public its commitment to clearly institutionalise the values of competitive multi-party system, civil and fundamental rights, human rights and the rule of the law.

5. The CPN (Maoist) has made the commitment to let the leaders, activists, and the people who were displaced during the armed conflict to be resettled in their homes. It has also committed that all land, houses and property seized unjustly will be returned. This will create an environment where people will be allowed to freely conduct their political activities.

6. Through self-criticism and self-evaluation of the past mistakes and shortcomings, the CPN (Maoist) is committed not to repeat those mistakes.

7. The seven political parties have realised they made mistakes when they were in parliament and in government and have committed that they will not repeat those mistakes.

8. Human rights and press freedom will be respected while moving the peace process ahead.

9. The talk of municipal elections and parliamentary polls is to trick the people and the international community and to legitimise the illegitimate and autocratic rule of the king. We will boycott these polls in our separate ways and urge the people to make such elections unsuccessful.

10. The people and their representative political parties are the real guards of nationalism. We are fully committed on the self-reliance, sovereignty, territorial integrity and national unity. It is our common duty to have friendly relations on the basis of the principle of peaceful co-existence with all the countries of the world, especially with our neighbours India and China. We urge all patriotic people to remain alert about Mandale nationalism that the king and the monarchists are preaching to the people. We also appeal to international powers to support the democratic movement against autocratic monarchy through all possible ways.

11. We urge civil society, professionals, people of all caste, communities and areas, the media, intellectuals and general Nepalis to actively participate in the people's movement that will be conducted on the basis of our agreement that has democracy, peace, prosperity, progressive social change, freedom, sovereignty and integrity of the country as the cornerstone.

12. Past misbehaviour of the parties will be investigated, and action taken against those found guilty and the findings made public. Any problems arising will be sorted out at the concerned level or through discussion at the leadership level. *(This is an unofficial translation of the original text in Nepalese provided by the The Pioneer.)*[17]

Analysts say that this dramatic turnaround has been due to the role played by India, the US and the UK the latter two in the background.[18] The UPA government is said to have hosted the meeting of the political parties and the Maoists in New Delhi in September followed by full fledged consultations in November 2005. Thus the proclamation by Comrade Prachanda, "__join pluralistic politics, allow unimpeded access to the heartland by the political parties, and seek UN involvement in overseeing the laying down of arms in the run-up to Constituent Assembly elections".[19] Indian efforts to coordinate diplomacy with other nations and successfully weave an agreement with both parties appear to have succeeded. However the move of Chinese weapons and equipment worth about 18 trucks is a matter of great concern.

The stoning of Crown prince's convoy on 2 December 2005 could be an indication of the people's mood on the street against monarchy but transforming it into a change in the affairs of the state necessitates a series of measures over a sustained period for which commitment of all constituents, the King, the political parties and the Maoists is essential. The signals coming from the establishment however are mixed. In a recent press conference the vice Chairman of the council of ministers, Mr Tulsi Giri categorically denied any intention by the government to come to an understanding with the political parties and the Maoists and out rightly rejected cease fire by the Maoists. He proclaimed instead elections to the municipal bodies and the parliament, a proposal which has been rejected by the political parties.[20] The pressure on the Nepali army is clearly shown by the nature of fratricide undertaken by a Nepali soldier who killed eleven devotees and injured nineteen at the Kali temple in the Nagarkot tourist resort after arguments with the local villagers in mid December 2005. Sage diplomacy and innovative acceptance of the new power equation within the state by the monarchy will alone provide the answer to the situation of flux in Nepal in 2006.

Measures to Check Movement on the Indo-Nepal Border

India has undertaken pragmatic measures to implement its plan of integrated check posts for recording movement of people across the Indo-Nepal border to include, customs, immigration and security forces on the spot. The aim is to keep a tab on illegal movement between India and Nepal but not all border movement. Nepal is also likely to introduce such a system. Special passes will be introduced for regular people and traders to avoid inconvenience and regular registration. On reaching the check posts, the travelers will have to register their name and address. Check posts were established at Rupaidiha in Bahraich District and Sunauli in Maharajganj distircit on 1 November 2005. 6 acres of land has been acquired in Rupaidiha.

20 percent money has been made available by Central government to the state.[21] The open Indo-Nepal border agreement was modified to introduce checks on immigration between the citizens of the two nations as a pilot project in Rupaidiha in Bahraich

District of Uttar Pradesh on 1 November 2005, ironically Deepawali Day, the most auspicious for citizens of both India and Nepal. The pilot project required cross border movement to be carried out after checking and recording of identity documents. Anurag Shrivastava, then District Magistrate of Bahraich and Superintendent of Police, R P Singh were present on the Indian side, while on the Nepali side, District Magistrate and Superintendent of Police of Banke District were present. The occasion saw lot of curious citizens reacting differently. Rupaidiha has been the transit trade point for many years and traders were the most affected. This had far reaching effect in areas of Gorakhpur District as well as, Sonauli, Ganeshpur, Barhni and Khuniyaon. The proposal seems to have political support as Yogi Adityanath, the Member of Parliament from Gorakhpur, said that this was a necessity keeping in view the ultra sensitivity of the borders between the two countries.

This process is nothing new but integration of check posts has been carried out now. All agencies were in different locations in Rupaidiha earlier. This should also be carried out in other check posts and will achieve better coordination. Since Indo-Nepal is an open border with large number of routes only vehicle bound traffic will be checked. These measures will only restrict movement on the main roads connecting the two countries; large scale movement takes place across the narrow tracks which crisscross the border at a number of places. This will carry on unrestricted. Large scale movement of material such as explosives and arms can also take place across the uncharted border in tractors to be transported later in trucks.[22] Slow process of land acquisition for central forces on the ground due to apathy of district administration further mars the process.

The Road Ahead

Political analysts as Dr Thomas Marks believe that the Maoists may be in the strategic phase of moving their revolution from the gun to the ballot which may result in the 'dictatorship of the proletariat'. The role of India will always be viewed with suspicion keeping in view skepticism of the so called, 'Sikkim solution'. The allusion by Mr Tulsi from India as interference in the sovereign rights of Nepal further substantiates this sentiment.[23] While local and general elections, the former being scheduled for 8 February 2006, could lead to democracy towards which all parties are inching at, its actual conduct as per Marks will be a difficult process given the lack of security which has raised the threats of resumption of violence at the end of the proposed cease fire.[24] The Maoists have raised a call for banning the elections and have said that they will ensure that these are thwarted. The Maoists have also threatened poll candidates with, "special physical actions" which spells a pall of gloom for the hapless people of Nepal. The signs at the end of the year, 2005 are thus not encouraging.

The creation of a common document of understanding and discussion between various parties in a negotiation is a first step. The 12 Point Charter evolved is a step in this direction but would involve many more concomitant measures to achieve lasting peace. A benign power structure in Nepal would imply that the King sees sense and offers concessions. Political parties build both policies and public support. Maoists deliver on their promise to return to mainstream policies. It could be an all party interim government backed by a, "democratically accountable military" as this would provide political leadership the muscle while the military will be provided political guidance without which it is likely to be a law unto itself. If the monarchy is forced to abdicate power this will create a power vacuum in Nepal's internal as well as external governance as the civil and military bureaucracy controls the state's structures which will collapse as these have always owed their allegiance to the monarchy and will not be able to adjust or provide centrality of power from any other authority. A better alternative is abdication of the absolute monarchy by the king and acceptance of a constitutional role. The King of Bhutan has provided an enlightened model of a monarch abdicating his throne in favour of his son in 2008 and holding the first national elections for parliamentary democracy under the new king in 2008.[25] The political parties lack the strength in numbers as well as good will amongst the people to run the government if they usurp power. They will need to run the government if they usurp power. They will need the support of the civil and military bureaucracy of which there is likely to be a possibility as they do have links with them. The Maoist victory will be facile as they lack the networking and the administrative ability to run a modern government. However they have the power of the barrel of the gun which has permeated to a large number of districts and the country side. A quiet recognition seems to have taken place amongst the palace coterie on the inevitability of devolution of powers of the throne, it is how this is translated into reality on the ground hopefully bloodlessly is the challenge. Though publicly it seems to be in a denial mode saying that the Maoists are militarily defeated.[26] The proposal to hold municipal and parliament elections in 2006 should provide indications of the path ahead. These elections have been designed by the monarchy as a demonstration of its sincerity towards evolving of a democratic structure. If there is a positive response of the political parties and the Maoists to these elections, a reconciliation within the present dispensation will be possible, If the elections are aborted, Nepal could well lead itself to mayhem and anarchy as the government is unlikely to be able to impose itself in successful conduct of such elections in areas other than Kathmandu and its surroundings. The alternative is return to a bloody civil war which is unwinnable for both the parties, the Maoists and the Royalists. This alone may not be enough to run a modern state. India has played its cards very well. It has links with all the three points of the star either overtly or covertly. It has garnered international support for its policy of peace through political restructuring and international mediation. How it succeeds to leverage this relationship to create an effective governance structure in Nepal to avoid the state falling to the wolves and veer the state towards a constitutional democracy is the challenge to the Indian leadership, political, bureaucratic, particularly the external affairs staff, intelligence and the civil society which has very deep links in Nepal. In 2006, it is expected that a consolidation of the forces of peace will occur to demonstrate the path to a more lasting arrangement which may come about many years ahead dependent on the progress made

India will undoubtedly benefit immensely from a resolution of the Nepal conflict in many ways; it will spell the end of Maoist insurgency in Nepal and in turn send the right signals to Naxalites at home. India's century's long traditional relationship with Nepal based on free people to people contacts with benefits for both nations will be restored. Economically the region has tremendous potential for providing power to India's most industrially under developed region, the Northern Gangetic plain. Nepal has some 43,000 MW of hydro power which can be shared with India in the following projects under consideration, West Seti Hydro Project, Upper Karnali, Pancheshwar, Sapta Kosi, Sun Kosi. Burhi Gandaki, Kamla Multipurpose and Bagmati. [27] India thus will never compromise its security concerns on Nepal.

References

1. The Economic Times Editorial. "Let the—" The Economic Times. 29 November 2005. New Delhi. p. 6.
2. Indian Express Report. "India worried—". The Indian Express. 20 December 2005. Lucknow. p. 5.
3. Datta Ray, Sunanda K. "Don't Ditch This Man" The Times of India. 27 September 2005. Lucknow. p. 4.
4. Mehta, Ashok K. "The King of Hard Times." The Pioneer. 14 December 2005. Lucknow. p. 6.
5. Mehta, Ashok K. "The King of Hard Times." The Pioneer. 14 December 2005. Lucknow. p. 6.
6. The Pioneer Report. The Pioneer. 14 December 2005. Lucknow. p. 8.
7. Chalmers, Rhoderick. "Nepal on the Brink." The Indian Express. 12 October 2005. Lucknow. p. 8.
8. Mitra, Chandan. Dangerous Liaisons, perilous drift. Sunday Pioneer. 18 September 2005. Lucknow. p. 12.
9. Roka, Hari. "Glimmer of Hope" The Times of India. 11 November 2005. Lucknow. p. 5.
10. Roka, Hari. "He'll Have to go" The Times of India. 26September 2005. Lucknow. p. 5
11. Report Sunday Indian Express. 27 November 2005. Lucknow. p. 5.
12. Indian Express Report. "India worried over China—". The Indian Express. 20 December 2005. Lucknow. p. 5.
13. Chakma, Suhas. "Breaking the logjam in Nepal" The Pioneer. 23 September 2005. Lucknow. p. 7.

14. Sahni, Ajay. The Pioneer. 24 September 2005. Lucknow. p. 6.
15. Ghimire, Yubraj. "Indian—" Indian Express 01 October 2005. Lucknow. p. 7.
16. P.G. Rajamohan. "The Stalemate that Isn't". Down loaded from South Asia Intelligence Review. September 2005.
17. Downloaded from Daily Pioneer.com. 30 November 2005.
18. Bose, Ajoy. "Red-letter day—". The Pioneer. 28 November 2005. Lucknow. p. 7.
19. Gupta, Kanchan. "UPA—" The Pioneer. 20 November 2005. Lucknow. p. 1.
20. Ghimire, Yubraj. "Nepal—". The Indian Express. 21 December 2005. Lucknow. p. 7.
22. Times of India Report. "People's Movement—" Times of India. 8 October 2005. Lucknow. p. 5.
22. Hindi Hindustan. 2 November 2005. Lucknow. pp.1, 11,15.
23. Ghimire, Yubraj. "Nepal—". The Indian Express. 21 December 2005. Lucknow. p. 7.
24. Marks, Thomas A. "Between Illusion and Reality". South Asian Intelligence Review. Weekly Assessments and Briefings Volume 4, No. 21, December 5, 2005 Downloaded from the internet 10 December 2005.
25. Hussain, Syed Zarir. "Bhutan King—". The Pioneer. 19 December 2005. Lucknow. p. 5.
26. Acharya, Yuvraj. Times of India. 21 December 2005. Lucknow. p. 9.
27. Gupta, Supriyo. "Alienating the King—". The Pioneer. 25 November 2005. Lucknow. p. 7.

7

Bangladesh-2006 A Year of Concern

"A deep pocket filled by oil rich hands, virtually unrelenting access to arms, an insidious nexus with mainstream political parties and the government's blind eye to them—— the deadly concoction that has made it possible for the religious terrorist groups to thrive in Bangladesh."[1]

Zayadul Hasan

Bangladesh the Year Ahead

The well entrenched Islamic groups led by Jamaat-e-Islami in the government of Khaleda Zia have made it virtually impossible for the security forces in the state to come down heavily on the terrorists who have been on a rampage since August 2005. The likes of Jamaat-ul-Mujaheedin, Jagrata Muslim Janata Bangladesh and Harkat-ul-Jihad are actively undermining governance in the state.[2] These modern day anarchists, who have no inclination to abide by the rule of law, have ensured that it is they who dictate agenda to the government, a program which is increasingly medieval and anti modern. The armed forces in Bangladesh are also assuming a degree of influence, witness the efforts to acquire fighter aircraft for the Bangla air force which was rightly questioned by the Indian Air Chief, Air Chief Marshal Tyagi as Bangladesh does not face any external threat. Perhaps Tyagi missed the point that such acquisitions are made to demonstrate power at home rather than abroad. In case the Armed forces align with the Islamists, the fate of Bangladesh will be no less than that of Afghanistan, a fear which has been expressed by many analysts such as Hiranmay Karlekar. A coalition of the power dyad, Begum Khaleda Zia and Sheikh Hasina appears the best solution for political stability in Bangladesh which will provide the government the will to break the back of a militancy which is slowly moving from the covert to the active phase with dangerous portends. However if Sheikh Hasina chooses to play politics, the state may well fall into the hands of the Army or even worse into anarchy.

Bangladesh thus faces internal turmoil in the year ahead led by the Islamic militants who are seeking rule by the Shariah. The spate of suicide bombers are thus likely to be increased, in 2005 these were only a handful. The nation is likely to face greater problems in checking this threat as it is ill prepared to combat it from the security as well as the political point of view. Politically the ruling establishment is dependent on the Islamic parties for its survival, while the security establishment has been soft pedaling the militancy over the years and lacks the strength, the will as well as the intelligence to check the growth of suicide bombers and other terrorists. Lack of governance is another area of concern. For India, cross border movement of people will be the key issue as this will result in turmoil in the North Eastern States as well as in West Bengal expected to go for elections along with Assam.

India should use its goodwill to foster an understanding between the two iron ladies of Bangladesh just as it is attempting reconciliation in Nepal. This will ensure that the hapless people of Bangladesh are provided some dignity in their lives. Let us hope that the Bengali intellectual analyst prevents a situation which will turn our Eastern states into a security nightmare. In case this does not happen, the Indian state will face a wide spread anarchical situation from Eastern Uttar Pradesh, Bihar and West Bengal to the North East all in turmoil fed by Bangladesh at the base.

Main Security Issues

Population Implosion. This implies large scale movement of people due to teeming population density of the country and a retreating land mass due to rise in sea levels and submergence of coast line and littoral islands. The populace lacking adequate means of subsistence is perforce flowing towards the unguarded borders with India, through West Bengal, Meghalaya, Assam and Tripura settling in the North East as well as flowing into the more prosperous, "metromerates" of Mumbai, Delhi and Kolkota. The attendant social and communal problems created by this population particularly in the North Eastern states will have to be addressed in the long term but even now its immediate impact is evident in many forms. The propensity of the politicians in Assam to allow in settlers as a source of vote banks is another contributor to the continued influx of Bangla population into this state with a large land mass and relatively sparse population. Over the years, some of the Bangla leaders have even considered it their right to settle in Assam. Some sources indicate that some elements of the Bangla state are in collusion with the inductees who flee to India with the support of the personnel of the Bangladesh Rifles, though these claims have never been substantiated.

Rise of Islamic Fundamentalism. The coalition of Begum Khaleda Zia's Bangladesh Nationalist Party with Jammat-e-Islami has led to the transformation of a secular country in the vision of its founder, Sheikh Mujib to an Islamic one. The rise of Wahabbism is a cause of concern particularly its more virulent form. After having targeted the opposition it is said that these forces are now literally, "gunning" for judges and advocates practicing modern law with the aim of imposing Islamic Sharia'h based on Quranic injunctions. An indication being explosion in a court in October 2005 and killing of two judges a month later in November.[3] The ruling junta has remained a mute spectator to these incidents thereby further emboldening terrorists. Thus the twin factors of a coalition of convenience between the ruling party and the Islamists and the growth of fundamentalism is a cause of concern.

Support to Indian Militants. Indian rancour at its Eastern neighbour is also due to the support it has been providing in terms of sanctuaries to the militants from the North East. Recent reports indicate that even Naxalites have held a three-day meeting in the Rajshahi division to discuss planning for the 2005 annual conference of the Coordination Committee of Maoist Parties and Organizations in South Asia (CCOMPOSA) to be held in Bangladesh. This meeting was reportedly planned near the border with India some times in December 2005.[4] Apart from this large sanctuaries are also provided to Indian militants in the Chittagong Hill Tract as well as in hotels in various towns of the country.

Antagonism against India. Adhikar, a Non Governmental Organization is reportedly propped by Bangladeshi intelligence agency to spread malicious propaganda against India and particularly the Border Security Force. Adhikar was the first to allege that India was behind the blasts in the country. Bangladesh has also alleged that it is a victim of terrorism by India and not its creator. Adhikar has also spread the canard that there is reverse infiltration from India to Bangladesh as its economy is in better shape than India's.[5] Such issues lead to avoidable acrimony especially since the Indian government is extremely vulnerable to public opinion and there are many shades of the same when these involve such a complex issue as cross border activities with our Eastern neighbour sharing its borders with a very vulnerable West Bengal, Assam and other North Eastern states.

Bangladesh Internal Polity as it Affects Indian Security

Animus between the Bangladesh Nationalist Party leader and the present prime minister, Mr Khaleda Zia and the Awami League leader, Sheikh Hasina Wajed has created political opportunity for the right wing Jamaat-e-Islami and the radical Oikya Jote to flourish. Bangla leader's denial of existence of Islamic fundamentalism has been a cause for its growth, leading to virtual Talibinisation of the society. Some indications were –

(a) Islamic fundamentalist parties and madarsas funded by Arab money flourishing in the country.

(b) Training camps where Pakistani and Bangladeshi ex servicemen are preparing terrorist cadres for service in Myanmar and South East Asia. Support and sanctuary agreements for Indian insurgent groups in the state.

(c) Open statements of Talibanisation of society.

(d) More than 1000 blasts in the country since 1999, politicians, journalists, teachers, professors and intellectuals are the targets. British High Commissioner of Bangladeshi origin was also targeted.

The route of Bangladesh to Islamic fundamentalism is denoted by the following steps –

(a) Sheikh Mujibur Rehman, the father of the nation believed in secularism but he had to succumb to the reality of Islamic symbolism and adopted the salutation, "Khuda Hafiz" instead of Joy Bangla. This indicates a marked shift to create an Islamic identity rather than a Bangla one.

(b) Zia-ur-Rehman and Ershad who followed were out and out Islamists who dropped the word secularism from the constitution and adopted Islam as the state religion respectively. This can be seen as a period of twenty years of Islamisation. Bangladeshi residents were reported to be fighting in Afghan jehad and are known to be inmates at Camp X-Ray in Guantanamo.

(c) Cultural policing by fundamentalists denoted by ban on cinema houses, music, and circuses, while compulsary beards and burqas for men and women respectively.

(d) 30 religious militant organisations have set up a country wide network with the aim of creating a jihadi state based on violence by trained cadres from Afghan, Lebanon and Palestine theatres. Demilitarisation of violence in some states as Palestine and Afghanistan may not necessarily mean good for others as there is migration of criminals and militants to states as Bangladesh where insurgency may be in a nascent state.

(e) Training in Chittagong Hill Tracts, districts of Naogaon, Rajshahi, Khustia, Bogra and Pabna bordering West Bengal are said to be favourite areas.

(f) Jagrata Muslim Janata Bangladesh is said to be the main organization in these areas with 30,000 activists while Jamaat-ul-Mujaheedin boasts of 10,000 full time and 100,000 part time workers.

(g) Chittagong districts include Rangamati, Cox's Bazaar, Bandarban and Khagrachari bordering Mizoram, Tripura and Myanmar in which main activists are Harkat-ul-Jehad Islami, a close associate of Pakistani HUJI and the Osama inspired International Islamic Front. It has 25,000 trained activists.

(h) Several NGOs received funds from Kuwait, United Arab Emirates, Saudi and Pakistani sources for opening mosques, schools, madarsas and hospitals diverted towards militancy. Earnings of these NGOs is Rs. 1200 Crore taka annually.

(i) Slogan by Al Qaeda and Taliban – "Amra sobai hobo Taliban. Bangla hobe Afghanistan" We will become Taliban and Bangla will become Afghanistan.

Corruption, radicalism, partisan fighting, rivalry between two principal political parties, poverty, lack of good governance has resulted in radicalization of society. The coalition partners of the ruling Bangladesh Nationalist Party (BNP), the Harkat-ul-Jihad-al Islam (HUJI) is said to be having ties with Al Qaeda, while Oikya Jote founded by Fazlur Rehman is said to be an associate of Osama Bin Laden. He is said to have signed the fatwa by Al Qaeda in 1998, dictated by Osama bin Laden which declared American civilians as legitimate targets. On the other hand Jamaat-e-Islami(JI) is said to be having ties with Siddiqui Islam or Bangla Bhai who has fought in Afghanistan and wants Taliban style government in border areas. Jemaah Islamiya (JI) Leader Hambali arrested in Thailand in August 2003 decided to shift JI elements to Bangladesh to save its personnel from counter terrorist activities in South East Asia.[6] The JI is banned by Bangladesh government.

The HUJI for instance is said to have members estimated from a few thousand to 15000. Madarsas are the main recruiting ground for terrorists as elsewhere. The links of terrorists from Bangladesh with global terrorism is evident with 16 Bangladeshis on 4 December 2003 apprehended in Bolivia planning hijack of plane to attack USA but were later released due to lack of evidence. 11 Bangladeshis were arrested on 14 August 2003 on suspicions of a terrorist act.

In the Chittagong Hill Tracts (CHT) adjoining India's North East, a large number of madarsas have come up with several terrorist camps of the HUJI. HUJI has also been active in Cox's Bazaar on the border with Burma. The Al Qaeda is reportedly recruiting Burmese Rohingya Muslims from refugee camps in south eastern Bangladesh to fight in Afghanistan, Kashmir and Chechnya. 150 Taliban and Al Qaeda were reported as early as in December 2001 aboard MV Mecca moving from Karachi to Chittagong.

The Rohingyas are a community which is easy to penetrate by any foreign intelligence agency. Rohingya Solidarity Organisation (RSO) is the largest organization representing over 120,000 Rohingyas in Bangladesh. These speak the same language as CHT Bangla residents and are said to be fertile for recruitment when under pressure from Myanmar. The United Nations High Commissioner for Refugees (UNHCR) had given them refugee status and these stayed in shelters in Teknaf, Ukhiya, and Naikhongchhari. A large number of these refugees were repatriated to Myanmar but Bangladeshi sources claim more than 27,000 illegal Rohingyas still live in the Bandarban district with risk of their involvement in crime and eventually terrorism.[7] Security analysts are also concerned about radicalization of the border district of Bandarban which due to its mountainous terrain with deep forests is ideal as a base for the marginal militant groups both from Bangladesh as well as Myanmar such as the Arakans. It also forms a convenient route of entry and exit for the Islamists. Myanmar is also a haven for gun-runners and the explosives and ammunition seized from Naikhongchhari are said to be similar to the explosives used in the August 17 and October 3, 2005 serial blasts. Poppy cultivation provides a narco terror dimension to the districts. Bangladesh's Army is reported to be destroying the poppy crop every year but is not said to be very effective in eliminating the same.[8]

Government policy is of appeasement and denial, thus Khaleda Zia announced on 1 July 2003 that no Al Qaeda terrorist was present in Bangladesh.[9] The Bangla leadership perhaps appears to be striving for a pan Islamic rather than a pan Bangla identity which has its roots in West Bengal. Islam provides it an alternative character. Even Pakistan has been going through this identity crisis. It wants to shake itself away from the Indic image but cannot fit into the traditional Islamic image giving up centuries of geographic and ethnic rooting with the Indic civilization particularly when it is the geographic epicenter of the Harappan civilization. Much as Pakistan tries to align itself with the Islamic states of the Gulf, the geographical separation of Central Asia and proximity to India denies it this facility. Bangladesh is also attempting to embrace a far more virulent form of fundamentalist Islam. In the case of Pakistan as well Bangladesh geographic, linguistic and ethnic similarities with the Indian sub continent cannot be wished away. The waters to these countries also emanates from India which is the harsh reality. It is when these nations reconcile to the reality of a Pan South Asian (nee Pan Indic civilisational) identity that perhaps lasting peace will emerge in the Sub Continent after decades of turmoil. The solution in the long term is Indian ability to persuade these states including its own marginal communities to identify with the Indic civilization and accept a South Asian identity without being a threat to their own individual character.

The Bangla Blasts – Manifestation of Terror

On 17 August, Bangladesh was rudely shocked by a series of blasts. The bombs were reportedly small IEDs, low on explosives, bombs made in the basement with four batteries and a switch attached by a tape. A switch activated the device which allowed escape by the individual planting it. The bombs contained saw dust with no splinters thus casualties were limited to two dead and 150 hospitalised though many exploded in crowded places. These blasts are likely to have been carried out by the activists of Jama'atul Mujahideen Bangladesh (JMB) and Jagrata Muslim Janata Bangladesh (JMJB) headed by Maulana Siddiquir Rahman alias Bangla Bhai. Bangladesh Home Minister Lutfuzzaman Babar alleged that the blasts were master minded by Bangla Bhai and Rapid Action Battalion (RAB) was entrusted the task of investigating these. It arrested younger brother of Bangla Bhai, Maulana Obadur Rahman Fazle from Jamalpur

District. Another report states that Industries Minister Matiur Rahman Nizami also Emir of the Jamaat-e-Islami of Bangladesh had plotted the blasts. Blasts were to demonstrate the third call for establishing of Islamic rule in the country. But some sources in the Government claimed that Bangla Bhai is a media creation.[10] These explosions did not cause major casualties but were an indication of how worse things had become, the direction in which the country was going and the ground support that fundamentalism had received. The extent of the planning, build up and support both in terms of money and movement of the explosives all over the country and the perfect timing achieved demonstrated effective organization.

In the series of blasts 9 people were killed and 66 injured when bombs went off in Chittagong and Gazipur near Dacca. One suicide bomber and two policemen were killed in bomb attack at Chittagong. The target of the bombers was possibly courts. Jumatul Mujahideen Bangladesh reportedly is behind the blast as its leaflets were found near these sites. The group plans to set up Islamic rule in Bangladesh.[11] A third blast by suicide bombers was carried out on 8 December 2005, in Netrokona, 360 km north of Dhaka, killing eight and wounding 50.[12]

Acceptance of conflagration of terrorist threat to Bangladesh by the government is indicative by the reports that a new law to empower the central bank to suspend and stop operations of any account for 30 days when any suspicious transaction is noticed has been proposed. A seven year jail term is being provisioned in this law for money laundering. A Financial Intelligence Unit and a Financial Crime Investigation and Prosecution office are also being set up under the same law. This should pose problems for the large number of Islamic organizations based in the Middle East to fund the terrorist organizations in Bangladesh.[13] However the proof of the pudding is in the eating and hence effective implementation is as important as the proposed legal provisions. Let us hope that these add teeth to the government's efforts of clamping down on terrorism.

Indo – Bangla Border Issues

Indo-Bangla border is a virtual maze of riverine terrain, enclaves and adverse possessions by both sides. India shares 4,095 km border with Bangladesh with more than half across the North Eastern states. 60 percent of the border remains unfenced with concrete pillars. There are 181 border posts along the Indo Bangla border with the North Eastern states where Border Security Force (BSF) troops are deployed in strength. Tripura's 865 km land border is also being patrolled jointly.[14] Trafficking of people has rendered these areas vulnerable to clash between the forces deployed to prevent movement of people and goods across the unfenced areas. Director General level talks held between BSF and Bangladesh Rifles commenced on 28 September 2005 to resolve the numerous acrimonious issues arising out of the imperfections of the Indo Bangla border. The main concerns were construction of border fencing and support to terror infrastructure by the Bangladesh Rifles. BSF handed over a list of suspected terrorist camps and killing of BSF officer Jeewan Kumar, extending of joint patrolling in 212 patches where Indian villages stretch up to the international boundary, unprovoked firing and awards of the Border River Commission.

Bangladesh officials argued that constructing the fence within 150 m of the zero line violates the 1975 informal agreement, which stipulates that no barricade can be set up by either country in close proximity of the border. The BSF sources stated that fence is not a defensive mechanism.[15] Major General Mohammad Jahangir Alam Chowdhury, the chief of the Bangladesh Rifles while addressing a joint press conference on 30 September alleged that the August 17 serial blasts that rocked 64 districts in Bangladesh were the handiwork of Indian agents and criminals. He also charged India with harbouring 700 criminals wanted in Bangladesh of which 200 were Indian officials. The officer also denied that more than 172 terrorist camps were there in Bangladesh and stated that not a single insurgent group was located there and denied that BSF officer Jiwan Kumar had been killed by BDR as alleged by Indian side. BSF Chief R S Moosahary brought out that the officer had been shot in the back and was in his shorts and unarmed. Indian intelligence agencies allege that Bangladesh has been harbouring a host of leaders such as Paresh Barua and Arvind Rajkhowa of ULFA, Ranjan Daimari of National Democratic Front of Bodoland (NDFB), Jeevan Singha of Kamtapuri Liberation Organization (KLO), Nayanbashi Jamatia and Biswa Mohan Debbarma of National Liberation Front and Ranjit Debbarma of All Tripura Tiger Force.[16]

The tensions between the two forces on the border continued as two Bangladesh Rifles (BDR) personnel are reported to have entered Bhimpur, 75 metres from the Indo-Bangla border on 15 October 2005 and raided a house of a villager Samsul Islam Mandal which stands in an isolated spot on the plea that his sister had crossed over to Bangladesh. During the scuffle, Mandal is reported to have snatched a BDR personnel's rifle. BDR personnel then returned with reinforcements and took away the snatched rifle. BSF posted at Bhaigarh post one km from Bhimpur rushed to the spot but by then the BDR personnel had returned back.[17] This demonstrates the type of activities that are regular occurrence on the border increasing the level of tension.

It is also reported that Inter Services Intelligence (ISI) of Pakistan along with certain powerful elements of the Bangladesh Nationalist Party and Bangladesh Rifles have propped up an international arms smuggling network to provide sophisticated arms to ULFA, PLA and ATTF all groups in the North East as well as terrorist groups in Kashmir and Maoists both in India and Nepal. Bandarbund, Khgarachari and Rangamati districts of Chittagong hills are used extensively for arms smuggling. Some intercepts have revealed:-

(a) In village Tajerpura over two lakh bullets and 200 kg of RDX were seized by the Bangladesh police.

(b) Near Chittagong, 1290 SMGs, AK 47 rifles, 100 Tommie guns, 400 Uzi guns, 150 Rocket Launchers, 2000 Grenade Launchers, 840 rockets, 25,000 hand grenades, 6932 magazines and 18.4 lakh bullets were seized as per an intercept. Part of the consignment belonged to ULFA, PLA, ATTF.

(c) SMGs are favourite weapon of the ULFA.

(d) Seizure made under international and US pressure after incontrovertible proof provided by India.

(e) These arms were reportedly smuggled in two ships from a post in Hongkong and were off loaded in two boats for ferrying to a designated spot in 12 trucks at the Chittagong Urea Fertilizer Ltd (CUFL) in two huge trawlers.

(f) ULFA chief Paresh Barua and commanders of NSCN (IM) reportedly present at the time of loading.

(g) Only 10 of the 12 trucks are reported to have been caught. 2 trucks were driven off by the ULFA and NSCN.

(h) Two boats ferrying the weapons are reportedly owned by brother of Salahuddin Qadir Chowdhury, the political advisor to the Prime Minister of Bangladesh, Begum Khaleda Zia. Cover up reportedly launched after this was discovered presumably on instructions from higher quarters.

(i) Initially 43 persons were held for investigations, 33 were accused but 23 let off including three of the four main accused terrorists.

(j) Khulna, Sylhet and Jessore are other districts which are hotbeds of religious terrorism.[18]

The blasts in Bangladesh from August onwards has led to heightened security on the Indo Bangla border especially after likelihood of the dreaded Bangla Bhai crossing over to the Indian side with a drive launched to apprehend terrorists. Malda, Murshidabad and Nadia are said to be active sites astride the Indo Bangla border and are hence under surveillance by the West Bengal police. The terrorists deftly shifted to the relatively quieter district, Birbhum as a safe corridor for transit. A conclave of Student's Islamic Organisation was held in a college near Malda attended by 10,000 SIO members. Efforts to raise the communal temperature have also been reported by the Intelligence Bureau.[19]

Security on the Wire - Indo-Bangla Border Fencing

Security is best ensured on the front line. Permitting infiltrators to pour inwards allows them the freedom to transit in wider areas mingling with multitudes. Fencing is considered a good defensive mechanism to prevent infiltration from Bangladesh. Government had decided that fence should be erected 150 yards or 135 metres from the International Border (IB) between India and Bangladesh along certain stretches. 4096 km of the border with 3286 km to be fenced by March 2006 and 1948 km already fenced can be effectively regulated. The remaining border is said to be unfencable due to riverine terrain and forests.[20] Delays in construction of the fence have been attributed to a multiplicity of factors: -

(a) Resistance from Bangladesh.

(b) Delays in land acquisition. For instance in West Bengal in the nine border districts the state government authorities are reported to have provided only 8 km of land at or more than 150 yards from IB. Land acquisition of 65 kms in North 24 Pargana, Nadia, Murshidabad, Malda, Dakshin Dinajpur, Uttar Dinajpur, Darjeeling, Jalpaiguri, and Coochbehar is still pending.

(c) In West Bengal over 463 km long border area is yet to be fenced though a total 108.3 km falls under difficult and riverine terrain which cannot be fenced.

Joint India-Bangladesh Guidelines for Border Authorities 1975 is the protocol which indicates the actions to be taken by border forces. Bangladesh is representing against Indian edifice of the fence based on para 8 (e) which prevents construction of any structure having defence potential. Thus unprovoked firing to prevent fencing work is also undertaken from time to time.[21]

The Border fencing was also said to be affected by flooding with approximately 365 kms of the 854 kms of fencing erected during Phase 1 damaged and resistance from the Bangladesh Rifles led to difficulty in checking infiltration by the floating posts of the Indian BSF. Additional posts, surveillance by boats on foot and vehicles including perhaps bicycles is essential during such circumstances. In a reply in the Rajya Sabha, Mr S Reghupathy, Minister of State for Home affairs said that the government has also sanctioned 3656 posts in various ranks for the Prevention of Infiltration of Foreigners and Mobile Task Force specifically designed for checking infiltration.[22] Phase II of the project of 65 kms in West Bengal's nine districts is being planned but is held up for want of provision of land by the West Bengal Government as indicated earlier despite reports of maximum infiltration from this area.[23]

There is a need to ensure that sufficient funds and engineering effort is made available after every monsoon for repairs which would be inevitable. The Army is understood to have such measures in place for repairs of the fencing in Kashmir after snow fall in winter. Approximately 25 % of the budget can be kept aside for this purpose. This apart contractors need to be available to execute the work alternatively army engineers can be commissioned for this task as this is a matter of national concern. The land transfer issue needs serious consideration at district level and should be made time bound. Land is not only required for fencing but also for establishment of posts, this is frequently delayed resulting in lack of proper facilities for troops to man the posts as well as live in reasonable comfort under inhospitable circumstances.

Seeking Peace in 2006

Bangladesh is turning out as a long term thorn in the Indian East with an inimical political party and leadership at the helm, rising Islamic fundamentalism, poor governance, failing law and order and lack of international values in the regime. Some of the issues which need to be considered for resolution of antagonism and peace within and with India are as per succeeding paragraphs.

Political Reconciliation – Main Parties. The main parties, BNP and Awami League should reconcile their differences and provide a combined political resistance to the fundamentalist elements in the state. While it may be difficult for the ruling BNP to dissociate itself immediately and openly from the Jamaat, it has to dissociate itself from the strident elements as the HUJI and the Jama'atul Mujahideen Bangladesh (JMB) and Jagrata Muslim Janata Bangladesh (JMJB) with which people continue to associate it.

Diplomatic Firmness in Dealing with the BNP Regime. Indian government's relationship with the current regime in Bangladesh is limited to exchange of occasional pleasantries interspersed by vitriolic conversations of the kind witnessed during the Inter border DGs meet held in September 2005. The diplomatic impasse with Bangladesh would have to be disentangled with great tact yet firmness of resolve against what is soon emerging as a threat in the East.

International Pressure for Political Reconciliation. International pressure from the United States and the European Union has to be brought upon the regime for a political reconciliation and joint political action by both the main political parties and suturing the political parties from the Islamic fundamentalists. This can be linked politically as well as economically with aid for the teeming millions of the state.

Network with South East Asian States. We also need to build networks with the South East Asian states for combating terror. This will also have salutary effect to check the crime and drug syndicates which are operating from these areas with impunity. Thus multi beneficial associations will facilitate destruction of the terror networks in the North East.

Economic Support. The regime in Bangladesh needs to be supported effectively in pecuniary terms through aid and assistance for rebuilding the economy, ecology and disaster avoidance infra structure. This will go a long way in improving subsistence at the grass roots thereby overcoming the need for transmigration to India. Bangladeshis are pioneers in micro management and weaving together effective self help groups whose talent can be exploited to advantage in reaching to the grass roots.

Strengthening the Indo Bangla border. The need to strengthen the surveillance and security system on the Indo Bangla border including border fencing is a primary security measure which needs attention, The Border Security Force troops relieved from the Kashmir Valley by the Central Reserve Police Force should be deployed on the Indo Bangla border in greater strength. A second tier of surveillance and blocking should be employed using forces such as local home guard if required in more vulnerable areas. Of concern is the slow pace of erection of the border fence. If General N C Vij, the erstwhile army chief could have the line of control entirely fenced in a period of just about a year, why the speed of construction of the fence along the Indo Bangla Border cannot be faster is unfathomable.

References

1. Hasan, Zayadul. Of the Daily Star. Quoted in, Sood, Vikram. "Dacca Comes to roost". Hindustan Times. 12 October 2005. Lucknow. p. 6.
2. Baid, Samuel. "Bangladesh—" The Sunday Pioneer. 11 December 2005. Lucknow. p. 5.
3. The Pioneer Editorial. "Bangla Bombers". The Pioneer. 1 December 2005. Lucknow. p. 6.
4. The Daily Star, August 11, 2005. Down loaded from South Asia Intelligence Review September 2005.
5. Singh, Pramod Kumar. "Dhaka—" The Pioneer. 02 October 2005. Lucknow. p.1.
6. The Pioneer Report. "Jihadi Train Gathers Speed". The Pioneer. 5 October 2005. Lucknow. p. 7.
7. Bibhu Prasad Routray. "Beyond the Bandarban Recoveries." Weekly Assessments and Briefings. Volume 4, No.18, November 14, 2005 South Asia Intelligence Review.
8. Bibhu Prasad Routray. "Beyond the Bandarban Recoveries." Weekly Assessments and Briefings. Volume 4, No.18, November 14, 2005 South Asia Intelligence Review.
9. Sood, Vikram. "Dhaka comes to roost" The Hindustan Times. 12 October 2005. Lucknow. p. 6.
10. Singh, Pramod Kumar. "Dhaka—" The Pioneer. 02 October 2005. Lucknow. p.1.
11. Times of India Report. 30 November 2005. Lucknow.
12. Ahmed, Nizam. "Bangladesh blasts—". The Indian Express. 9 December 2005. Lucknow. p. 7.
13. Indian Express Report. "Bangladesh to pass—". The Indian Express. 19 December 2005. Lucknow, p. 7.
14. Hussain, Syed Zarir. "Alert Sounded—". The Pioneer. 2 December 2005. Lucknow. p. 4.
15. Indian Express Report. "BSF-BDR Talks: Border terror on agenda". 28 September 2005. Lucknow. p. 6.

16. The Pioneer. Lucknow. 1 October 2005. Lucknow. p. 1,3.
17. Hindustan Times Report. Sunday Hindustan Times. 16 October 2005. Lucknow. p. 16.
18. Pramod Kumar Singh. "Arms smuggling—" The Pioneer. 19 October 2005. Lucknow. p. 3.
19. Sengupta, Saugor. "Post Bangla—". The Pioneer. 2 December 2005. Lucknow. p. 4.
20. Singh, Pramod Kumar. "Swirling waters—". The Pioneer. 16 December 2005. Lucknow. p. 1.
21. Singh, Pramod Kumar. "Indo-Bangla border fence work moves at snail's pace". The Pioneer. 19 September 2005. Lucknow. p. 3.
22. Singh, Pramod Kumar. "Swirling waters—". The Pioneer. 16 December 2005. Lucknow. p. 1.
23. Singh, Pramod Kumar. "Swirling waters—". The Pioneer. 16 December 2005. Lucknow. p. 1.

8

Pakistan-Reducing The Confrontation in 2006

"The truth is, a power shift has occurred in Pakistan, and the state now appears far more fragile and vulnerable to the threats currently confronting it."

Ajay Sahni, Director Institute
for Conflict Management

INDO - PAK DIALOGUE – 2006

Hope is the key to success in international relations howsoever vexed these may be. The Indo Pak dialogue spread over a number of wars between the two states and over five decades of acrimony perhaps highlights the statement above very succinctly. The relations between the two nations have improved considerably after the low in December 2001 which carried on till the end of 2002. This was Operation Prakaram when both sides hammered each other across the line of control and were face to face across the wire of the international border. However the peace process has continued thereafter. For India the key issue is cross border terrorism. Stopping the interminable flow of youth across the line of control is an essential step for placing the negotiations on a sound footing. While India claims Pakistan has control over this flow, the same is vehemently denied by the other side. The US has a powerful stake in the region, increased even further after the revelations of clandestine nuclear proliferation in Pakistan. Thus Indo – Pak relations are of great interest for the USA. For Pakistan, Kashmir is the core issue and is striving to reduce troop levels in the Indian state. Some concerns of the US, India and Pakistan in Indo-Pak relations are as follows:-

(a) American interest in Musharraf's political future.

(b) India's apprehensions on Musharraf's credibility on steps to prevent terrorism.

(c) Musharraf's fear that India will ignore Pakistan and achieve peace in Kashmir.

(d) Continuing instability in Afghanistan. Indian and Pakistani dabbling in the country.

(e) Global and Indian Kashmir linkages.[1]

Musharraf is reported to have undertaken effective steps to curb terrorism the main one's being restructuring of the Inter Services Intelligence or ISI organization dealing with Kashmir primarily based on the likely threats being posed to the President himself. US is preferring a low key approach and this is proving to be successful.[2] To understand the peace process the broad contours of the composite dialogue process between India and Pakistan which commenced in 2004 need to be considered. These issues are covered in the Joint statement of the Foreign secretaries on February 18, 2004 the excerpts are as given below.

"Both sides agreed that they would approach the composite dialogue with the sincere desire to discuss and arrive at a peaceful settlement of all bilateral issues, including Jammu and Kashmir to the satisfaction of both sides. They reiterated their commitment to promote progress towards the common objective of peace, security and economic development for their peoples and for future generations.

They agreed to the following schedule of meetings:

(i) Foreign Secretaries would meet in May/June 2004 for talks on peace and security including CBMs; and Jammu and Kashmir.

(ii) Talks on Siachen; Wullar Barrage/Tulbul Navigation Project; Sir Creek; Terrorism and Drug-trafficking; Economic and Commercial Cooperation; and Promotion of Friendly Exchanges in various fields would be held at the already agreed levels, in July 2004.

The following technical level meetings would be held earlier:

(a) Meeting between the Director General, Pakistan Rangers, and the Inspector General, Border Security Force,

(b) Expert level talks on nuclear CBMs in the latter half of May 2004.

(c) Committee on Drug-trafficking and Smuggling in June 2004.

They reviewed the existing links between the Directors General, Military Operations of Pakistan and India, and agreed to consider further strengthening these contacts.

The Foreign Minister of Pakistan and External Affairs Minister of India would meet in August 2004 to review overall progress. This would be preceded by a one-day meeting of the Foreign Secretaries".[3]

While the negotiations are expected to continue, there are hopes in achieving solution of some issues such as the Sir Creek, Baglihar, improved trans movement routes and trade. Thus the peace process is in a positive trajectory, though the more contentious issues, Kashmir, cross border terrorism, Siachen and so on remain on the conflict radar of both nations. Inasmuch as Pakistan, containment of the state less the cross border terrorism facet is seen to have worked well so far. The next phase is containment of cross border terrorism and continuous engagement both economic and political, this alone will bring peace in South Asia. The diplomatic temper will continue to be high and should create a number of moments of anxiety particularly with indications of India likely to adopt a aggressive diplomatic policy vis a vis the happenings in Pakistan. This was evident with Indian foreign spokesperson expressing concern on the situation in Balochistan on 27 December 2005 and the acidic repartee from his counter part.[4]

The Key Negotiations during the Year - 2005

The key event in Indo-Pak negotiations during 2005 was the visit of Pakistan President Pervez Musharraf to India from 16 to 18 April 2005. Excerpts of the Joint statement highlight the main issues which are under discussion between the two countries' and the growing commitment at the highest level on bringing about peace commitment at the highest level on bringing about peace in the region. While there would be many hiccups in the process, it confirmed commitment of the leadership and their sincerity to bringing about peace in the region. Excerpts from the joint statement will highlight the major issues:-

1. Commitments made in the Joint Press Statement of January 6, 2004 and the Joint Statement issued after their meeting in New York on September 24, 2004 were reaffirmed and satisfaction was expressed on the progress in the peace process and the improvement of relations between the two countries.

2. Increased frequency of the bus service and allowing trucks to use this route to promote trade. Operationalising additional routes, the next being the Poonch-Rawalakot link. Early start of the bus service between Amritsar and Lahore and to religious places such as Nankana Sahib.

3. Re-establish the Khokhrapar-Munnabao route by January 1, 2006.

4. Consulates of the two countries in Mumbai and Karachi respectively would be opened.

5. On the issues of the Sir Creek and Siachen, existing institutional mechanisms should convene discussions immediately with a view to finding mutually acceptable solutions to both issues expeditiously.

6. Ministers of Petroleum and Natural Gas would meet in May to explore cooperation in the sector including on the issue of pipelines.

7. It was accepted that enhanced economic and commercial cooperation would contribute to the well being of the people of the two countries and bring a higher level of prosperity for the region. The two leading economies of South Asia should work together for the greater prosperity of the region.

8. Reactivation of the Joint Economic Commission as early as possible and early meeting of the Joint Business Council.[5]

A major review of the Composite Dialogue Process (CDP) was carried out on 3 October 2005 between Pakistani

External Affairs Minister Natwar Singh who met at the Nathiagali resort. The eight points under discussion were covered to include peace and security including CBMs; Jammu & Kashmir; Siachen; Wullar Barrage/Tulbul Navigation Project; Sir Creek; Terrorism and Drug Trafficking; Economic and Commercial Cooperation and Promotion of Friendly Exchanges in various fields[6] . A very realistic appraisal of the progress made was carried out and is summarized herein. On Siachen the problem of verification of actual ground positions was accepted. India has commanding positions hence is unwilling to vacate till verified and agreed upon by both sides. Mechanism to work out the actual ground position was arrived at during the Meet on 3 October 2005. Maritime Boundary at Sir Creek is to be discussed in third round in January. Pre notification of ballistic missile tests which each country carries out was agreed upon. Hotline between Coast Guard and Pakistani Maritime Security Agency (PMSA)agreed upon by Coast guard Director, A K Singh and PMSA Director General, Rear Admiral Bakhtiar Mohsin. Indo-Pakistan Joint Commission is also to be revived.[7]

Significant agreements were reached on missile testing and it was accepted that no test will be carried out within 40 km on either side of IB or LOC, the planned impact area will not be within 75 kms of IB or LOC, the horizontal distance of trajectory will be 40 kms from the IB or LOC and

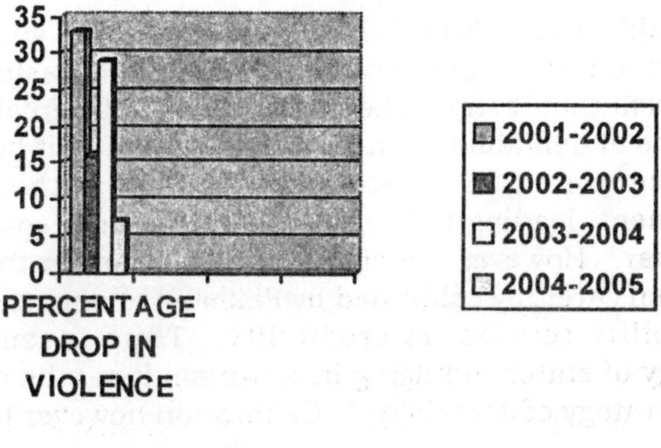

distance of trajectory will be 40 kms from the IB or LOC and 72 hours ahead of 5 day launch window for a missile warning will have to be given and pre notification will be by means of a special format through foreign offices. The agreement is said to be valid for 5 years from 2005 – 2010.[8]

Reopening of Jhelum Valley route (JVR) has brought about positive changes. Five meeting points have been iden-

(a) Teetwal-Karnah.

(b) Sonavali-Hathlanga-Uri

(c) Balnoi-Mendhar

(d) Digwar-Tarorah.

(e) Pachanti-Bagh.[9]

The New Years day 2006 began well for Indo-Pakistan relations with both sides exchanging a list of nuclear installations, based on the special agreement between the two nations proscribing attacks on each other's nuclear facilities. A statement from the Foreign office of Pakistan stated, "The governments of Pakistan and India Sunday exchanged lists of their respective nuclear installations and facilities in accordance with Article II of the Agreement on Prohibition of Attacks Against Nuclear Installations and Facilities between Pakistan and India of December 31, 1988," This simultaneous exchange took place in Islamabad and New Delhi.[10]

Pakistan – Support to Terrorism

Pakistan has been following the strategy of substantial support to fostering terrorism in Jammu and Kashmir with the caveat that it should be at a level of being deniable. The calculus of deniability can go awry at times as it happened in December 2001 with the attack on the Indian Parliament, leading to the two nations almost going to an open war. However the simmer of terrorism in the Valley has been carefully calibrated by Pakistan to ensure that the deniability retains its credibility. Thus inasmuch as strategy of states indulging in terrorism it can be called as the, "strategy of deniability". Calibration however has to be observers of the situation as Mr. K P S Gill believe that the tap of terrorism has receded at a much slower pace in 2005 than in other years as is evident from the graph below[12]

India needs to be more demanding in concrete measures for reduction of violence in Jammu and Kashmir such as a drop in the percentage of violence could be one of the indicators though difficult to perceive commonly by both states but it would at least have some standard being adopted rather than none at present.

Kashmir

Pakistan has repeatedly emphasized on demilitarizing of the LOC as a solution to the Kashmir issue well knowing that this would be unacceptable to the Indian side and used it as a bargaining chip in the Indo Pak dialogue process. Recently on 1 November 2005, Pakistani President reiterated this demand of demilitarizing the line of control. A similar demand was made earlier by the Pakistan Ambassador to the United States, retired General Jehangir Karamat for demilitarizing Kupwara and Baramulla Districts of Kashmir both having an active line of control with Pakistan. India also apprehends that demilitarization would provide free pathways to the jehadis to move into Kashmir. This counter combined with the reports of flow of terrorists infiltrating into Kashmir should be effectively used to counter Pakistan's information warfare campaign.

Pakistan had floated a new proposal for self governance in Kashmir on both sides of the LOC, during the meeting of the Prime Minister Shaukat Aziz with Manmohan Singh in Dhaka. But the same was not acceptable to India which dismissed it as it felt that the people in Jammu and Kashmir enjoyed perfect autonomy while that on the Pakistani side lacked the same.[13] Details of the proposal are not available however it may be one of the trial balloons floated by Pakistan from time to time. Pakistani President, Pervez Mushraff has the habit of announcing important diplomatic proposals through the media as a form of loud thinking or even proactive perception management constantly demonstrating initiative, for it is important for the demonstrating initiative, for it is important for the Pakistanis to be seen as those possessing enterprise and the upper hand.

India finds Pakistan proposals on Kashmir lacking sincerity. This facet is reasonably supported by facts on ground for instance 143 foreign nationals mostly of Pakistani origin have been detained under public safety Act in Kashmir. Detention of persons completing their 24 month term under law is being extended in order to regulate their continued presence in the country for facing trials or make arrangements for expulsion. Counselor access is likely to be given to these detainees who due to security reasons were in prisons outside the state. State officials also claimed Islamabad was reluctant to admit that its nationals were busy in sabotage and did not claim detainees as it would have weakened its position diplomatically.[14]

We are thus on a slippery slope as far as Indo- Pak dialogue on Kashmir is concerned. Nothing much can be expected in the form of an understanding. What we should however hope for is the continuance of the peace process with cease fire on the line of control. This itself will provide much needed succour to the hapless people on both sides of the line of control.[15]

Siachen Glacier. India will not give up the heights unless there is a credible guarantee that Pakistan won't do a Kargil in the glacier. That is why it is insisting on authentication of the actual ground position line. (AGPL). However authentication creates two problems for Pakistan –

(a) Legitimise what it has been calling Indian aggression in 1984 when India landed a brigade on Saltoro ridge preempting Pakistani moves.

(b) Pakistan Army will have to admit that it has been lying to its people since 1984, claiming it had the heights of Saltoro.[16]

A solution will rest on the acceptance of the actual ground position as the effective line of control by Pakistan. This is going to be a difficult process as it would necessitate a come down by the country's ruling elite, the army top brass. Unless a face saving formula is offered no progress in this forthcoming in 2006. India should evolve a solution which enables the Pakistani regime to back off with reasonable dignity. Why should India do so without corresponding reciprocal gestures by Pakistan is a contentious issue?

Sir Creek. Joint survey of the horizontal section of the boundary has been done in the Creek and Indian officials admitted that the disagreements are narrower than what both sides had thought. We should now undertake a joint survey of Sir Creek itself and start by the end of the year so that the third round can discuss ideas relating to drawing of the maritime boundary.[17] In the negotiations held in December 2005, the survey of the horizontal line has been completed and boundary pillars erected before 1947 are reported have been identified. Further significant discussions are likely to be held during the third round of composite dialogue process slated in January 2006. On Sir Creek, the possibilities of an agreement in 2006 are very bright and can be envisaged based on the proposals for equity in division.

Baglihar. Problem of Baglihar is that of gated spillways. India wants eight spillways to avoid silting while Pakistan feels these gates amount to storing water thereby depriving it of its share of Chenab water as well as leaving it open to the risk of flooding. Thus Pakistan feels that this violates the Indus Water Treaty. World Bank, neutral expert Raymond Lafitte and his team visiting Roorkee after the project site in Jammu and Kashmir's Doda district to see live running model of Baglihar project developed by the Irrigation Research Institute are expected to give a decision during 2006.[18] This will be an interesting point in relations on this vital issue.

Pakistan – Clandestine Nuclear Proliferation. The greatest chink in Pakistani nuclear armour is the clandestine network run by AQ Khan, and its links with Iran which should be played up to heighten US apprehensions of this facet. Dr A Q Khan is said to have offered critical technical as well as material help as far back as 1987 when a multi million dollar deal was signed with Iran.[19] In fact networks as that of A Q Khan are said to be more dangerous than the Iran's state led nuclear build up. Detailed monitoring and surveillance of such networks by our intelligence agencies assumes as much priority as the terror networks. Diplomatically too India needs to play the Nuclear Card with Pakistan to greater effect than at present.

PAKISTAN INTERNAL ISSUES

Pakistan Terrorism Structure

There are hardly any indications of dismantling of the terror infra structure in Pakistan. A detailed survey by Anil Bhat reveals startling facts. Madarsas rose from the 700 in 1980 to 7000 in a few years and today are reported to be 10,000. Hafiz Saeed, former Chief of the Lashkar-e-Toiba is said to have reiterated the determination of continuance of Jihad. Jihad's success in Afghanistan has probably spurred its proponents to further it in other states including Kashmir. Suicide squads come from the ranks of seminary students at Muridke, the Jamaat-ud-Dawa's main centre. Jamaat-ud-Dawa is Lashkar's political patron. Binori town Near Karachi has also fostered suicide volunteers. Jihadi media mainly vernacular continues to spew venom against Jews, Hindus and Christians. Bhat has listed jihadi publications and their place of publication as given below:-

(a) Akhbar-i-Jahan weekly, Daily Islam, Daily Jasarat, Ummat all from Karachi and K2 from Northern Areas.

(b) Majjalla-tul-Dawa– Jamaat-ud-Dawa's publication-Lahore.

(c) Moon Digest – Monthly - Lahore, Monthly Ghazi-Karachi. Gulabdin Hekmatyar and former ISI chief Hamid Gul are on its editorial board.

(d) Monthly Shahadat – Rawalpindi.

(e) Nida-e- Millat – Weekly - Lahore.

(f) Nawa-i-Waqt. Lahore

(g) Taloo-e-Islam Monthly.

(h) Voice of Islam –Lahore –English Monthly

(i) Weekly Ghazwa – Lahore.

(j) Wadi ki Awaz – Srinagar.

(k) Weekly Naqqara – Northern Areas.

(l) Weekly Takbeer – Karachi.

(m) Weekly Wadi – Northern Areas.

(n) Weekly Zarb e Momin –Karachi.

(o) Zarbul Mujahideen – Fortnightly publication of Hizbul Mujahideen.[20]

A newly emerging threat from the Earthquake relief operations in Pakistan Occupied Kashmir is the growing influence of jihadi organizations in relief work in concert with the Pakistan Army.[21] Popularity of the Jehadi organizations in Pakistan and particularly POK has increased greatly with their effectiveness in organizing relief operations much faster than the Pakistani government including the Army. Pakistan's human rights groups have however alleged that militants are exploiting this influence by taking orphans of the quake into training camps for fighting the war against India. Ansar Burney Welfare Trust has raised serious reservations on this issue and has even alleged that government officials were also participating in this process.[22] Radicalization of Pakistan Occupied Kashmir in the light of the speed with which the militant cadres fanned out and provided aid to victims as other agencies looked on is thus felt imminent. The US establishment is also aware that the vacuum in aid deliverance is being filled up by groups inimical to US interests in the region. These jihadis seem to be ironically applying the lesson of winning the war of hearts and minds, standard counter insurgency tactics.[23]

Pak Politics – Army in Retreat?

Ajai Sahni's observations quoted in the heading above seem more ominous than they appear in the first place as these are portraying a shift in the power calculus in Pakistan from the military driven state model to a people driven mold. While in a globalised World, it was inevitable that such a transformation will take place even in feudal areas of Pakistan, the pace at which it is occurring is significant, for even the more enlightened parts of Pakistan, the Punjab and urban Sindh have yet to embrace a globalized, democratic world view. Perhaps the changes which are occurring in neighboring Afghanistan are rubbing off in Balochistan. India can draw some relief from the discomfort of the Pakistani state to the extent that this will bring about larger changes in the Pakistani society, bringing it at par with modern democratic states with rule of the people rather than the uniform, overcome the feudal governance structure, reduce corruption thereby encouraging democratic reforms, bring equality in human and gender rights and reduce the sway of Islamic fundamentalists on the society. Such a change however will not be easy to come by and will possibly involve great turbulence, possibly even a civil militancy in Balochistan and the Northern Areas. For the year ahead however it entails a turbulent Pakistan.

The signs of an Army-mullah self perpetuating dyad with mutual interest in keeping power within is demonstrated by the following factors –

(a) Lower ranks of the Pakistani army till the colonel or major dominated by religious extremist elements from a lower middle class financial background were well seeped in the Islamist culture and thus would be difficult to turn around in the long term till the army itself was ousted.

(b) Muttahida Majlis-e-Amal (MMA) an umbrella organization of religious parties is surviving with support of the army.

(c) Extremist organizations as the Lashkar-e-Toiba or Jaish-e-Mohammad were not fringe groups but had a lot of hold on the low income, unemployed madarsa educated youth in Pakistan.[24]

Total hold of Pak army on the country's polity is likely to weaken with President Musharraf facing problems of loyalty as well as integrity within the Army. Traditionally loss of public face has led to the Army falling from the public eye and a change of regime in Pakistan in the past be it 1971 or later. Continued post of Pervez Musharraf as the Army Chief has caused consternation amongst the Army top brass. Involvement of Pak top brass in arms deals also causing loss of trust in the Army establishment in the populace in Pakistan. Chasing terrorists at the US behest in Waziristan is irking a number of Pakistani army leaders so is the growing warmth in relations between the US and India. Kashmir as a core issue is being diluted as per feelings in the Pak higher circles particularly with the peace process moving positively, opening of greater points of contact and transit between the two countries and delay in settlement. Indian insistence on no redrawal of boundaries is another vexatious issue for the Pakistanis. Analysts as Wilson John feel that India should keep its options open as far as dealings with other Pakistani leaders including generals are concerned.[25]

Pakistani religious leaders, the mullahs have been saying that India is shortchanging Pakistan. If a solution in Kashmir is prolonged, the people may become frustrated and castigate Musharraf for putting Kashmir on the back burner. If Musharraf is seeing to be giving in too much to Indians, his position will become weak. Presently they feel that control over military is complete and also because if he is taken off, there would be instability. Gap between Musharraf and his corps commanders is widening as those who had put him in the chair after the coup have retired and those in command were brigadiers or major generals then. "Every chief works with a crop of lieutenant generals who are actually buddies-mostly of the same age group. The team today is much junior and younger to him and would rarely have communicated with him directly throughout their army life. So you cannot expect them to have the same wave length with him as the ones in 1999. That makes a lot of difference in the army", says a Pakistani analyst.

Musharraf is seen to be keeping these in good humour by assuring post retirement ambassadorship or corporation chairmanship. The vocal minority of Islamic radicals can make a difference in time of crisis. Vocal minorities matter the most hence one must pay heed to them.[26] However Musharraf continues to have the confidence of the ruling elites in Islamabad including the Prime Minister. Thus reacting to the castigation at the Commonwealth summit in Malta, Pakistan Prime Minister Shaukat Aziz stated that President Musharraf will shed his army uniform in 2007 as the country was facing many challenges due to the war against terrorism and other security issues.[27] This provides for stability in Pakistani polity as there are no political challengers, a benign corps commanders hierarchy and so on.

Pakistan – Weak Areas of Governance – Gilgit, Baltistan, Balochistan and Frontier Areas

Pakistan is continually facing a crisis of governance in the Gilgit and Baltistan areas in the North, Balochistan and the Federally Administered Tribal Areas (FATA). Indus flows through the area of Gilgit and Baltistan. Karakoram highway a vital strategic link passes through the area and is used for supply of clandestine nuclear and other missile material from China and North Korea. China is also provided a link through the Karakoram highway to Gwadar port close to the Gulf of Oman. Acute deprivation of the people has been seen in areas of Gilgit and Baltistan or Balawaristan.

60 per cent of population lives below poverty line. Illiteracy rates are the highest in these areas. No infra structure development and Shia – Sunni divide has been further heightened with the effort of administration to induct Sunni Pashtuns and formally annex the area. Chitral has already been similarly annexed by making it a part of North West Frontier Province recently. Reportedly Shias formed 85 percent of the population in 1948, but only 53 percent in 2004. This is referred to as the World's last colony and any criticism of the Punjabi-Pashtun bureaucracy leads to instant reprisals. The administration of Northern Affairs Legislative Council is said to be totally ineffective and a puppet in the hands of the loyalists. Frontier Corps has been inducted to brow beat the Shias in the region. 4000 persons have been killed in sectarian clashes in the last decade. 80 persons died in collisions with Pakistani forces in the region in 2005 (November 2005). Shia religious scholar killed recently and attempts at Wahhabising of education are known.[28]

Pakistan is also facing a lot of resistance in the Frontier areas bordering Afghanistan. Pakistan Army is actively engaged in Waziristan with reports of Taliban and al – Qaeda militants fighting bloody battles with troops.

There are claims that of the 500-600 al-Qaeda terrorists in the South Waziristan area in 2004 approximately 400 have been eliminated. But the remainder continue to be effective against US troops in Afghanistan. The situation in North Waziristan is equally alarming with reports indicating that between August 15 and September 15, 2005, over 100 persons were killed in battles between the militants and the Army. President Musharraf has called for a border fencing in the area but the proposal is not likely to be accepted by the Afghan government as it involves the delicate issue of the Durand line which has never been formally accepted as the official border between the two states but a line drawn by the British to suit their convenience.[29] Analysts as Kanchan Lakshman state that the Pakistani state has very limited control in the FATA. The tribal areas bordering Afghanistan are likely to pose serious challenges to the Government in the year ahead. As it will impinge on the governance and stability in Afghanistan, the international community will also have to take a closer view of the state of affairs prevalent in these areas and not be lulled by the establishment of a parliament in Kabul in December 2005.[30]

Militancy in Balochistan is reportedly brewing on a large scale, the fourth time such an occurrence is taking place on Pakistan's Western most province. Balochistan Liberation Army is said to be active in the state. In 2005, 261 bomb blasts and 167 rocket firings have been reported while at least 111 civilians and 23 security forces are reported to have been killed upto 15 December.[31] A number of terrorist camps have been noticed named as, "Farrari camps" or camps of the fugitives. The need for a federal dispensation keeping in line with the resource contribution of the state to the economy has been a long standing demand of the Balochis. Thus related issues as the enhancement of gas royalties to the province, clearance of arrears, development of gas in the area and greater provincial autonomy dominate the demands for which unrest is brewing.[32] The awakening of the peripheral areas is thus likely to be a cause of concern for the Pakistani Army and will engage it in the year ahead.

Shia – Sunni strife in Pakistan is likely to be on the increase as per a report in The Daily Times, Lahore quoted in the Indian express. Indications are induction of some suicide bombers in the predominantly Shia, Northern Areas from South Punjab. The vulnerable areas are said to be the Northern Areas, North and South Waziristan Agencies in the Federally Administered Tribal Areas (FATA) and all of Balochistan, which comprises 40 percent of Pakistan territory.[33] The portends as per the Daily Times report are that sectarian violence will continue in Pakistan as the Sunni militias led by the Lashkar – e – Jhangvi and Sipah Sahaba funded by Saudi riyals will continue to play on the sectarian strife in the state to create insecurities.

Pakistan as a state will have to embrace a more democratic federal structure overcoming the feudal tribal nature in the outlying provinces as Balochistan and the Northern Areas, while overcoming the new feudalism in areas as Punjab and Sindh, where tribalism has been replaced by feudal agro-industrial overlordship through control of agriculture and industry by a coterie of ex landlords loathe to renege their privileges of power.

Pakistan Building The Armed Might

Pakistan has continued to build up its military capability relentlessly despite the economic crunch in order to attain a semblance of parity with the Eastern neighbour, India. However Pakistan's main area of focus remains missile capability which was seen to be considerably enhanced in 2005. Pak has carried out tests of the Babur Land Attack Cruise missiles in August 2005 and is expected to field one regiment, 18 Road Mobile autonomous launchers in 3 batteries of 6 launchers by 2008. Indian Brahmos Land version is slated to be inducted by 2017.[34]

The Shaheen 1 or Chinese M 9 is a joint Pakistan and Chinese integrated weapon and is said to be superior to anything that India possesses. Shaheen II, a Chinese M 18 version is a two stage missile. While the M11 has a range of 300 km thus not violating the Missile Technology Control Regime (MTCR), this appears to be the red herring to facilitate transfer of M9 to Pakistan. M9 will be the back bone of Pakistani threat to India. M 9 is violative of MTCR. China's long term strategy appears to be that Russia, India, USA are collaborators, competitors, long term adversaries in that order of chronology. During the primary period of China's emergence it will cherry pick a foreign policy based on needs of time for instance for economic requirements, collaborate with USA, for military needs collaborate with Russia. India appears the weakest link in this power chain due to lack of strategic focus. China has used Pakistan as its paw to undermine India. Noted strategic analyst, Raja Menon has proposed an axis of powers with India and Vietnam to undermine China.[35]

Pakistan is pressing for $ 4 billion deal to purchase 77 F 16 fighters and also signed on 18 October a deal for 6 Saab airborne early warning aircraft from Sweden worth $ 1 billion even as it is bidding for $ 580 million aid for earthquake relief. On 3 November US announced $ 62 million worth Harpoon missiles to Pakistan. Thus in Geneva, it received only 12 percent of the aid it requested for perhaps resulting in postponement of the F 16 deal, announcement for which was made on 6 November.[36] The Saab Ericcson AEW system will replace the Fokker planes of the Pakistan Air Force. Two third of the money is for the aircraft while one third will go to Ericsson to provide the Erieye Airborne radar. The integration work will be carried out entirely in Sweden. Saab Chief Executive, Ake Svenson was contemplating a number of contentious issues which could be easily resolved.[37] Pakistani purchase of this equipment will alter the arms balance in the sub continent particularly as it would restore some sort of air parity as at present India is enjoying absolute air superiority against Pakistan both qualitatively as well as quantitatively. Internally too as far the power dynamics within the country is concerned the focus on acquisitions for the Pakistan Air Force and the Navy may provide greater power to these services and reduce the influence of the Army in Pakistan which would be a welcome development.

For the first time perhaps, Pakistani opposition has criticized the government for its arms shopping while the earthquake victims are still suffering. The Pakistan People's Party spokesperson, Faratullah Babar demanded that the purchase of Saab AEW aircraft be deferred. Babar emphasized the need for diversion of resources for human security to prevent deaths from starvation and cold. Musharraf has ruled out cuts saying that earthquake and defence are two separate matters.

Pakistan is also slated to build a modern combined general headquarters in Islamabad for the Pakistan Army, Air Force and Navy. Babar has called for suspension of this construction for two years. Pakistan human rights group such as the Human Rights Commission of Pakistan secretary general, Iqbal Haider has clearly brought out that this will not be appreciated by the authorities considering aid to Pakistan and also alleged corruption in the rehabilitation efforts which were being led by army generals.[38]

References

1. Rajamohan, C. "Triangular Ties—". The Indian Express. 4 October 2005. Lucknow. p. 8.
2. Rajamohan, C. "Triangular Ties—". The Indian Express. 4 October 2005. Lucknow. p. 8.
3. Downloaded from hinduonnet.com on 23 December 2005.
4. Raja Mohan, C. "Third Time—". The Indian Express. 29 December 2005. Lucknow. p. 9.
5. Provided by the PTI and downloaded from the Rediff.com site on 16 Sep 2005-09-20
6. Downloaded from hinduonnet.com. 23 December 2005.
7. Hindustan Times Report. Hindustan Times. 4 October 2005. Lucknow. p. 1,13.
8. Samanta, Pranab Dahal. "India, Pak—". The Indian Express. 4 October 2005. Lucknow. p. 1.
9. Husain, Masood. "Government—" The Economic Times. 29 September 2005. New Delhi. p. 2.
10. Varma, K J M. "India, Pak exchange lists of nuke installations, facilities" rediff.com. Islamabad | January 01, 2006 15:37 IST. Downloaded rediff.com 01 Jan 06.
11. Gill, KPS. "Containing ideological violence." The Pioneer. 24 December 2005. Lucknow. p. 6.
12. Gill, KPS. "Containing ideological violence." The Pioneer. 24 December 2005. Lucknow. p. 6.
13. Times of India Report. The Times of India. 22 November 2005. Lucknow. p. 8.
14. Hussain, Masood. Economic Times. 4 October 2005. New Delhi. p. 2.
15. Detailed review of the Kashmir peace process also carried out in the chapter on Kashmir.
16. Prasannan, R. "Peace overdrive". The Week. 16 October 2005 p. 52.
17. Prasannan, R. "Peace overdrive". The Week. 16 October 2005 p. 52.

18. Jain, Sonu. "And in Roorkee—". Indian Express. 5 October 2005. Lucknow. p.1,2.
19. John, Wilson. "Investigate Pakistan-Iran—". The Pioneer. Lucknow. 23 November 2005. p. 6.
20. Bhat, Anil. "The Tip of the Jihadi Iceberg" The Pioneer. 22 September 2005. Lucknow. p. 7.
21. The Economist. 5 November 2005. p. 30.
22. Nelson, Dean. "Quake orphans—". The Times of India. 14 November 2005. Bangalore. p. 12.
23. Reddy, Murlidhar B. "Calamity mitigation—" The Hindu. 16 November 2005. Hyderabad. p. 10.
24. Interaction of Farooq Hassan organized by Security and Political Risk Analysis (SAPRA) quoted in The Pioneer. 24 October 2005. Lucknow. p. 4.
25. John, Wilson. "Failure divides Pakistan". The Pioneer. 28 September 2005. Lucknow. p. 7.
26. Prasannan, R. "Peace overdrive". The Week. 16 October 2005. p. 52.
27. Times of India Report. The Times of India. 29 November 2005. Lucknow. p. 10.
28. Sood, Vikram. "The World's Last Colony". Hindustan Times. 9 November 2005. Lucknow. p. 6.
29. Mir, Amir. "Janus faced Counter terrorism". Extracted from weekly news letter of SAIR as at SATP.org.
30. Lakshman, Kanchan " Searching for Order in Waziristan" South Asia Intelligence Review Weekly Assessments & Briefings Volume 4, No.23, December 12, 2005.
31. Sahni, Ajai. "Pakistan's Province of fear". The Pioneer. 21 December 2005. Lucknow. p. 6.
32. Sahni, Ajai. "Pakistan's Province of fear". The Pioneer. 21 December 2005. Lucknow. p. 6.
33. The Indian Express Report. The Indian Express. 9 December 2005. Lucknow. p. 9.
34. Pravin Sawhney. "Dawn of Land Attack Cruise Missile". Force September 2005. NOIDA. p. 16.
35. Menon, Raja. "The road to Vietnam" The Indian Express. 6 October 2005. Lucknow. p. 9.
36. Khera, P N. "They can—" Hindustan Times. 10 November 2005. Lucknow. p. 6.
37. Times of India Report. The Times of India, 8 November 2005. Lucknow. p. 10
38. Indian Express Report. Indian Express. 4 November 2005. Lucknow.

9

Sri Lanka – Redefining Peace or Continued Strife

"I do believe that it is in our national security interest to ensure that our neighbours evolve as viable states with moderate and stable political and social environment and a robust economy."

Indian Prime Minister Manmohan Singh

Sri Lanka has posed a challenge for preservation of unity of a society which is pluralistic yet atavistic, homogenous yet divisive, a feature which is unique to the post colonial states of South Asia, be it India, Pakistan or Sri Lanka. Unlike the expectations on which the vast Indian sub continent was divided on a flawed two nation theory, the differences in the people did not disappear with creation of Pakistan, India and later Bangladesh. As human society tends to coagulate in small groupings, there is always a tendency to seek smaller factional identity within larger clusters, thus in India, people sought to identify with their tribe, Nagas, religion, Kashmiri muslims, ethnicity, Gujaratis and Tamils or language, Mahrashtrians and so on. Within the sub groups they continued to identify themselves as Marathas, Brahmins and Kolis a few of the sub castes, if we just take the example of Maharashtra. Despite these differentiations, it is a marvel that societies as India and Sri Lanka have prospered and can truly be regarded as the success stories in South Asia, democracies which are fostering pluralistic proclivities opposed to insular tendencies in other parts of South Asia, Pakistan, Bangladesh, Nepal, Myanmar or Afghanistan. The latter is however emerging as a model democracy if we overlook the continued dominance of the southern provinces by the Taliban. Bhutan which is a gentle monarchy is attempting pluralism in a small way with growing space being given to the Nepali ethnic population in the Southern region and elections promised by the King a few years hence.

Sri Lanka is slated to see turbulent political upheaval in the year ahead. While simmering violence in the island nation will continue, there are possibilities of a full blown return to a civil war unless the new dispensation in Colombo along with the principal players, India, the international community and Sri Lanka Truce Monitoring Mission (SLMM) effectively engage the Tamil leadership in general and LTTE in particular in a positive manner. In Sri Lanka, the nation is divided on ethnic lines, Tamils and Sinhalas. Muslims, Buddhists and Hindus reside peacefully while there are ideological variants communists, socialists, capitalists and so on. The main division is of course between the Tamils and the majority Sinhalas. The simmering conflict which has been ongoing over two decades now is seen to be tapering albeit at a very slow interminable pace. Liberation Tigers of Tamil Eelam (LTTE) continue to play hide and seek with serenity of its own community by blatantly violating the cease fire agreement with the Government inked in February 2002. The LTTE has suffered heavily in terms of casualties to its cadres reported at 17,903 killed between the period 27 November 1982 to 15 November 2005.[1] It is not likely to therefore give up its aims very easily unless offered a face saving formula. At the same time political pressures from within the Tamil community can be brought to bear on the LTTE to give up its path of violence as the same has achieved only marginal gains. The LTTE's determination to use violence as a strategy for change is highlighted by its continued campaign commencing with elimination of antagonistic leaders as Kadirgamar, the charismatic and defiant Tamil Foreign minister of Sri lanka followed by violation of the Cease Fire Agreement by launching attacks on Sri Lankan troops in December 2005, which has resulted in heavy casualties by employing its favourite arsenal the improvised explosive device. In fact the SLMM has recorded over 3000 violations of the Cease Fire Agreement by the LTTE as against only 150 by the security forces.[2] Political expediency of the LTTE is also evident by its proscribing the Tamils from participating in Presidential elections held during 2005 leading to rise in power of the relatively hard line Rajpakse. A third dimension to the conflict is the growth of rebel LTTE leader Karuna's group and others such as the

Roaring Tiger Force and Trincomalee Tamil Consortium. Such pseudo gangs have complicated the violence as well as politics in the Island further.

What is required in Sri Lanka immediately is continuing the Cease Fire Agreement at all costs. Towards this the accord by both sides on continuance of the Agreement and proclivities for talks under the Sri Lanka Truce Monitoring Mission (SLMM) are welcome signs which gives rise to suspicions that the present attacks by the LTTE are not a sustained effort to break the cease fire but bargaining chips on the parley table.

There is no doubt that sovereignty of the state has to be maintained at all costs. A pluralistic society within the sovereign state needs to be concomitantly built up with equity between the Sinhalese and the Tamil to satisfy aspirations of both the communities. Accepting minimal Tamil aspirations without hurting Sinhala pride is the key to this transformation. Since Tamils seem to be held hostage to the LTTE physically if not ideologically, the need to provide the LTTE with a honorable exit policy in the form of greater autonomy appears to be the way ahead. On the other hand the Sinhala extremist opinion led by the leftist *Janathâ Vimukthi Peramuna* (JVP) and the predominantly Buddhist *Jâthika Hela Urumaya* (JHU) needs to be factored in any solution being evolved. This is the political challenge before the state and the international interlocutors who are increasingly getting impatient with continuing violence in the country. The boundaries of a solution are very narrow, between maximum autonomy proposed by the Sri Lanka government to a federalism demanded by the LTTE. But these are within range of reasonable negotiations by both sides. This provides hope. In case India is able to shed its inhibitions on participation in the peace process, it would receive the necessary impetus and drive it to a viable solution in the years ahead. For this the government must persuade Ms Jayalalita the Tamil Nadu Chief Minister to engage in the dialogue as the Tamil diaspora within India does have some influence over the LTTE.

Election of the new President, Mr Mahendra Rajpakse, has resulted in posturing by both sides, more so by the LTTE, in the power game in the island territory. Rajpakse who comes from rural Sinhala in the South does not bear the cross of being from the elite Bandarnaike dynasty which has been in the seat of power over the last many decades. The election plank of Rajapakse had been anti federal and thus he had the support of Sinhala nationalists both from the left and the right. A shrewd calculation is seen to have been made by the master power politics practitioner, V Prabhakaran of the LTTE who is said to have wanted a hardliner in power so that he could attain maximum gains for the LTTE by proving that the Sri Lankan government was unitary and hence unfair to the people of the North and the East.[3] The Sri Lankan government in power has to adopt a strategy of fostering the aspirations of the Tamils for regional autonomy in the North East. Federalism based on, "internal self determination" is the option for which Sinhalese establishment under the new president should be persuaded, to marginalize the LTTE at home as well as abroad. The LTTE and the Tamil masses seem to be at a divergence with the Tamil populace willing to accept federalism but for the physical stranglehold of terror of the Tamil Tigers.[4] The LTTE had stopped the Tamils from voting in the presidential elections in Sri Lanka which is said to have led to the moderate Ranil Wickremesinghe losing the elections and Mahindra Rajpakse's coming to power. LTTE's calculations seem to have been that it would be easier for Mahindra to gain concessions for the Tamils by being able to rein in the chauvinist Sinhalese elements in South Sri Lanka than the moderate Ranil. The LTTE demand of self determination, national liberation and establishment of self government of the Tamil homeland appears to be a dilution of the more stringent self determination and national liberation stand made earlier as per J K Sinha, a former special secretary with Research and Analysis Wing.[5]

27 November is celebrated by the LTTE as Heroes Day and the speech by LTTE supreme leader, Vellupillai Prabhakaran on this occasion gives a good indication of whether LTTE is thinking of confronting or cooperating with the new President, Mahindra Rajpakse. Prabhakaran announced that he would be forced to resume the armed

struggle unless the new President delivered peace on the terms of the LTTE. While no specific indications were given, LTTE watchers believe, that Prabhakaran's demands are likely to be on the following lines :-

(a) Federalism – Hence moves to transform from a unitary structure to a federal one will gain importance.

(b) Weakening of the International Safety Net seen as a trap by the LTTE.

(c) Removal and checks on the Sri Lankan Army backed Tamil para militaries from the East as per the Cease Fire Agreement.

(d) Vacation of Jaffna which is seen as LTTE stronghold and political heartland.[6]

While there is no likelihood of acceptance of these maximalist demands of the LTTE, there is ample scope to consider these as negotiating instruments based on which further talks can be held and a final solution arrived at. Thus acceptance of these as a opening move rather than an end state will greatly facilitate the process of peace in the country.

End of the year, 2005 saw increase in tension between the LTTE and the Sri Lankan forces with alleged attacks by the LTTE on Sri Lankan troops including a navy patrol and a troop carrying bus.[7] Though the LTTE has denied the attacks, the signs for 2006 are ominous. The LTTE is apparently attempting to up the ante for negotiations with the newly formed government of Rajpakse. This is a standard practice for guerrilla groups who play shadow boxing with a new ruler. Management of the political power play by both parties at this stage will be crucial to continuance of the cease fire as the most important issue in Sri Lanka in 2006. All players including India should use the leverages that they have to ensure that the conflagration is controlled and political dialogue resumed.

The intransigent attitude of the LTTE has greatly antagonized the international community involved in the peace process. The Co chairs of the Aid Sri Lanka conference, the US, EU, Norway and Japan have expressed that the LTTE should be admonished for its continued violence particularly after the recent attacks on Sri Lankan forces in December 2005. The violence was also marked with a reported attack on a helicopter carrying the Italian deputy foreign minister. The Sri Lanka Truce Monitoring Mission (SLMM) is also anguished at the spate of violence and has called for stricter action against the LTTE.[8] Since the international community has considerable leverages with the Sri Lankan expatriates in particular, measures as freezing of LTTE assets and political pressure should wean away the LTTE from the path of fresh violence that it has set for itself of late. The international community and Sri Lankan Prime Minister Mr Rajpakse will have to deftly hit the LTTE ball out of the sand bunker that a short sighted Prabhakaran seems to be eternally placing it over the years. The year 2006 thus promises to be that of a fractured peace and possible open confrontation in Sri Lanka. The solution lies in active catalyzing of the peace process by India by nudging the LTTE to accept a federal system with greater autonomy rather than total independence which will not be acceptable to Sinhalese majority and also not in the interest of the Tamils at large. Greater Indian involvement has been sought by Mr Rajpakse who emphasized this need during his visit to the country in December for over three days. He needs India's support which can be garnered not only by the Foreign office in New Delhi but also through the good officers of Ms Jayalalitha in Chennai.

References

1. Mehta, Ashok K. "Missing". The Pioneer. 28 December 2005. Lucknow. p. 6.
2. Mehta, Ashok K. "Missing". The Pioneer. 28 December 2005. Lucknow. p. 6.
3. Venkataramanan, K. "Tigers". 27 November 2005. Sunday Pioneer. Lucknow. p. 2.
4. Venkataramanan, K. "Tigers". 27 November 2005. Sunday Pioneer. Lucknow. p. 2.
5. Sinha, J. K. "War Clouds over Lanka". The Times of India. 14 December 2005. Lucknow. p. 9.
6. Balachandran, P. K. "Federalism tops". Hindustan Times. 4 December 2005. Lucknow. p. 17.
7. Gardner, Simon. "Tigers attack". The Indian express. 23 December 2005. Lucknow. p. 7.
8. Balachandran, P. K. " No support". Hindustan Times. 25 December 2005. Lucknow. p. 17.

10

The Regional and International Dimensions of The New Great Game

"Madmen in authority, who hear voices in the air, are distilling their frenzy from some academic scribbler of a few years back. I am sure that the power of vested interests is vastly exaggerated compared with the encroachment of ideas. Sooner or later it is ideas not vested interests, which are dangerous for good or evil."

Keynes

SAARC - A Regional Economic Confederation - The Way to Peace

South Asia is a sub continent full of continental sized problems. It is the least integrated region, thus indicating that even in this age of globalization, blending between neighbours is far fetched, a sad commentary on the state of affairs in one of the least developed and highest populated regions of the Earth. While the reasons for the same are in the historical division of the sub continent in 1947 and its subsequent polarization on ethnic, religious, linguistic and other divides through deliberate policies of regional isolationism followed by many of India's neighbours due to trust deficit and an ever increasing fear of being swamped by the larger nation, India. These fears were at times deliberately fostered by the rulers of these states for survival of their regimes as the Indian state has always been unwilling to proselytize lacking national power and will to go beyond the borders, the so called Goa or Sikkim examples cited by India's detractors in the region are mere examples of consolidation and not proselytizing by the larger power.

The way out for South Asian peace is the prescription offered by globalizers, as World Bank vice president for South Asia, Praful Patel, increase economic activities between states. Patel cites that the intra regional trade was less than one percent of GDP in 2003, less than half of any region. The region has the fewest people to people contacts in the World. Patel has advocated increase in infra structure between states and positive trade policies to improve this situation. Energy can be one of the key exchange currency for intra regional trade as both electricity and gas can provide major benefits to the states of the region. To do so, Patel feels that trust and transparency along with creation of infra structural linkages of highways, skyways and roads are essential.[1]

Indeed much of this appears to be underway albeit at a slow pace. Few points were opened across the line of control in Kashmir apparently for movement of aid material after the earthquake, but these could soon become permanent features as routes once opened are difficult to close down. As also the Gadra - Munnabao rail and road links are slated to be opened shortly. With Tibet and China, the Nathu La route is to be opened in 2006. This would greatly open up the region economically as well as culturally. If we can in the longer time frame convert these economic benefits into political ones to evolve a confederation of states modeled on the European Union, it would be a great boon to the vast multitudes living in poverty and anarchy in the region. The defence budgets of states could straight away be halved as the main threats are envisaged and directed at each other.

Importance of Processes of Peace

In the initial nation building process in South Asia after the end of the colonial rule creating a nation state from a patchwork of feudal land lordism necessitated a unitary federal approach in entire South Asia from the 1950's to 1980's. The period from 1980's to 2000 was that of turmoil when unitary approach was questioned and challenged while the period from 2000 to 2020 is seen as a period of growth towards federalism. While propagating peace strategies, we need to make clear distinctions between groups adopting violent methods of change and those preferring the parliamentary process. The key to transformation of the people's movement is to convert it to adopt the non violent, democratic path rather than the insurgent or terrorist course. There should be no reason in the 21st Century particularly with emphasis on information age tools as media, public opinion polls, transparency in all spheres of public as well as private life for people to adopt the violent path to change. However we need to understand that this will not come about very easily on its own, but would require a sustained, incremental approach which may be strewn by violence.

The process of peace however has to ensure that equating democratically elected governments with groups which propagate violence and the non parliamentary route to power such as LTTE in Sri Lanka or Hurriyat in Kashmir needs to be reviewed. The peace process should distinguish between politics of peace and politics of violence and foster the former while ruthlessly defeating the latter. The peace process itself should promote subtly plural values, egalitarian society, non violent and parliamentary route to power. The population should be made to understand the dangers of supporting ethnic chauvinism though it takes time for people to realize the hazards of the path of violence adopted by terrorist groups. Initially there will be sympathy, followed by support leading to greater violence by terrorist groups till realization sets in that the violent path is not the one which will bring about change or happiness to the people. The example of the support of the people of Tamil Nadu to the militancy in Sri Lanka can denote us some of the salient steps on this path, in 1980's it was sympathy followed by support. In the 1990's realization came that the path of violence was tainted with blood, which in the 2000's has resulted in alienation of the people of Tamil Nadu from the destiny of Sri Lankan Tamils.

Sino - Indian Relations

Sino Indian relations are held hostage to the boundary dispute after the ignominious war of 1962. India has claimed that China is illegally occupying 43,180 sq. km. of Jammu and Kashmir including 5180 sq. km. illegally ceded to Beijing by Islamabad under Sino-Pakistan Boundary agreement in 1963. China accuses India of possessing

90,000 sq. km. of Chinese territory mostly in Arunachal Pradesh. In Second phase of the Sino – Indian border talks the Special representatives are mandated to work out an agreed framework for a boundary settlement based on mutually agreed political parameters and guiding principles which had been evolved during the visit of the Chinese premier Wen Jiabao to India on 11 April 2005. The special representative mechanism to address the border issue was created during the June 2003 visit of then Prime Minister Atal Bihari Vajpayee to China.

Prime Minister Manmohan Singh and Chinese President Hu Jintao, met on 14 September 2005 on the sidelines of the UN General Assembly. They reached an agreement to seek a reasonable solution to the boundary question with greater urgency. Guiding principles and political parameters should form the basis of solution for long standing disputes.[2]

First round of talks under the second phase were concluded with a bid to find an agreed framework for a boundary settlement based on mutually agreed political guiding principles between National Security Advisor M K Narayanan and Chinese Vice Foreign Minister and Special Representative for boundary talks, Dai Bingguo from 26–28 September 2005 at Beijing. The Chinese foreign ministry spokesman Qin Gang said that China and India are making efforts to find a fair and reasonable solution to the border issue. The solution has to be acceptable to both sides.[3] The next round of talks are slated for January 2006 during Dai's visit to India.

Indian Prime Minister, Mr Manmohan Singh had a discussion with Chinese Premier, Mr Wen Jiabao on the side lines of the ASEAN and East Asia summits in Kuala Lumpur on 14 December 2005. The meeting was reported to be fruitful though negotiations are expected to be prolonged due to the complicated nature of the problem.[4] The joint working group set up to explore the possibility of a Sino-Indian preferential trade agreement has also submitted its recommendations and the next steps will be taken for implementation shortly. The Prime Minister thanked China for support on India's entry into the ITER for development of thermal energy.[5] The Indian Prime Minister also had a review of economic cooperation with the Japanese Premier, Mr Junichiro Koizumi. He thanked Japan for its support on the ITER. Japan has assured additional measures on cooperation on a global scale on existing and emerging issues particularly on infrastructure cooperation in disaster management.[6] This Indo – Japanese axis is also significant as China and Japan are major constituents of the World economy as well as active competitors in the North Asian power sphere.

The Chinese are known to be elusive about their intentions on the border issue. A general consensus amongst observers is that China having determined its minimum interests and claim areas will follow through to maintain its stand regardless of what negotiations are undertaken concurrently. This was evident with reports of Chinese incursions on the 470 km border with Bhutan in November 2005 violating the 1998 Sino Bhutanese border treaty of peace and tranquility.[7] What is the Chinese intention in this case is difficult to assess except the need to maintain long term claims on the burner.

India needs to leverage the presence of Dalai Lama in India as a bargaining chip by highlighting the Tibet card, instead it is said that Indian policy makers are trying to soft pedal the issue to avoid hurting Chinese sensibilities. China has undertaken major developments in Tibet to include -

(a) Construction of railway line from Golmud in China's Qinghai province to Lhasa.

(b) All weather roads near the Indian territory.

(c) Oil pipeline across Tibet.

Corresponding development of Indian infra structure in Arunachal Pradesh has been recommended by foreign secretary, Shyam Saran.

Sino Indian Border Trade

Chinese Ambassador to India, Mr Sun Yuxi, brought out on 13 October 2005 that border trade between India and

China was to be reopened in April 2006 after infrastructure such as wide roads and customs establishment on the Chinese side is constructed on a war footing. While the Indian side had hoped that the Nathu la route would be opened in October 2005, the Chinese claimed that this would not be desirable as the infra structure would not support movement during the winters which was to commence by end November or early December therefore the route would have been closed two months after opening. The Chinese thus had proposed that trade be revived only after full infra structure was in place. If what the Chinese Ambassador has said is true than the Chinese have a point as without infra structure to support move during the winters the opening in October would have been merely symbolic, however inter state relations particularly between two estranged neighbours as India and China progress as much on symbolism as on factual advancements on the ground or perhaps are a mix of symbolism and facts. Volume of trade five decades ago when the pass was open was said to be $1 billion per annum, hence it was expected that this will be considerably higher once the pass was reopened in April. This was also a welcome development as it would lead to large scale economic activity and create employment opportunities in Sikkim.[8]

In terms of some antagonist developments in Sino-Indian relations, China's delay in opening the trade route through Nathu La on 1 October 2005 for a trial period of one month, at the last minute may also have been to demonstrate dissatisfaction at Indian parleys with America. China has also deployed CSS 5 missiles for regional targeting and also ballistic missiles in Tibet. Chinese assistance to Pakistan's nuclear programme is also said to be with the aim of Indian encirclement. A letter of credit has also been opened to sell arms to Nepal.[9]

Chinese Strategic Capability

China's strategic capability can be reviewed with the help of the yearly US document Annual Report to Congress assessing, "The Military Power of the People's Republic of China 2005" published by the Office of the Secretary of Defence.

US Department of Defence.[10] The report states that Chinese focus on building "comprehensive national power," with emphasis on economic development continued. China is slated to complete its 10th Five Year Plan and is preparing to undertake the 11th Five Year Plan (2006-2010) this year. The philosophical exclamations of Chinese leader Deng's, "24 character" strategy: "*observe calmly; secure our position; cope with affairs calmly; hide our capacities and bide our time; be good at maintaining a low profile; and never claim leadership.*" Later modified with addition of the phrase, "make some contributions (*you suo zuo wei*)" aptly sums up Chinese approach to attaining strategic capabilities in the long term. China continues to place strategic reliance on asymmetric means to achieve parity with advanced states as the United States and will focus on, "asymmetric, non-linear, and "leap ahead" technologies through the 1990s – and for the foreseeable future" to close the gap with the United States. Chinese reliance on information to achieve strategic defence goals is also evident with the new term introduced in the Defense White Paper which exhorts the People's Liberation Army to fight wars adapting to, "local wars under conditions of informationalization." This is also reflected in long term capability building with emphasis on acquisition of command and control, communications, computers, intelligence, surveillance and reconnaissance (C4ISR) assets. Networking is also being emphasized along with institutional changes.

Of particular concern to India is China's missile capability. Details of Chinese missile forces including China's missile inventory, total launchers/missiles and estimated range in that order is as given below.

(a) CSS-4 - ICBM - 20/20, 8,460+ km.

(b) CSS-3 - ICBM - 10-14/20-24, 5,470+ km.

(c) CSS-2 - IRBM - 6-10/14-18, 2,790+ km.

(d) CSS-5 - MRBM - Mod 1/2 34-38/19-23, 1,770+ km.

(e) JL-1 - SLBM - 10-14/10-14 1,770+ km.

(f) CSS-6 - SRBM - 70-80/230-270 - 600 km.

(g) CSS-7 - SRBM - 100-120/420-460 - 300 km.

(h) DF-31 - ICBM DEVELOPMENTAL - 7,250+ km.

(i) DF-31A - ICBM DEVELOPMENTAL - 11,270+ km.

Significant accretion is seen in Chinese SRBM capability with the Second Artillery having five operational SRBM brigades with another brigade deployed along with PLA ground forces. This however may not affect India directly to that an extent as the short range determines a focus towards Taiwan.[11]

Considerations Chinese Strategic Capability - 2006

China ostensibly is not a major threat in 2006. However it will emerge as a cooperative competitor in the economic and energy as also in the military field in the years. Long term trends of Chinese military capability need to be observed and prognostications on what threat it can pose needs to be made accordingly. Of particular concern is the build up of long range aircraft and missile as well as nuclear capability. The factors which need consideration are as follows:-

1. Chinese strategic missile capability.
2. Chinese nuclear capability.
3. Chinese economic appetite and growth of national power.
4. Chinese defence modernisation plan and the time frame of its impact on India vis a vis Chinese deployment of surplus assets from Taiwan and its impact on South East Asia.
5. Chinese indulgence of South Asian states particularly Pakistan and Bangladesh and a benign role of late in Nepal.
6. Chinese interest in Mynamar and the Bay of Bengal.
7. Chinese sensitivity to Indo-US cooperation – Was it the reason for postponement of the Nathu la route?
8. How will Sino – Indian peace talks progress and what will the impact be on the state of security?

Some suggestions for positive relations -

(i) Develop the ongoing border dispute dialogue to a logical conclusion.

(ii) Underplay the military implications of the Indo-US Strategic cooperation.

(iii) Develop cooperative interests in energy development.

(iv) Prompt China towards non military and non nuclear cooperation with Pakistan in particular and Bangladesh in general.

(v) Limit China's role and involvement in Nepal.

Afghanistan - The Frontiers of The New Great Game

"Wars waged abroad are often lost at home; and that may be starting to happen in Iraq" says an Economist quote. Well what is true in Iraq for the USA, should be true in Afghanistan for India, for though the country has not deployed its armed forces there, it has a sizeable number of medical personnel, road construction engineers and workers who have now been threatened with the killing of M R Kutty, the Border Roads driver. But the stakes in Afghanistan for India are high enough to denote the need for continued stay in the country. The issues in Afghanistan are complex. They entail rebuilding a nation from the symbols of nationhood to the construction of a parliament, uniting the Tribal-Federal state, satisfying warlords, caring for the needs of minority ethnic tribes who had a major role in creating a modern nation state and defeating the proponents of anarchy, the Taliban and the Inter Services Intelligence (ISI) of Pakistan, which is accused as a major catalyst of violence in the region. For India a democratic Afghanistan means a secular friend in South Asia, reducing one hot spot in this troubled region wrecked by strife in the past five decades. It means access to Iran and Central Asia, markets for goods and services and also undermining Pakistan's influence in the region. The resistance from Pakistan also implies that India would have to demonstrate substantial fortitude in sustaining its soft campaign of aid and development to the war ravaged state bringing about considerable human security benefits to the people of the state as well as raising India's stake in the international comity of nations. It is the first foray of display of soft power by an emerging power. There is no room for complacency and India and Afghanistan are well set to reap the benefits of this strategic friendship.

Afghanistan has proved an easier area for control than Iraq. It had clearly defined groups of opposition before the war, Taliban, Northern Alliance, Hekmatyar group and so on. There was also clear leadership alternatives aligned to various groupings, castes and clans, well known and easily identifiable, who could be approached for a compromise.

It had low density of population as compared to Iraq. Thus conventional wisdom which denotes that there is a need for a specific number of troops deployed for counter insurgency operations based on space and population was not applicable in Afghanistan and the state could be quelled using a mix of hard and soft power in the central areas, while the peripheral quarters continue to be under varying degrees of independence based on tribal loyalties which may take many more years to fall in line.

Internal Situation

Elections for 249 seat Wolesi Jirga or the Lower House of Parliament from 34 provinces under Afghan-UN Commission were held on 18 September 2005. 12 million Afghans of a 25 million population were registered to vote. 10 percent of 5800 candidates were women. Taliban and Al Qaeda reportedly attempted to disrupt these elections just as they had tried to do so during the Presidential elections in October 2004 but were unsuccessful. Pakistan's ISI is once again reported to be employing unidentified terrorists and criminals to sabotage political stability in Afghanistan.[12] Successful conduct of elections demonstrated the commitment of the nation to a new path of democracy and peace despite continued presence of disruptive elements. The new parliament building was also inaugurated in December 2005 giving flesh to the Constitution. The security situation continues to be precarious particularly in the South where Pushtun warlords remain in control of many areas.

Afghanistan – Controlling the Country Side

The US Armed forces have deployed 17,000 troops mainly in the South in a counter insurgency role while NATO has deployed 9,000 troops in a policing role in the

North and the Western parts of Afghanistan. NATO operates as the International Security Assistance Force. The Pushtuns in the South are continuing to resist the Americans and have already killed 59 Americans and over 1000 Afghans in insurgency related violence in the area. The US has evolved a new concept of PRTs or Provincial Reconstruction Teams in the southern provinces which are garrisons dedicated for reconstruction. NATO forces will be deployed in the South for the first time in the PRTs likely to face the ire of the Taliban which is continuing to run a low simmering insurgency there. When deployed in the South it will operate under the British run Allied Rapid Reaction Corps or ARRC. Each PRT will have a garrison of almost 1000 troops. In Lashkargar, the British will deploy a strengthened British Battalion likely the Royal Anglican Regiment. A mobile reserve of 1000 troops and an American aviation battalion comprising of 12 NATO Apache attack helicopters, six Dutch and six British will also be under the ARRC. This will need redefinition of the rules of engagement under which NATO forces operate in Afghanistan, as they would have to be prepared to fight if not undertake offensive counter insurgency operations as the Americans are doing. Britain is already talking of undertaking counter opium missions in the South. The US aims at merging the US and NATO forces in Afghanistan may take some time as NATO countries are reluctant to undertake a more active role. Taliban can upset US aims by the very crude method as suggested by the Economist, of killing more NATO troops which will dissuade NATO governments from participating actively.[13]

The concept of PRTs is however sound and would provide the much needed security grid in Southern Afghanistan in the shadow of which development and build up can take place.

The Great Game in Afghanistan

Maniappan Raman Kutty, a driver with the Border Roads Organisation working in Afghanistan was kidnapped on 19 November 2005 and his body with throat slashed was found in Southern Afghanistan on 23 November 2005. Taliban claimed to have killed the individual on the plea that the Border Roads Organization did not comply to their demand of pulling out of Afghanistan. However Indian Embassy in Kabul claimed that they had never been contacted by Taliban.[14] This killing represents the mindless regression strategy followed by most fundamentalist organizations as the Taliban. Is it an anti India action or only an anti development action or a combination of both remains to be seen. In Kashmir, the terrorists have very rarely attacked Border Roads Organization personnel or assets as a mark of understanding of the contribution of this organization to development in the State. 38 Indo Tibetan Border Police (ITBP) personnel are reported to be deployed for security of personnel working on the road in Afghanistan and their strength is reportedly being beefed up.[15] It is however very difficult to provide security to drivers working on the highway construction as poor Kutty. Since they have to be constantly on the move from one place to another transporting road material and labour, there is no fixed point security or individual security which can be provided to such personnel. They are also unarmed and probably not even trained to handle small arms. Thus they are the most vulnerable. In such situations as Afghanistan perhaps one answer would be deploy drivers in pairs or buddy system and provide them at least minimal training for self defence as the threat will be ominous even in the days ahead and perhaps would even increase as India's commitment enhances over the years in pursuit of the Great Game.

The killing occurred during the construction of the 219 km long road from Delaram in Afghanistan to Zaranj in Iran which will provide access to Iranian ports of Chabahar and Bandarbass, to Afghanistan shortening the route by over 600 kms. Perhaps this was a thorn in Pakistani strategic plans for the region as links with Iran would have reduced dependence of the Afghans with it. An Indian force in its backyard including its links with Iran would also have been a matter of concern. An Iran-Afghanistan-India linkage will work against Pakistan's long as well as short term interest. Thus some reports state that the killing had a Pakistani hand. The Taliban is also reported to have denied the killing of the Indian BRO driver and also reports of the National

Security Advisor (NSA), Mr M K Narayanan, castigating Pakistan for the killings may have been made against this background. This thread is also supported by the fact that the kidnapping was not followed by any calls for negotiations by the kidnappers and was carried out virtually in cold blood. Indians are engaged in a number of projects in Afghanistan to include the 220 KV double circuit transmission line from Pul-e-Khumri to Kabul at a cost of $111 million; a $ 80 million project of reconstruction of the Salma Dam Power Project in Herat and reconstruction of the prestigious Habibia School.[16]

There are also said to be approximately 700 Indians working in Afghanistan in various capacities particularly para medics and doctors.[17] The security of these and over 290 Indians in road projects and many others in scattered projects across Afghanistan is thus very important. At Herat, Mazar-e-Sharif, Shebargan and Kandahar the only decent hospitals are said to be run by small teams of 4 to 6 doctors, nurses and para medics from India.[18] The Afghan guerrillas can be fought psychologically by denoting them that they are encouraging casualties of their own kith and kin by forcing out medical teams. Such cases of killings of our personnel deployed abroad on tasks in overall national as well as human interest may be expected in the future as well particularly in Southern Afghanistan. Protection of Indians deployed in the area needs to be undertaken either by deploying greater military or para military troops or in conjunction with the PRT nodes with an understanding with the NATO and US troops in Southern Afghanistan. Nations do not abandon their strategic objectives due to killing of individuals as the brave Kutty. All sympathy is due to his family Bindu, sons Ajay 8 years old and the little 3 year old to, Akshay. They are all valiant soldiers in this great game.

A strategic relationship is also being built between the Afghan leadership in Kabul and beyond and the Indian government across all its dimensions to include diverse leaders from Qanooni to Karzai, the Pushtuns and the Tajiks as well as other ethnic communes. India has to balance relations with the US and Russia as well as understand the sensitivities of Pakistan which is affected by a serious dent in its area of influence losing primacy in Afghan polity which it had enjoyed for over a decade and a half. In the internal polity of Afghanistan there are said to be four players, the Afghan government, the main ethnic groupings like the Northern Alliance, the break away Pashtun groups and the renegade Taliban.[19] Pakistan is likely to have some control over the renegade Taliban as well as some splinter groups. How we play our cards with these players will affect our stakes in this vital region.

In this context a quote by US Vice President, Dick Cheney needs some consideration. "It is a dangerous illusion to suppose that another retreat by the civilized world would satisfy the appetite of the terrorists and get them to leave us alone – such a retreat would convince the terrorists that free nations will change our policies, forsake our friends, and abandon our interests whenever we are confronted with murder and blackmail".[20] Nations always have to take their international responsibilities and commitments seriously and go for the long haul. Any commitment has to be made for a period of 10 to 15 years and no less. This was perhaps the fundamental mistake when India deployed in Sri Lanka in the 1980's. It should be very clear that no foreign presence will be welcome in any alien country for long, even Indians greeted with open arms in Bangladesh were reviled in a few months, the Allies were welcomed in Paris but were loathe to stay there any more than required so were the Allies in Germany after its conquest. A model needs to be evolved, to prop up confidence and capabilities of indigenous forces and governments with foreign troops operating in the background. Use of soft power as being done by India with local protection is another facet which can be employed to extend influence in the desired area.

Indo - US Cooperation

Indo – US Nuclear Cooperation

18 July 2005, US President George W Bush and Prime Minister Manmohan Singh signed a land mark agreement on civil nuclear cooperation. It envisaged separation of

India's strategic programme into separate civilian nuclear enterprises and its sub sets from military nuclear installations and place the former under safeguards in exchange for global access to nuclear commerce. This move has invited a number of diverse responses summarized as given below:–

(a) The antagonists feel that this is an asymmetrical agreement as it binds India without reciprocal US commitments. Congressional approval in the days ahead as per US legislative procedure may perhaps lead to some commitments by the Bush government as any concessions at this stage is not legislatively prudent and will also make it difficult to gain approval of the legislators influenced by the strong non proliferation lobby in America.

(b) Separation of civilian and military facilities would impact ability to produce requisite quantity of weapons grade fissile materials and tritium is another critique offered. Government sources do not agree with this surmise and claim that Tritium can also be produced as it is required in gram quantities and has suffered due to lack of irradiation spaces in research reactors.

(c) Separation will be difficult, costly and untenable. This is a problem as sequestering organizations and personnel will be more difficult that physical facilities.

A pragmatic appraisal will reveal, that India is in dire need of nuclear supplies particularly new sources of natural uranium to run its nuclear plants and also produce weapons grade plutonium. It would thus be safe to agree with Ashley Tellis that the Manmohan-Bush agreement is a major victory for India.[21]

In the ongoing parleys, a series of statements by US officials and law makers voicing new benchmarks and placing the burden of meeting conditions associated with the deal entirely on India has heckled India's ambassador to the United States, Mr Ronen Sen. US officials had suggested that India should separate its civilian and military nuclear reactors before Washington fulfills part of the deal. Some US law makers have also said that approval will hinge on additional steps by India such as implementing a moratorium on fissile material production. This was not acceptable to the Indian side as it would imbalance the pact. US – India nuclear agreement was a public document hence it should not be renegotiated or reframed. Opposition from non proliferation lobby in the Washington is surprising given that it had been a mute witness to A Q Khan's clandestine proliferation in Pakistan while ignoring India's strong legacy of non proliferation and commitment to international laws and regulations. Nicholas Burns, Chief U S negotiator had in September 2005 presented Indian officials with a blue print suggesting how the Americans might go about separating Indian nuclear facilities, but the Indians felt that they will be able to carry this out without any external help.

A slow pace of progress can be expected during the year ahead as the internal political dynamics of two very vibrant democracies will come into play.[22] But 2006 will certainly see India forging ahead in its quest for acquiring nuclear energy resources in tune with its long term energy requirements.

Indo-US Defence Cooperation

A new landmark in Indo – US Defense relations was the signing of the, "The Defense Framework - New Framework for the U.S.-India Defense Relationship" by Minister of Defense of India, Pranab Mukherjee and Secretary of Defense of the United States, Donald Rumsfeld on 28 June 2005 in Washington DC. This spelt out refurbishing of the US-India defence relationship which has come out of the cold war mode into that of active engagement. The document has been included at the end of the chapter.

US Defence Security Cooperation Agency (DSCA) is the nodal agency for fostering defence cooperation by the USA with other countries. Indo – US Defence Cooperation received a phillip during the year 2005. Indo US Defence Policy Group met on 21-22 November 2005 in Washington after a gap of 16 months to discuss sale of military hardware including missile defence systems to India. The meeting concluded on 24 November 25 at Washington DC. The three day meeting of DPG was co chaired by Indian Defence Secretary Shekhar Dutt and Under Secretary for Defence and Policy Eric Edelman. Views on international strategic and security situation and on the further development of bilateral defence cooperation as envisaged under the Indo U S Defence Frame work agreement inked in June 2005 were exchanged. The Military Cooperation Group met at Honolulu, Hawaii on 17-18 October where India requested participation by the IAF in the international Red Flag Exercises.[23] At the end of seventh round of talks importance of service to service ties, series of joint exercises between the armed forces of both countries including recently held Cope India 2005 exercise between November 7 – 17 2005 was reviewed. The sub groups established for defence cooperation include military cooperation group, joint technology group, senior security technology group and senior technology security group and defence procurement and production group.[24]

In terms of defence sales to India from the US, these have tripled over the past few years from $5.6 million in 2003 to $ 17.7 million in 2004 and are slated to be $ 64 million in 2005.[25] This shows considerably enhanced interests of American companies in India. A Technical Assistance Agreement outlining the legalities and processes of technology licensing and transfers between the USA and India is however essential before the Indian industry can benefit from contracts by the US defense industry. Such an agreement thus needs to be worked out on priority during the year 2006.

While the cooperation in training is progressing well, arms and weapon procurements are not going apace. Establishment of a protocol for processing arms procurement requests is essential. Indian officials are particularly irked that while sanctions were lifted in September 2001 and a wish list was given by India to the United States in November 2002 to include Patriot anti missile systems, radars, guidance and propulsion systems for ballistic missiles, satellite communications, imagery, jammers, electronic warfare systems, submarine rescue and thermal sights no progress has been made except for the last two items on the list.[26] The sticky point appears Indian insistence on co production of all arms being procured through foreign agencies given its experience of lack of alternative sources of supply during the Soviet dismemberment followed by US sanctions.

Indo US Technology Cooperation

The Indo-US High Technology Group had its fourth meeting during the year on 30 November and 1 December 2005 in New Delhi. An area of prime concern is a technology safeguard agreement between both the countries which would allay American fears of transfer of sensitive technology to countries such as Iran and Libya. This apart there was general agreement on the need for progressive cooperation in extending technology benefits to India with greater involvement of Indian companies to join the supply chains of global vendors.[27]

Health is the next opportunity for future cooperation between the USA and India by 2020 feels the Ranbaxy chairman, Mr Harpal Singh. US is slated to spend 20 per cent of its GDP in health care. Collaboration between the US and India involving hospitals and laboratories would reduce healthcare costs for the United States with great savings for its economy while for India it will virtually replicate the benefits that accrued from the IT revolution.[28]

Russia- Renewed Opportunity

Russia has been severely undermined in the international community with the republics of the erstwhile Soviet Union gradually leaving its orbit to embrace Western and European nations politically as well as militarily. Its economy is also floundering as the manufacturing base which was heavily dependent on a thriving arms industry, nuclear and space technology finds itself at sea in the information age of bits and bytes. The Rose Revolution in Georgia and the Orange revolution in Ukraine have undermined the efforts made by Russian leaders to reintegrate these separated states and driven these newly formed nations and their pro Western governments out of the Russian sphere of influence. Though the economic consequences of such moves have been unfortunate, with slow growth of economies and increase in level of poverty as linkages with Moscow which underwrote a large amount of the economy particularly oil of these states have been severed, the pro West leadership of Saakashvili in Georgia and Yushchenko in Ukraine has been unmoved.[29]

Russia is countering these influences by removing subsidies on gas and other economic aid been provided to these states. Internally this has led growth of xenophobes in Russia along with Eurasianist views favouring a look east policy of stronger ties with Eastern nations as well as with Middle East countries as Iran.[30] A Reuters report quoted in the Sunday Express has stated that Russia plans to sell more than $ 1 billion worth of tactical surface to air missiles, modernize the air force and supply patrol boats to Iran. The missiles include 29 TOR-M1 systems designed to bring down aircraft and guided missiles at low altitudes. Russian sources claimed that there was no international restriction to sell arms to Iran and all the weapons were essentially defensive in nature. Typically, Rosoboronexport, Russia's state defence supplier and Russian Defence Ministry declined to comment on the issue.[31]

Great nations never die or even fade away; they only rise from the ashes of each demotion over decades and centuries. It is apparent that Russia is undergoing just such a turbulence in its status and will rise from these depths, garnering its strengths particularly the arms industry and soft nuclear capability. In this it is exploiting the pariah states, such as Iran which have been isolated by the United States and other Western nations, to sell arms as well as nuclear technology. The Western embargo in fact is being used by Russia as a stratagem to exploit its proximity with such states while at the same time gaining concessions for the international community on their irrendicitism, Iran's nuclear whittling down recently being a classic example. As Russians feel increasingly isolated in the international community, it is an opportunity for long time friends as India to engage it economically as well as in defence and security relations. Russia remains a powerhouse in all respects and will reemerge as one of the great powers if not in the orbit of six by 2050; United States, European Union, China, India, Russia and a possible conglomerate of Islamic states led by Iran or Egypt.

Energy Security – The Need Of The Future

The theme of 2006 for security and international relations would be Energy security. It will drive Indian relations with other states beyond as well as within the periphery of our national interest. Even relations with Pakistan are set to be catalyzed by the need for energy. Thus Pakistan has assured full support to the $ 7 billion gas pipeline between Iran and India terming it as the Pro-Poor Gas Pipeline for affordable and sustainable supply of energy to benefit the poor of both India and Pakistan. This came about during the third meeting of the India-Pakistan joint working group(JWG) on 17 December 2005.[32] The time frame visualized for the start of the project is by 2007 and completion by 2010. Drawing 60 million cubic metres, India will increase it to 90 million cubic metres in the next 2-3 years while Pakistan will double the 30 million cubic metres being drawn initially. The key dates of this proposal in 2006 will be as follows:-

(a) Monthly meeting of the technical sub working groups to finalise the transportation tariff, transit fee payable to Pakistan, system configuration, pipeline route and pricing mechanism.

(b) February 2006 - The first trilateral meeting between Iran, India and Pakistan. Visit of Pakistani petroleum minister was also scheduled.[33]

(c) March 2006 - Next JWG meeting.

(d) April or May – Finalization of the Project Structure and Framework Agreement between Iran, India and Pakistan.

India needs to improve relations with Nepal as it can be a major source of hydro power for India some 43,000 MW which include the following projects under consideration[34]

(a) West Seti Hydro Project.

(b) Upper Karnali.

(c) Pancheshwar.

(d) Sapta Kosi.

(e) Sun Kosi.

(f) Burhi Gandaki.

(g) Kamla Multipurpose.

(h) Bagmati

Diplomacy Of Military Training

The Year 2005 saw India undertaking vigorous defence diplomacy through joint training with a large number of nations from the United States to Mongolia. This apart Chinese military observers were slated to witness tank maneouvres in deserts in November.[35] This has certainly been a great leap forward for our defence forces who are seeing a new era of glasnost which will see them emerging as the finest fighting force in the World. Some of these joint training activities are covered in the succeeding paragraphs.

USA - India Joint Training

Indo – US joint training is based on a structured defence cooperation agreement comprising of a Defence Policy Group and ten year frame work. The Indian Armed forces are able to share their knowledge with US forces being deployed in a variety of roles including conventional wars, low intensity conflict and disaster management. This is the typical, "three block war", concept talked of by US military thinkers as Krulak envisaging an army having to fight a conventional, sub conventional and civil assistance role all at one time. The benefit of experience of both sides is therefore mutual.

Joint training with US defence personnel of the US Army Pacific was carried out in the Counter Insurgency and Jungle Warfare School (CIJW School), Vairangte in September 2005. CIJW School began as an ad hoc jungle warfare school in Munkree in Meghalya 1967 and shifted to Vairangte in Mizoram in 1971. A 42 member team of 7 officers and 35 soldiers was the third batch of personnel to be trained in the school. Training was limited to two weeks. Col Arnold Marcus said that as the US Armed Forces were called for deployment in different countries and situations hence there was a varied training requirement. 50 percent of the US team was from Guam island, the Western most territory of US and half from 25 Infantry Brigade both of the

Pacific Command. 40 officers and jawans of 22 MARATHA LI also participated in the exercise. The training was typically carried out in three phases, class room, operations in semi urban areas and special operations in jungle terrain. Mongolian and Uzbek officers are also likely to be in trained in the CIJW School shortly.[36]

Indo – Russian Military Training

Joint military exercises between Indian and Russian troops were carried out from 11 to 19 October 2005. The airborne exercise codenamed, "Indra" was conducted in a mechanized environment with para troops dropped along with mechanized Armoured Personnel Carriers, heavy guns and related equipment. Anti terrorist operations were also practiced. Russian defence minister and other top ranking officials witnessed the exercises.[37]

Indo – US Air Force Air Exercises November 2005

The aim of the Indo – US Air exercise in November 2005 was to understand the operational concepts through closer interaction, familiarize fighter controllers with each others procedures and train together with AWACS. This would facilitate joint operations during contingencies including the tsunami disaster.[38] 81 U S Air Force personnel landed in Kolkata and proceeded towards Kalaikunda air force station for the drills slated to begin on 7 November 2005. Communist Party Marxist activists had protested landing of US Air Force personnel in India on 03 and 04 November at the Kolkata airport. An F 16 squadron of the USAF along with AWACS participated in the joint exercise.[39] Air Commodore Abdul Saikia AOC Kalaikunda led the Indian and Nelson Cabot, the US team. Nelson is the commander of the 36 Operations Group of the United States Air Force. The 300 strong crew included 50 US officers and three women officers. Sukhois, F16, Jaguars, MIGs and AWACS took part in this exercise.[40]

A USAF transport aircraft with 28 wheels and 12 F 16 Falcon fighters also reported to have arrived on 06 November 2005. Protests by CPI(M) cadres led by Dipak Sarkar, district secretary were mounted at the Kalaikunda air base against the use of AWACS which as per the cadres would expose our facilities to US radars who can destroy our facilities in case of a confrontation. Fears were also expressed that the US could take over the air base as it had done so in as many as 130 countries.[41]

The joint exercise at Kalaikunda, in West Bengal between the Indian and US Air Force marked a new chapter in the Indo – US joint relationship. For the first time, AWACS and the F 16's in approximately a squadron strength participated with the IAF which fielded the MIG 21, MIG 27, MIG 29, Sukhoi 30 and Mirage 2000.[42] With the acquisition of Isreali developed AWACS, the IAF would have greatly benefited from this exercise. Kalaikunda is developing in a state of the art base for training with the Singapore Air Force also bidding for training facilities there due to the large area available for exercises around it including an air to ground range in close vicinity.[43]

Indian Armed Forces – Defence Relations Myanmar

The Indian Army Chief of Staff, General J J Singh visited Myanmar from 29 November 2005 for three days during which joint operations on the border are said to have been finalized. This has perhaps seen launching of operations by the Myanmarese Army against camps of the Naga Khaplang faction in Northern Myanmar in December 2005. The visits to Myanmar had commenced with the Chief of Air Staff visiting Myanmar in November 2004 wherein he is said to have proposed upgradation of the Myanmarese air force.[44] In third week of January, Indo Naval defence relations are said to be raised to a new level, with the visit of Navy Chief, Admiral Arun Prakash visiting Myanmar.

Myanmar's military junta is headed by the head of state, Than Shwe and his second in command, General Maung Aye who will be engaged by the Naval Chief and Chairman of Chiefs of Staff Committee and possibilities of supply of BN 2 Islander maritime surveillance aircraft, deck based air defense guns and training exchange progammes are expected to be discussed.[45]

Indian engagement of Myanmar has a number of connotations. Ideologically the military junta should be anathema for Indian democratic leanings now forming part of international or global values. India has been propagating democracy and release of Aun Sang Kyii but it is emphasized that this should be done by the country at its own pace and manner. Breaking off ideology and foreign relations based on realistic politics is a new trend in Indian relations and this has seen engagement of the Myanmar's junta. In addition to abandonment of purely ideological considerations, the impetus has probably been Chinese engagement of Myanmar to consolidate its relationship and reach the Bengal seas. An advantage gained with improved military relations with Myanmar is that joint operations can be launched in conjunction with the Army on the other side to destroy bases for North East militants in Myanmar. Such an operation has been launched in January 2005 as well as December 2005 and has seen mixed results. A similar operation launched in Bhutan by the Royal Bhutan Army had resulted in lowering insurgency levels in Assam and bringing the ULFA cadre to the negotiating table.

THE DEFENSE FRAMEWORK. New Framework for the U.S.-India Defense Relationship, Signed on June 28, 2005 in Washington DC by Minister of Defense of India, Pranab Mukherjee and Secretary of Defense of the United States, Donald Rumsfeld 28 June 2005.

1. The United States and India have entered a new era. We are transforming our relationship to reflect our common principles and shared national interests. As the world's two largest democracies, the United States and India agree on the vital importance of political and economic freedom, democratic institutions, the rule of law, security, and opportunity around the world. The leaders of our two countries are building a U.S.-India strategic partnership in pursuit of these principles and interests.

2. Ten years ago, in January 1995, the Agreed Minute on Defense Relations Between the United States and India was signed. Since then, changes in the international security environment have challenged our countries in ways unforeseen ten years ago. The U.S.-India defense

relationship has advanced in a short time to unprecedented levels of cooperation unimaginable in 1995. Today, we agree on a new Framework that builds on past successes, seizes new opportunities, and charts a course for the U.S.-India defense relationship for the next ten years. This defense relationship will support, and will be an element of, the broader U.S.-India strategic partnership.

3. The U.S.-India defense relationship derives from a common belief in freedom, democracy, and the rule of law, and seeks to advance shared security interests. These interests include:

— Maintaining security and stability;

— Defeating terrorism and violent religious extremism;

— Preventing the spread of weapons of mass destruction and associated materials, data, and technologies; and

— Protecting the free flow of commerce via land, air and sea lanes.

4. In pursuit of this shared vision of an expanded and deeper U.S.-India strategic relationship, our defense establishments shall:

(a) Conduct joint and combined exercises and exchanges;

(b) Collaborate in multinational operations when it is in their common interest;

(c) Strengthen the capabilities of our militaries to promote security and defeat terrorism;

(d) Expand interaction with other nations in ways that promote regional and global peace and stability;

(e) Enhance capabilities to combat the proliferation of weapons of mass destruction;

(f) In the context of our strategic relationship, expand two-way defense trade between our countries. The United States and India will work to conclude defense transactions, not solely as a means to strengthen our countries' security, reinforce our strategic partnership, achieve greater interaction between our armed forces, and build greater understanding between our defense establishments;

(g) In the context of defense trade and a framework of technology security safeguards, increase opportunities for technology transfer, collaboration, co-production, and research and development;

(h) Expand collaboration relating to missile defense;

(i) Strengthen the abilities of our militaries to respond quickly to disaster situations, including in combined operations;

(j) Assist in building worldwide capacity to conduct successful peacekeeping operations, with a focus on enabling other countries to field trained, capable forces for these operations;

(k) Conduct exchanges on defense strategy and defense transformation;

(l) Increase exchanges of intelligence; and

(m) Continue strategic-level discussions by senior leadership from the U.S. Department of Defense and India's Ministry of Defence, in which the two sides exchange perspectives on international security issues of common interest, with the aim of increasing mutual understanding, promoting shared objectives, and developing common approaches.

5. The Defense Policy Group shall continue to serve as the primary mechanism to guide the U.S.-India strategic defense relationship. The Defense Policy Group will make appropriate adjustments to the structure and frequency of its meetings and of its subgroups, when agreed to by the Defense Policy Group co-chairs, to ensure that it remains an effective mechanism to advance U.S.-India defense cooperation.

6. In recognition of the growing breadth and depth of the U.S.-India strategic defense relationship, we hereby establish the Defense Procurement and Production Group and institute a Joint Working Group for mid-year review of work overseen by the Defense Policy Group.

The Defense Procurement and Production Group will oversee defense trade, as well as prospects for co-production and technology collaboration, broadening the scope of its predecessor subgroup the Security Cooperation Group.

The Defense Joint Working Group will be subordinate to the Defense Policy Group and will meet at least once per year to perform a midyear review of work overseen by the Defense Policy Group and its subgroups (the Defense Procurement and Production Group, the Joint Technical Group, the Military Cooperation Group, and the Senior Technology Security Group), and to prepare issues for the annual meeting of the Defense Policy Group.

7. The Defense Policy Group and its subgroups will rely upon this Framework for guidance on the principles and objectives of the U.S.-India strategic relationship, and will strive to achieve those objectives. Signed in Arlington, Virginia, USA, on June 28, 2005, in two copies in English, each being equally authentic.[46]

Secretary of Defence	*Minister of Defence*
FOR AND ON BEHALF OF THE GOVERNMENT OF THE UNITED STATES OF AMERICA	FOR AND ON BEHALF OF THE GOVERNMENT OF THE REPUBLIC OF INDIA

References

1. Patel, Praful. "For an Integrated South Asia" The Economic Times. 2 December 2005. New Delhi. p.16.
2. Economic Times. 16 September 2005. p. 3. new delhi.
3. Joseph, Anil K. "India, China conclude 6th Round of Dialogue" The Economic Times. 29 September 2005. New Delhi. p. 2.
4. Pioneer Report. The Pioneer. 15 December 2005. Lucknow. p. 2.
5. Pioneer Report. The Pioneer, 15 December 2005, Lucknow, p. 2.
6. Pioneer Report. The Pioneer, 15 December 2005, Lucknow, p. 2.
7. Hindustan Times Report. Hindustan Times. 28 December 2005. Lucknow. p. 11.
8. Economic Times Report. "China creating". Economic Times. 14 October 2005. New Delhi. p. 8.

9. Shukla, Saurabh. "The Dalai Lama" India Today. 17 October 2005. p. 44, 46.

10. This portion of the chapter is adapted from Annual Report to Congress. "The Military Power of the People's Republic of China 2005". Office of the Secretary of Defense. United States of America. Downloaded from web site. Pentagon.gov. Down loaded 23 October 2005.

11. This portion of the chapter is adapted from Annual Report to Congress. "The Military Power of the People's Republic of China 2005". Office of the Secretary of Defense. United States of America. Downloaded from web site. Pentagon.gov. Down loaded 23 October 2005.

12. Baid, Samuel. Pak Role in Afghan Democracy. Sunday Pioneer. 18 September 2005. Lucknow, p. 5.

13. The Economist. "Southward, ho!" The Economist. 5 November 2005, p. 32.

14. Times of India Report.The Times of India. 24 November 2005. New Delhi, p. 1.

15. The Indian Express Report. The Indian Express. 2 December 2005. New Delhi, p. 6.

16. Lakshman, Kanchan, "Reframing 'Strategic Depth"South Asia Intelligence Review. Weekly Assessments and Briefings Volume 4, No. 20, November 28, 2005.

17. Saksena, Rashmi. "Indians unsafe" . The Hindustan Times. 16 December 2005. Lucknow. p.1.

18. Bajeli-Datt, Kavita. "Terror Highway". The Week. 4 December 2005. p. 36.

19. Shukla, Ajai. "Small start to the Great Game". The Indian Express. 30 November 2005. Lucknow. p. 9.

20. The Economist Report. T he Economist. 26 November 2005. p. 35 .

21. Tellis, Ashley. "Enriching Agreement" India Today 17 October 2005. p. 47.

22. Chiddanda Rajghatta. Times of India. 25 November 2005. New Delhi. p. 6.

23. Aroor, Shiv. India, US. Indian Express. 29 September 2005. New Delhi. p. 5.

24. Times of India Report. Times of India. 25 November 2005. New Delhi. p. 6.

25. Parthasarthy, G. "US looks to India in a new light". The Pioneer. 15 December 2005. Lucknow. p. 6.

26. Raghuvanshi, Vivek. "India irked", Defense News. 2 May 2005. p. 22.

27. Raghuvanshi, Vivek. "India, US ", Defense News. 12 December 2005. p. 34.

28. Parthasarthy, G. "US looks to India in a new light". The Pioneer. 15 December 2005. Lucknow. p. 6.

29. Shaumian, Tatiana. "Not everything is orange", The Sunday Pioneer. 4 December. 2005. Lucknow. p.11.
30. Shaumian, Tatiana. "Not everything is orange", The Sunday Pioneer. 4 December. 2005. Lucknow. p.11.
31. The Sunday Express. 4 December 2005. Lucknow, p. 5.
32. The Times of India Report. "It's a Deal ", The Sunday Times of India. 18 December 2005. Lucknow. p. 1.
33. The Times of India Report. "It's a Deal ", The Sunday Times of India. 18 December 2005. Lucknow. p. 1.
34. Gupta, Supriyo. "Alienating theKing". The Pioneer. 25 November 2005. Lucknow. p. 7.
35. Pioneer Report. "Hectic Training on cards for Indian jawans" The Pioneer. 17 September, 2005. p. 2. Lucknow.
36. Kashyap, Samudra Gupta. "Mizoram", Indian Express. 27 September 2005. Lucknow. p. 6.
37. Pioneer Report. "Hectic Training on cards for Indian jawans" The Pioneer. 17 September, 2005. p. 2. Lucknow.
38. The Pioneer Report. The Pioneer, 18 November 2005. Lucknow. p. 2.
39. Times of India Report. Times of India, 06 November 2005. Lucknow p. 7.
40. Bandopadhaya, Krishendu. "Flying", The Times of India. 8 November 2005. Lucknow. p. 7.
41. Nagchoudhury, Subrata. "Mock battles", The Indian Express. 7 November 2005. Lucknow. p. 1,2
42. The Pioneer Report. The Pioneer, 18 November 2005. Lucknow. p. 2.
43. The Pioneer Report. The Pioneer, 18 November 2005. Lucknow. p. 2.
44. Aroor, Shiv. "India to firm up", The Indian Express. 16 December 2005. Lucknow. p. 2.
45. Aroor, Shiv. "India to firm up", The Indian Express. 16 December 2005. Lucknow. p. 2.
46. Downloaded from newdelhi.usembassy.gov on 30 December 2005

11

Rationalising Islam – The Conflict Within

"Islam is in its origins an Arab religion —— Islam is not simply a matter of conscience or private belief. It makes imperial demands —— His (Islamists) holy places are in Arab land; his sacred language is Arabic. His idea of history alters. He rejects his own, he becomes whether he likes it or not, a part of the Arab story."

V S Naipaul

" —— the principles of traditional Islam can concur with the best of Western values on many critical issues —— "

King Abdullah of Jordan

Naipaul and Abdullah are apparent contradictions in interpretation of the great religion of Islam. Ironically the traditional Muslim fails to acknowledge and appreciate the minions of both these savants. Naipaul's summary of Islam is the essence of how it is resisting the two dominant trends of our times, localization as well as globalization, the Muslim continues to be an Islamite first and then a global citizen or even a citizen of his country. To remind them of their umbilical link with Mecca there is the yearly Haj and of their sacred duty to their religion Ramzan. Abdullah sees a closer linkage between Islamic and western values which he feels are universal in nature. Increased globalization and influence of the West in all walks of life, political, social, economic and cultural has led Islamists into characteristic isolation due to perhaps the loudness of Western hedonism. International values as democracy, freedom of speech, gender rights, rule of law are relatively alien to the Islamic World beset by medieval feudal values in many ways. In their struggle to adopt to newer realities, Islamists are embracing the Shariah, the ancient laws of Islam which they are comfortable with and with which they bench mark. These evidently clash with modern laws espoused by rest of the civilizations including the measured Chinese and Indic cultures.

Islam is beset by a crisis within its three main branches, Sunni, Shia and Ibadi and eight schools of jurisprudence or madhhabs.[1] The main clash is between the two prominent strains, Sunni Wahabbism and Shia Sufism. Wahhabism the militant strain in Sunni Islam has been the most belligerent as its followers, mostly simple, uneducated folk, unable to make a living in the modern World, feeling greatly threatened and hence waging a war in the manner which is easiest to adopt, terrorism. But Islam is rapidly adjusting to the new realities of global political and social order, modernizing states as Jordan are no longer silent mutants to the mayhem of terrorists and loud protests were heard against killing of innocents in Amman on 9 November 2005. Other states are not too far behind. It is said that the global jihadis have created many enemies within Islam through their, "self goals" in Istanbul, Casablanca, Sharm el-Sheikh and Riyadh alienating Muslim masses.[2] Surprisingly Afghanistan which suffered under the most virulent Islamic rule of the Taliban has been recovering speedily with a new constitution, a new parliament and a new democratic government with equal rights and opportunities to all including women. The Afghan senate has 50 percent of its members as women, while there are equal rights enshrined for all minorities, Hindus, Sikhs and so on. Ironically Indian experiment with democracy which is in its sixth decade now has yet to grant equality in parliamentary seats for the fairer sex.

In other places in the World, Islamic preachers are said to have become more moderate, such as the public admonition of the jihadists by preachers as Shiekh Abu Muhammad al-Maqdisi who warned that excesses by terrorists has defiled the image of Islam.[3] Iraq under American containment for over two years now has been regarded as the fountainhead of the Islamic revolution against western dominance but a quiet realization has forced a rethink in many countries including Egypt and Saudi Arabia who see the tide of terrorism engulfing their countries. Thus their leadership is engaged with the Iraqi

Sunnis to thrash out a compromise formula for participating in the Iraqi administration.[4]

Radicalization and dehumanization of the struggle within Islam is best exemplified by emergence of women Islamic suicide bombers in the Middle East, Chechnya, the Central Asian states, Iraq and Palestine in the recent past. In a survey by the Newsweek, there have been a number of suicide bomb attacks by Muslim women. The Al Qaeda leadership is reported to have assured women, martyrdom when death is attained through the suicide route, a perverse justice after relegating them for centuries to the oblivion of the burqa and the chaddar. As the Belgian director of police, Glenn Audenaert has said to the Newsweek, "It's a new generation, and perversely emancipation allows women to aspire to martyrdom".[5] Ayman Al Zawahiri, the Egyptian physician and Al Qaeda ideologue is said to be in favour of emancipation of women through education as well as a role in the military. However as the women suicide bomber takes off on her mission of death such esoteric issues are intermingled with more grass roots ones as revenge for bereavement of a near and dear one. The dilemma within Islam is best underlined by the predicament of the Bin Laden family. Osama's son, Hamza Bin Laden is reported to have featured in a film, "The Mujaheedin of Waziristan" fighting the Pakistan security forces at the tender age of 14.[6] On the other hand his niece, Wafah Dufour is modeling with nothing on but ostrich feathers to cover her nymphet body and has even abdicated the Laden surname.

Abdullah II Bin Al-Hussein, the King of Jordan has very succinctly put forth the struggle within Islam which he calls a process of reaffirmation rather than reformation for Islam's fundamentals need no reformulation. The extremist view which is dominant today belongs to a small minority which has gained prominence both amongst Islamic thoughts as well as in the West as these are considered a threat not only physically to Western structures but more so ideologically and culturally to the West's value system.[7] Abdullah states that the principles of traditional Islam and Western values as human rights, liberties, women rights, ban on terrorism, non aggression in the name of religion, and respect for other religions and so on are congruent and not divergent as is given to believe today. It is popular perception in Islamic countries that the West is trying to influence the core beliefs of Islam which is creating antagonism which can be easily avoided by shedding the path of perceived dissonance.[8]

Many modern Islamists as Abdullah are attempting to break away from the shackles of misinterpretation of their religion. Whether they are enlightened feminists as Irshad Manji or heads of governments as Karzai, each in his own way is trying to establish a linkage between Islam and the rest. Manji's rebellious voice within Islam represents the dilemma faced by ardent Islamists who want to stay inside but are offended by its virulence against other religions. Manji says, "I refuse to join an army of automatons in the name of Allah". She represents what should have been done and accepted long back, questioning of the scriptures. Fortunately Christianity had its Reformation which saw this great religion emerge as the magnet to galvanize vast multitudes of humanity through its liberal yet human values which could be easily related by the common man. Hinduism has overthrown the manacles of brahminical tyranny long back to emerge again as a galvanizing force for the people of South and South East Asia, other religions as Buddhism, Sikhism or Judaism had always been intrinsically egalitarian. The movement for reformation of Islam has perhaps just started and the fight within is manifesting as all such struggles do, as a fight without with the outside World. The movement for ijtihad, of independent reasoning is set forth in the Amman Message of November 2004, the full text of which is included at the end of the chapter. Writings of authors such as Manji and more scholastic renditions by Mahmood Mamdani will no doubt reform this great religion, Islam.[9] How much time it will take and how many lives it will cost will depend on the Islamists ability to transcribe their Operation Ijtihad into a non violent movement of change.

Amman Message

In the name of God, Most Merciful, Most Compassionate; Prayers and Salutations upon His chosen Prophet, upon the Prophet's household, his courageous companions, and all the apostles and prophets: *God Almighty said: "Mankind! We created you from a pair of a male and female, and made you into nations and tribes that ye may know each other. The most honoured of you in the sight of God is the most righteous of you" (Al Hujurat: 13).* Amman, the capital of the Hashemite Kingdom of Jordan, seizes the opportunity of this Holy Month of Ramadan, in which the Holy Quran was revealed, to issue a statement to the public, to our brethren in Muslim lands and in this whole world. We are aware of the dangers and challenges the Islamic Nation is facing today at this difficult juncture of its course. Evils threaten its identity, incite disunity, tarnish its religion and assail its tenets; they attack fiercely the very message of Islam. Some who attack Islam imagine it is their enemy. But it is not their enemy. Others, who claim to belong to Islam, have done gruesome and criminal acts in its name. The message that is under attack is the message of tolerance, revealed by the Almighty to His prophet Muhammad, God's prayers and salutations be upon him, and carried after him by his orthodox successors and household members: a message of brotherhood and humanity; forming a righteous religion that embraces the entire sphere of human life, upholding what is good and forbidding what is wrong, accepting of others, and honouring all human beings. Over many years, the Hashemite Kingdom of Jordan has sought to repel assaults on Islam by halting the fallacies against it and promoting true understanding of the faith. These efforts are inspired by the religious and historical legacy of the Hashemite monarchy, honoured as direct descendants of the Prophet, the Messenger of God. For five decades, his late Majesty King Hussein Bin Talal, God rest his soul, persisted tirelessly to reform the image and support the unity of the world's

Muslims. His Majesty King Abdullah II has continued this effort with the same steadfastness since the day he held the flag. Today, His Majesty is determined to ward off Muslim marginalization and isolation in the global movement of human society. His goal is to assert what the world's 1.2 billion Muslims expect themselves to be: full partners in the development of human civilization, and in the progress of humanity in our age. The Muslim faith is based on belief in one God and the message of His Prophet; the daily prayers by which we connect to our Creator; the Ramadan fast in which we resist and discipline the desires of the body; the Zakat charitable tax by which we help others; and the Haj pilgrimage to God's House, Mecca, which represents the unity of the Nation (the Ummah), and is performed by those who are able. These obligations, regulating human behaviour in all its dimensions, have created a strong and cohesive Nation and a great civilization. Equally important, they reflect deep principles that are needed for humanity's own good: unity of the human race, equal rights and obligations, peace, security, social equality, the honouring of pledges, neighborliness and respect for others, and the protection of belongings and property. Islam's principles also provide common ground among different faiths and peoples. The origin of divine religions is one, and Muslims believe in all messengers of God; denying the message of any of them is a deviation from Islam. This furnishes a wide platform upon which peoples of different faiths can meet together, with respect for others' ideas and faiths, and act in common in the service of human society: *"The messenger believeth in that which hath been revealed unto him from his Lord and (so do) the believers. Each one believeth in God and his angels and His scriptures and his messengers – We make no distinction between any of His messengers – and they say: We hear, and we obey. (Grant us) Thy forgiveness, our Lord. Unto thee is the journeying" (Al Baqara: 285).* Islam honours every human being, without distinction of colour, race or religion: *We have honoured the sons of Adam, provided them transport on land and sea, sustained them with good things, and conferred on them special favours above a great part of our creation (Al Isra'a: 70)* Islam also affirms that Muslims, when spreading the call of God, are called to act gently on earth. *Invite to the way of the Lord with wisdom and beautiful preaching and argue with them in ways that are best and most gracious (Al Nahl: 125).* Because the Islamic mission is based on reason, Muslims are to shun violence and cruelty, and speak with kindness and respect: *It is part of the Mercy of God that thou dost deal gently with them, wert thou severe or harsh-hearted, they would have broken away from about thee. So pardon them and ask forgiveness for them and consult with them upon the conduct of affairs. (Aal Imran: 159)* Islam clarified that its message is to bring mercy to all peoples: *We sent thee not save as a Mercy for all creatures. (Al Anbiya'a: 107)* Prophet Muhammad, Peace Be Unto Him, emphasized the concepts of compassion and tenderness in Islam when he said, "Mercy from the Most Merciful is bestowed on those who have mercy on others, and those who have mercy on creations of God on earth, The Almighty in the Heavens will have mercy on you." Islam calls for treating others as one desires to be treated. It urges tolerance and forgiveness, qualities that elevate human life: *The recompense for an injury is an injury equal thereto in degree, but if a person forgives and makes reconciliation, his reward is due from God (Shura: 40) Nor can Goodness and Evil be equal. Repel (Evil) with what is better: Then will be between whom and thee was hatred become as it were thy friend and intimate (Fussilat: 34)* Islam calls for treating others justly, safeguarding their rights and possessions: *And let not the hatred of others to you make you swerve to wrong and depart from justice. Be just: that is next to piety (Al Maida: 8)*

God commands you to return trusts to their owners, and if you judge between people, you shall judge with justice (Al Nisa': 58)

"So give full measure and full weight and wrong not mankind in their goods, and work not confusion in the earth after the fair ordering thereof" (Al A'raf: 85) Islam dictates respect for conventions and pledges, and condemns treachery and treason: *Fulfill the Covenant of God when ye have entered into it, and break not your oaths after you have confirmed them, indeed you made God your surety (Al Nahl: 91)* Islam upholds human life. There is to be no fighting

against non-fighters; no assault on civilians and their properties, on children in their mothers' laps, on students in the schools, on older men and women. To assault the life of a human being is equivalent to assaulting the right to life of all – and this is one of the gravest sins, for life is the basis for the continuation of humanity.

If any one slew a person – unless it be for murder or for spreading mischief in the land – it would be as if he slew the whole people. And if any one saved a life, it would be as if he saved the life of the whole people (Al Ma'ida: 32)

Islam respects balance, moderation, and equanimity: *Thus have we made of you an Ummat justly balanced, that ye might be witnesses over the nations, and the Apostle a witness over yourselves. (Al Baqara: 143)* The Prophet Muhammad, Peace Be Upon Him, said: *"Facilitate and don't hesitate, augur well and don't shun away" (Hadeeth Shareef).* This is the faith that made historic advances in science, scholarship and intellectual life – achievements that empowered a great civilization, in whose achievements non-Muslims had their share, and which became the vehicle to bring knowledge for the West as well. Islam calls on Muslims to demonstrate tolerance and delight in human life; it opposes extremism, exaggeration, and intransigence. These phenomena are veils against right thinking – they conceal the repercussions of one's actions, and encourage a reckless disregard for religion, reason, and civilized behavior. Indeed, Islam rejects extremism as a deviation from true faith and a form of injustice. Furthermore, it is not a trait that characterizes a particular nation; it is an aberration that has been experienced by all nations, races, and religions. We denounce extremism today, just as our forefathers relentlessly did throughout Islamic history. Time after time, they insisted on the importance of one clear truth: the ends do not justify the means. We speak this truth again today. Islam is a religion of ethics that seeks what is good for people in the entire world. Its principles are those of honour. The means for spreading Islam are ethical means. And Islam can only be defended through ethical means. The foundation of relations between Muslims and others is peace. In Islam, war is only justified by necessity and challenges. No fighting is permissible when others pose no aggression. Even then, the duty of Muslims is to treat others with justice and benevolence: *God forbids you not, with regard to those who fight you not for your Faith, nor drive you out of your homes, from dealing kindly and justly with them: For God loveth those who are just. (Al Mumtahina: 8) But if they cease, let there be no hostility except to those who practice oppression (Al Baqara: 193)* On religious grounds, on moral grounds, we denounce the contemporary concept of terrorism which is associated with wrongful practices wherever they come from – including assaults on peaceful civilians, killing prisoners and the wounded, unethical practices such as the destruction of buildings, and ransacking cities. These despotic attacks on human life transgress the law of God, and we denounce them. As the Qur'an says: *Take not life which God hath made sacred, except by way of justice and law. (Al Anaam: 51)* Fighting injustice and realizing justice should be a legitimate undertaking through legitimate means. We call on the Nation (Ummah) to adopt what is necessary to achieve the strength and steadfastness needed to build itself and ensure the preservation of rights. No human whose heart is filled with light could be an extremist. We decry the campaign that portrays Islam as a religion that encourages violence and institutionalizes terrorism. Throughout history, extremism has caused the destruction of great civilizations. The tree of civilization wilts, and hearts close, when malice takes hold. It is an evil alien to Islamic values of moderation and tolerance. Today, we call on the international community to work seriously on implementing international law and ensuring respect for U.N. conventions and resolutions, ensuring that there are no double standards, that injustice is uprooted and that people's rights are returned. Achieving this will contribute to uprooting the causes of violence, exaggeration, and extremism. The Islam that we are honoured to belong to calls on us to be involved in modern society and contribute to its progress. To achieve that, Muslims reach out in brotherhood to all those who love justice, reason, and righteousness. Islam guides us to express, earnestly, the realities of our lives, and to share the soundness of our faith and beliefs. This is God's call for coexistence and piety. Islam guides us to work on reforming the religious discourse of civilization in our countries, through well-designed, practical scientific plans that focus on rehabilitating preachers. These priorities will ensure broad public awareness among these preachers of the true spirit of Islam and its methodology in building human life, as well as providing them with knowledge of contemporary culture and how to deal with their communities. *Say, 'this is my way. I, and those who follow me, call for God with a clear vision of the truth.' (Yusuf: 108)* Islam guides us to deal with the communication revolution, by utilizing the media in a sound, scientific manner, without weakness or emotional outbursts. Thus, we may respond to accusations stirred by enemies of Islam, while reaching all those who receive the messages of global media. Islam guides us to build up the Muslim individual through the best of education. Those who are confident in their knowledge and abilities are secure in their personalities, and through this self-confidence, present the distinguished outlook of Islam to the whole world. Islam guides us to benefit from and contribute to the achievements of this age. Islam encourages science and technology; it is a pioneer in its approach to comprehensive development. The Islamic approach provides a balance in spiritual, economic, and social life; provides for human rights and basic liberties; ensures the individual's right to live in dignity and security, guarantees basic needs, and administers society's affairs in accordance with the principles of justice and consultation. Such an approach both benefits from and strengthens the mechanisms of modern democracy. We attach great hope to the scholars of our Nation. It is they who will enlighten our youth – the generation that adorns our present age and will create and become our future. It is our scholars who will keep our youth from sliding down the paths of ignorance, corruption, close-mindedness and subordination, into the abyss of extremism. And it is our scholars who will hold a beacon to a different path – a path of tolerance, moderation, and goodness; guiding young people to the way of Islam and instituting its great values in their young hearts. Indeed, as role models in their religious manners, conduct, and speech, our scholars can contribute to the renewal of the march of our entire Nation.

By their exacting standards of science, positive visions of politics, and the grace to take all matters wisely and meticulously; and by bringing people together, not dividing them, by uniting hearts, not turning them away, and by raising humanity's eyes to the horizons of fulfillment: in all these ways, our scholars will help our whole Nation meet the challenges of the 21st century. Through such wisdom and achievement, Islam's goodness, peace, and love will flow to all the peoples of the world. We pray to God: to provide our Islamic Nation with means of renaissance, prosperity and advancement; to shield it from the evils of extremism and closed minds; to preserve its rights, sustain its glory, and uphold its dignity. He is the best Lord and the Best Aid. *God Almighty says: "And (He commandeth you, saying): This is My straight path, so follow it. Follow not other ways, lest ye be parted from His way. This hath He ordained for you, that ye may ward off (evil)" (Al An'aam: 153).* We conclude, thanking God, Lord of the worlds, Amman The Hashemite Kingdom of Jordan Ramadan 1425 Hijri November 2004 AD[10]

References

1. Al Hussein, Abdullah II. "Islamic Reaffirmation". Newsweek December 2005-February 2006. p. 26.
2. The Economist Report. The Economist. 26 November 2005. p. 29.
3. The Economist Report. The Economist. 26 November 2005. p. 29.
4. The Economist Report. The Economist. 26 November 2005. p. 29.
5. Dickey, Christopher. "Women of Al Qaeda". The Newsweek. pp. 28-29.
6. Dutt, Vijay. "Osama son". Hindustan Times. 25 December 2005. Lucknow. p. 17.
7. Al Hussein, Abdullah II. "Islamic Reaffirmation". Newsweek December 2005-February 2006. p. 26.
8. Al Hussein, Abdullah II. "Islamic Reaffirmation". Newsweek December 2005-February 2006. p. 26.
9. Rehman, Mujibir. "Calling all" Review of the Book, "The Trouble with Islam Today " by Irshad Manji in The Sunday Times of India. 11 December 2005. New Delhi. p. 4. Mahmood Mamdani quoted is the author of the book, "Good Muslim, Bad Muslim".
10. Downloaded from embassyofjordanus.com on 22 December 2005.

12
Internal Governance and Security Managment Issues of Concern - 2006

"We don't have the political will to fight terrorism".

R C Lahoti, Ex Chief Justice of India

State of Law and Order in Bihar and Uttar Pradesh

A deteriorating law and order situation is indicative of near collapse of state administration and consolidation of subversive forces in the area. These are opposite ends of the law and order spectrum at the extremes of the poles of balancing the conflict. The initial indications are reach of basic needs, power, water, health, education and roads to the populace through a process of effective, non corrupt governance. If it is the victim of a system driven by the politician-contractor nexus as in Uttar Pradesh, growth of criminalism will be followed by emergence of the phenomenon of naxalism. The state of law and order in Uttar Pradesh and Bihar raises dangers of anarchy and violence in 2006 unless the situation is not effectively dealt with. Law and order experts as Ved Marwah state that the government had ignored the signs of impending build up by Naxalites in Bihar as indicated by the attacks in Madhubani on the Indo-Nepal border in June 2005 and Home Guard Training Centre in Giridh, Jharkhand on 11 November 2005 in which 185 rifles were taken away by force. These linkages could possibly be as per Marwah, transformation of the movement from the positional warfare stage to mobile warfare spreading, "liberated zones" systematically by mobilizing civilians. As per Marwah, a successful counter naxalite strategy entails a synergy between all agencies based on a broad political consensus, integrating the social, economic, political and ethnic issues with the active support of the people. This has to be supported by the counter terrorism infra structure comprising of exceptional laws, special forces, intelligence network, improved weaponry and communications.[1]

The Emerging Criminal, Communal and Political Coagulation

1000 plus people mainly children killed in the Japanese Encephalitis virus epidemic from September to November, riots in Mau in November, naxal menace and Nepali Maoists across the International border, Eastern Uttar Pradesh is simmering at the seams. Colloquially called as Purvanchal , the area is divided in two distinct communal divides by the Ghaghra river. North of the Ghaghara the Hindu Yuva Vahini led by Yogi Adityanath is said to control the political as well as economic activities in districts as Gorakhpur, Basti, Deoria, Maharjganj, Kosinagar and Siddharthanagar. South of the River, the distiricts of Mau, Azamgarh, Varanasi, Balia, Jaunpur and Gazipur are controlled by mafia of the Mukhtar Ansari group tacitly supported by the ruling Samajwadi Party. The division on communal lines is all about control, "of contracts and other money-making projects".[2]

Mau which witnessed hostility in 1969, 1983 and 2000 saw a higher degree of violence, more venal and religiously potent than previous times in 2005. It has created ghettos in the region which is the most dangerous trend in communal politics. An effort was also made to destroy economic activity by damaging power looms and ransacking colonies which was never known in the past. This new trend is creating economically driven communalist violence wherein one community systematically destroys the infra structure of the other society to deny it sources of livelihood thereby resulting in destitution and out of area refuge, with corresponding benefits to the antagonists with however very grave long term socio-political impact, the contours of which are not easily discernible at present.

Polarization of the populace on communal lines has virtually fossilized with Mukhtar Ansari and Yogi Adityanath groups consolidating their respective positions on both sides of the religious divide. A political analyst, Ghosh has brought out that similar violence has been noticed in the recent past in other Uttar Pradesh towns of Barabanki, Chandauli, Sitapur and Agra creating a, "new DNA of riots".[3] The district administration has to be alert to prevent rioting in the first place and quickly controlling it if it emerges to nip it in the bud. This is the crux of all anti communal violence measures at the grass roots. An effective district administration headed by an alert deputy commissioner and superintendent of police who is not politically motivated is the answer to these ills. Police and district officials should not be concerned about the political impact of their impendent actions as promotion is guaranteed in these cadres in any case.

In Bihar the Politician-Criminal-Contractor all in one has replaced the nexus of yesteryears denoting concentration of negative power in a single entity. Criminals are assuming the mantle of political control rather than through proxies which is the most disturbing phenomenon difficult to check in the year ahead despite all the hype generated by the change of government which per se is the saving grace as under the previous dispensation even hopes of change would have been lost. These politician-criminals have no loyalty and are adept at changing colours based on the flow of political current and self gains. A Sunday Indian Express Survey has clearly highlighted the emergence of the political don giving out 11 of Bihar's most wanted men, some of whose photographs too are not available on the police rolls –

(a) inar, Vaishali and controls kidnapping and extortion in a wide swathe of territory in North-India.

(b) Rajen Tiwary operates along the Bihar-UP border running the transport network in the area.

(c) Bhangar Yadav is the leader in the West.

Champaran area and is a noted kidnapper, controls contraband, sugarcane and other contracts. No photograph of Yadav is available.

(f) Surendra Yadav is the underworld don of Gaya, controlling assets worth Rs. 5 Crore.

(g) Dhumal Singh is the coal mining contractor con trolling contracts in Jharkhand and has been victorious in politics for three times.

(h) Ashok Mahto is from Nawada and Sheikhupura and is known to target the upper caste bhumihars.

(i) Bindu Singh is the don of Patna controlling trad ers, doctors and other people with disposable in come.

(j) Shankar Singh runs the so called Northern Lib eration Army and controls the Rupauli region of Purnea.

(k) Rajesh Kumar alias Babloo Dev is a 29 year old don and a MLA from Kesaria in East Chamaparan.[4]

Such a trend is also visible in Eastern Uttar Pradesh where the recent killings of the Bhartiya Janata Party legislator allegedly under the directions of a Muslim MLA, Mukthar Ansari is said to be essentially for lucrative government contracts in the area.

Bihar's need hierarchy is inverted. Social and caste mobilization resting on pride and ego had a higher priority than development and poverty eradication, governance and law and order, basic facilities and infra structure. Lalu Yadav gave the Bihari lower castes, the Yadavs, the Kurmis, the OBCs pride in being what they were after centuries of social ostracization. This phase lasted for 15 long years and came to an end in 2005 when the population in Bihar truly came into their own and selected leaders of choice throwing away the shackles of Lalloism symbolized by the deprecating lantern. Initially social mind sets and later Laloo's successful manipulation of the bureaucracy, police and law and order machinery sustained the autocracy of non development.

There are many other challenges before the new Bihar leadership led by Mr Nitish Kumar today, recasting society fed on narrow caste and communal divisions based on vote politics will be a long term objective, preventing social backlash after the November Jehanabad jailbreak seen as a strike by the Maoists representing the backward castes against the Ranvir Sena in support of the forward castes is an urgent necessity. Communist Party activists are said to be well entrenched in Central Bihar, South Bihar and the Nepal border and are attempting to establish new links in other states with increase in recruitment and weapon acquisitions. They have a central command and are able to plan and execute operations with an effective network.[5]

Communal Riots in Europe - Affecting the Indian Diaspora

France, England and Australia, three nations known for their tolerance and secular values saw communal violence in the year 2005. The causes for these acts of hatred are many and need some consideration as a large part of those affected are from India, Pakistan and Bangladesh as also migration of people from South Asia is an ongoing phenomenon which will generate critical conditions of discord unless adequate checks are not instituted at the nascent stage of strife. Emergence of Islamofascism as per Sunanda K Datta Ray is the reason for the upsurge of communalism in France in particular and Europe in general in the year 2005. Islamofascism is a blend of Islamic bigotry with Western fascism due to implementation of laws such as ban on the head scarf, turbans, skull caps and outsize crosses. France has 5 million Muslims of Arab and African descent that had reasons to protest implementation of measures as the skull cap ban a religio-cultural symbol. Unemployment is high amongst these youth at 30 per cent. In the case of Clichy where riots first broke out in the suburb of Paris when two Muslim youth were electrocuted while allegedly fleeing the police the rate of unemployment is much higher at 40 per cent. The Mullahs started to move around the streets to quell violence, in turn giving them immense power over the youth in the year ahead. This is a new crusade or Eurabian civil war which will simmer until brought under control quickly by law and order, social and economic measures.

The trouble and riots in France have very limited overtones of religion as per renowned political analyst Fareed Zakaria, noting that there were no green flags and crescent signs during the demonstrations, only a sense of lack of dignity and respect, jobs and discrimination.[6] The apt designation of the root cause being a cocktail of unemployment, underemployment and stagnation is said to be a typically French problem with high unemployment rates in Muslim dominated areas varying from 15 to 30 percent. The societies in Western Europe are also said to be very insular and homogenous as opposed to say the United States of America. Integration of large number of foreigners whose numbers will increase as the population ages will be the essence of survival for Europe as per Zakaria. There is a need for affirmative action to integrate these foreigners and create a nation based on ideas and values rather than deeply rooted indigenous society based on the sons of the soil concept, unwilling to accept any foreigner trudge on their valued land. France and rest of Europe should as per Zakaria look for a solution which honours the past, embraces the present and prepares for the future.[7]

Birmingham won the prestigious European City of the Future award due to its vibrant and unique multi cultural mix with 30 per cent of its population being non whites, 20 per cent of it being Asian and 6 per cent blacks, 56,000 Indians, twice the number of Pakistanis and 21,000 Bangladeshis. Brown on black race rioting broke out in the city supposedly a model of European multi cultural harmony on 22 October 2005, when the Jamaican community accused Asian youths thought to be from Pakistan of raping a 14 year old Black girl. 100 strong Asian and Black youths organized in gangs carried out pillage and arson of shops and kiosks. Lozells, which is a poor area with history of bloody Handsworth riots of September 1985, was the centre of the riots. A week of rising tension preceded the riots. There has been open hostility in the past between Black and Asian gangs over drugs and crime.

The following conditions were existent in Birmingham which could have possibly resulted in the riots:-

1. A stable-unstable balance of communities.
2. Poor areas are the scene of loot and arson due to

poverty, limited stakes in the economic infra structure whether private or government, unemployment or under employment thereby the participants have plenty of time and energy to indulge in violence. In fact hostility acts as an outlet of dis ruptive destruction for energies which have no outlet.

3. Organized crime in terms of violent gangs already operating and based on communal lines readily available to create disruption.
4. History of riots.
5. Lack of effective political control on violent behaviour by organized groups.

It is common experience that such uprisings, if we may call the rioting in France and other parts of Europe and the Cornulla Beach in Sydney, Australia are non ideological movements arising from social and economic inequities, but it is only a matter of time that ideology and polity takes over. Once power brokers see this as another opportunity to achieve fame and fortune, they quickly seize it to colour the sufferings of the multitudes in ideology of the moment and veer them away to a path of gory violence thereby achieving their central aim of power for themselves. We can only pray that the deviants in France do not seize this opportunity to start another Islamic jihad in the heart of the land of liberty.

A varied multi cultural model is followed by the British where people are allowed to follow their own personal laws. However this invariably results in ghettoisation which creates threats of riots in times of tension between communities. The French follow a model of secularism which does not recognize ethnic or religious differentiation and all citizens have to live by a common code and culture. Thus French citizens cannot wear head scarves, display large crosses or wear turbans regardless of their religious customs. This does not seem to have solved the problem. The need is for commonality to extend beyond culture and religion to housing, employment and equal economic opportunity. Value based integration will be successful in case we are able to develop the economic and social standing of individuals and groups. Thus strategies for assimilation should include socio-cultural-economic emancipation leading to egalitarianism, a tall order indeed as human society is structured on a hierarchy of achievement.

The problem of integrating culture, religion and modernity has been with the Indic civilization since time memorial. India is a nation of migratory people, some have criss crossed our continental sized country while others have restricted themselves to only trans border migration. Thus India could well offer Europe a model wherein which the Indian nation state has over the ages learnt to assimilate vast multitudes of invaders as one of their own, the Moguls, the British, the French and the Portuguese, in their culture and built a unique society of secular credentials in a evolutionary rather than a revolutionary way. This process of integration is now ingrained in the Indian psyche and has been the real strength of the modern Indian nation state. While there are many problems faced by India in homogenizing its society as is wrought in the large number of militancies fostered throughout the length and breadth of the country, France may be able to learn a few lessons from the Indian model.

Darjeeling – Autonomy Achieves Peace

Creation of the Gorkha Hill Council, Darjeeling, an autonomous self governing council under the Sixth Schedule of the Constitution heralds to bring peace to hill districts in the East situated amongst the idyll surroundings of the Eastern Himalayas astride the strategic Siliguri corridor. A memorandum of settlement was signed between the Union Home Secretary, V K Duggal, West Bengal Chief Secretary, A K Deb and the Darjeeling Gorkha Hill Council administrator, Subhas Ghishing on 06 December 2005.[8] The issues of geographical and legislative jurisdiction of the Council will be settled by the concerned parties and a Bill will be introduced in the State Assembly and Parliament. The Council is scheduled to comprise of 33 members of which 10 will be from the Scheduled Tribes, 15 from non tribal communities and 3 all communities with 5 members nominated by the Governor of West Bengal. Term of the members will be for 5 years. The three subdivisions of Darjeeling, Kurseong and Kalimpong will be governed by the Council. The Council is slated to deal with issues such as land, forests, canals, water courses, agriculture, public health, tourism, vocational training, public works, construction and maintenance of roads, transport, live stock, irrigation, fisheries, education, small scale and cottage industries. The details are still under negotiation.

The issue of ethnic and cultural divide between the plains and the hills people has been brewing in many parts of North East India. Creation of the Hill Council will assuage the demands of the Gorkhas of the hill areas of West Bengal where trouble had been brewing for the past one and a half decade. Similar demands in other areas such as Bodos in Assam are long pending negotiations. The Gorkha-Darjeeling model could perhaps provide the way ahead. On the other hand there could be rising demand for greater autonomy which may become difficult to handle given the nature of interlocking union of tribes, ethnic communities and so on in the North East. This snow balling effect needs to be controlled in the larger perspective. The dual nature of State and Centre control implies that there are three parties to every issue which need to see eye to eye, the Centre, the State and the demanders. In the instance case, the alliance of the communist parties with the Congress in the Centre could have played a major role in its resolution along with some enlightened leadership at the state level namely the West Bengal Chief Minister, Mr. Buddhadeb Bhattacharjee. Such a congruence of interests is not achieved many times with vested political issues preventing an understanding or in extreme cases even subverting negotiations.

Security Blanket – Bihar Elections – Oct-Nov. 2005

The success of the Elections in Bihar in October – November 2005 needs to be studied in detail to demonstrate the effectiveness of policing when the state is determined to ensure law and order. There are a total of 243 assembly seats in Bihar. The threat of disruption of the elections were ominous, CPI (Maoists) had given call for poll boycott and arms were being smuggled into milk and curd containers from Nepal, hence SSB also enhanced vigilance on the borders of Nepal especially West Champaran districts. An area domination exercise was launched to effectively check inter state movement of extremists and criminals set out to disturb polls in the state particularly the Bihar-Jharkhand border. 174 companies of Central para military forces were deployed in Bihar during the elections each comprising of 74 personnel assisted by local police, this included 65 companies of CRPF plus 24 companies already there, 75 companies of BSF and 10 companies of ITBP. 104 of the 174 companies were deployed in Maoist affected districts. Well trained forces with experience in anti extremist operations were also reportedly redeployed from Jammu and Kashmir. Maximum deployment was in Rohtas, Gaya, Aurangabad, Bhabhua, Jehanabad, Buxar, Bhojpur, Jamui, Patna. In Gaya there were 28 companies of PMF incl 10 CRPF, 10 BSF and 5 ITBP while in Rohtas there were 16 companies including 7 CRPF and 9 BSF.[9]

The successful and peaceful conduct of elections in the Indian state of Bihar, notorious for booth capturing and manipulation by the politician-police nexus by deployment of police under the Election commission without any reference to the local government appears to provide a model for other parts of the country. In Bihar the para military forces were deployed after due assessment a month before the vote to instill confidence in the people. 1.5 lakh non bail able warrants were executed during one month with policemen waiting at nomination centers for candidates dodging bail. The commission even changed thana level officers when complaints were received against them. Communications were provided to the polling stations which were linked to police stations, magistrates and control rooms. Direct, "agents" also reported to the election commission for counter checking booth capture reports. Special observer of the Election commission, Mr. K J Rao ran the whole operation. Bogus voters were scared off by using 4000 digital cameras on the 57,000 polling stations, with Sagem Face recognition system to recognize even features altered through cosmetic measures.[10] Replication of such a model across the country is not difficult and would involve the simple practice of giving independence to the police to function at the ground level, free from the shackles of local pressures in the interest of maintenance of law and order. Alas! The simplest things are perhaps the most difficult.

Communal Violence (Prevention, Control and Rehabilitation of Victims) Bill

Communal Violence (Prevention, Control and Rehabilitation of Victims) Bill seeks to define communal disturbance, provides for punishment to offenders and also seeks to provide relief and rehabilitation to the victims of communal violence. The need for such a Bill was perhaps felt seeing the course of violence post Godhra in Gujrat in 2002.[11] Draft of the Bill circulated earlier by the home ministry which contained a provision wherein the Centre was free to deploy the armed forces at its discretion in a state where it felt that the area was communally disturbed without the consent of the state government has since been reviewed. Initial draft had provided for concurrent powers to the centre and the state to declare a state communally sensitive. The Bill lays down the condition that the Centre should draw the attention of the state government to the communal violence and direct it to take immediate steps to control the situation within a reasonable period thereafter the State government is required to take appropriate action to prevent and control the communal violence. In its latest form this provision has been amended to state that it can be done only after a request from the state government has been received and the Centre can intervene further only if it is of opinion that the directions issued in turn by the State government are not being followed.[12]

This will virtually restore the status quo ante as the Centre will not be able to effectively intervene when a state government, as has happened many times in the past is seen as not taking adequate action to control the situation going out of hand, the Centre will not be able to intervene effectively to reduce the level of violence.

Political commentators as Anil Narendra, have stated that it does not define communal violence or what is communally sensitive and it is the will to prevent communal riots that will be the main factor rather than laws and that reformation of the law and order agencies to act fast rather than laws will be more important.[13] The laws he feels are not to blame it is the politicians. More over even where the forces are deployed actual employment is based on the perceptions of the District Magistrate concerned. Should we amend laws to give independent authority to the district administration in communally sensitive areas and periods, as given to army columns when deployed in aid to civil authorities?

Overcoming the Tyranny of Communal Violence

When ideologically driven social and political organizations are in control of the government, hatred against the minorities is systematically fanned as a result of which they are isolated socially and economically as per Harsh Mander a social activist and writer.[14] The problem in Gujarat, a state wracked by communal violence for the past five years or so, as per the author is that the government not only lacked the will to act but also wanted that communal violence should continue.[15] This a dangerous trend which cannot be accepted casually as there are adequate laws using which the state can control violence if it decides to implement these in full. Thus the Communal Violence (Prevention, Control and Rehabilitation of Victims) Bill should empower the citizens particularly the minorities to be able to force the government to come to their aid and be even criminally liable for acts of omission and commission on the failure to protect or rehabilitate them or punish the guilty.[16] As per Mander, the State should prevent the build up to violence to include control and punishment for hate speeches and mobilization, ensure adequate, early, impartial and timely use of force when the first signs of violence break out, and provide relief and rehabilitation and justice. The state should be required to act rather than be merely enabled to act. The failure to protect citizens should be punishable and where as in Gujrat state complicity is widely believed the riots can be classified as genocidal with greater powers of punishment on the state authorities.[17] While Mander's suggestions are no doubt worth considering, their practical implementation even in the best of times is difficult for no standard code for defining state failure in carrying out its duties can be practically evolved, as mere public perception cannot be enough for judicial action. While the public can bring to notice the wrongs committed by state authorities, since the power of prosecution still remains with the state, prosecution is extremely difficult particularly in states as Gujarat and Uttar Pradesh where the government, the police and the offenders are all in a nexus. We should however be able to establish and codify certain common standards which should be observed by law if practicable which all public authorities must adhere to such as :–

(a) Use of temperate language – offensive words should be identified and their use should automatically lead to prosecution. Words such as kafir or satan or reference to any religion of any individual in the public or private domain and so on can be codified.

(b) Similarly language which can incite violence, which leads to recalls of past history of communal violence, vile mouthed leaders and so on should also be cognizable offences.

(c) Where there has been any act of omission by the law enforcing authority such as the superintendent of police and in charge of thanas which leads to loss of life, this should lead to automatic suspension with the rights to revocation of suspension with a public body and not merely the administrative chain.

(d) Greater participation of the public in direct law and order issues can also be deliberated upon such as organization of local peace committees should gain legal acceptance.

Police Reforms in India

The urgent need for police reforms in India has been

an oft quoted plea by many analysts, political leaders, retired and even serving police officers. However no one appears to be taking the first step. Perhaps the rot in the system is so deep that even thinking of reforms is considered anti establishment. Thus transformation oriented officers as the charismatic Kiran Bedi find themselves side tracked in non professional channels of limited significance and when they are seen to be making a difference there such as the changes Bedi brought about in the Tihar jail, they are kicked upwards to the United Nations on deputation. Individual police officers have reportedly become adept at influencing politicians in urge for personal progression and then share the spoils with the masters, thus creating a police-politician nexus of sorts. Politician's power lies in ability to transfer police upto the Superintendent of Police (SP) by the home minister. A SP in turn can transfer lower officers and men. This system of appointments by favour creates demotivation amongst those who are not included in the list. Appointments can also be made on extraneous considerations of political, caste and clan affiliations rather than purely professional ones. National Police Commission Report in 1981, advocated setting up of state security commissions to address the problem of arbitrary postings and transfers and depoliticize the police. This was never accepted. Amendments to the Indian Police Act 1861, particularly to ensure participative or community policing where local leadership in every locality is involved in getting the police to implement the law fearlessly is another measure which can improve policing in the country. Creation of community cooperates between police and local polity involving the people at the local level in a partnership surpassing sectarian, communal and partisan politics would thus be a welcome measure.[18]

Utilisation of funds allotted for modernization by the police is also very tardy and at times wasteful. Rs 16 Crore was diverted from police modernisation fund in Jharkhand in 2003-04 as per the objections raised by the Auditor General's Office. 18 Indigo cars were purchased using police modernization fund for bureaucrats and ministers of the state. In 2004-05 also a large sum was diverted from the same fund and five IED jammers, 20 bullet proof Tata Safari, 11 Tata Safari, 21 Boleros, seven Mahindra Scorpio, five ambulances and 16 Endeavour Utility Vehicles were purchased and given to ministers, the assembly speaker and the chief minister.[19] This when Jharkhand is in the front line of the Naxalite threat.

"It is necessary to organize bodies of women police in every country for the purpose of collaborating with the welfare services in combating trafficking and other crimes against women" said the International Criminal Police Commission way back in 1930. In 1995 women accounted for 1.21 percent of the police force while in 2005 women account for just 2.44 percent while total recorded crime against women is 7 percent. Critical mass represented should be a third of the total strength. Some states have put a target varying from 10-33 percent may be in another 30 years. Tamil Nadu has 8868 police women in a total of 36,552 police as well as a women commando force. Jammu and Kashmir also has a similar higher profile for its women police probably due to the needs of militancy in the state. Women should also be given mainstream role of crime prevention and investigation. 75 percent have never arrested any person. Gender audit and gender budgeting for women is essential. Commission to look into issues concerning women to suggest procedures for induction, training, deployment and work environment needs to be convened. Network of women police forums and mentoring programmes need to be designed for sharing experiences and guidance involving researchers as Jaya Indiresan who has been working on women in police from time to time. The Home Ministry has proposed to raise the force level to 10 percent in the next three years.[20]

Reforming Security Administration

There is a need to ensure other nominal security related checks such as restriction on issue of gun licences and control on explosives. Recently 100 tons of explosives were reported to have sunk as the ship carrying it for the Border Roads Organization's road project linking Afghanistan and Iran had capsized. The police as well as customs were unable to confirm whether the explosives had actually sunk with the ship or diverted for some other purpose. The company which had booked the cargo was also difficult to trace immediately, thus demonstrating the lack of concern on transporting explosives in the country. Similarly gun licenses have to be strictly controlled. Reports indicate that in the crime prone city of Lucknow, the police have been regularly recovering illegal arms. The availability is likely to be much greater than the proportion of recoveries. Stringent checks will ensure that criminals and then terrorists do not have access to arms. A table showing recoveries is as given below.[21]

TABLE

Recovery of Arms – Lucknow

Year of Recovery	*Number of Arms Recovered*
2002	313
2003	419
2004	407
2005 (Upto 30 November 2005)	313

The need to reform jail administration cannot be over stated. This is a part of the police-judicial system, wherein all jails in India are over populated due to long time taken in judicial decisions. These have also become a refuge for criminal dons and politically criminalized leadership who are known to run their empire from the safety and comfort of lockups with ease of access through cell phones. By ensuring that jails are run as restrictive institutions rather than safe houses for dons, these will be able to serve the purpose of reformatories. Simple measures as electronically jamming cell phone signals will ensure that the incarcerated do not have access to the outside World. Such innovative measures need to be undertaken to ensure that prisons are detention centers with true effect.

Police Reforms in Bihar

On taking over as Chief Minister, Mr Nitish Kumar and perhaps also in the light of the Jehanabad jail break by the Naxalites on 11 November 2005, a programme to reform the Bihar police has been put underway with the confidence of the Union Home Minister, Mr Shivraj Patil. The first demand to the Centre has been request for 50 more companies of para military forces in addition to the 24 companies already deployed in Bihar. Modernization of the police force would also be undertaken in right earnest, with surprisingly Rs. 100 Crore budget allotted lying unspent with the Bihar police so far since 2000. This would be spent to improve mobility, arms, ammunition and communication, construction of buildings and so on. Two additional battalions of the Bihar Military Police (BMP) would also be raised to fill up around 10,000 vacancies in the police force. In addition raising of India Reserve Battalions would also be considered.[22] It is apparent that apart from gross mis governance, the Lalu-Rabri regime in Bihar is guilty of criminal neglect by failing to reform and modernize the police force to make it effective in fighting not only the naxalite threats but also the law and order in the state. We must use the Right of Information act in future to seek the utilization of funds to effect in future.

Disasters 2006 – Nature's Fury or Callous Management

The tsunami disaster on December 26, 2004 left 10,273 people dead and 5,823 missing or feared dead in India, most of them from Nicobar Islands. 530 children were rendered orphan.[23] Disaster struck India once again in another geographical and ethnic fault line, the state of Jammu and Kashmir. The death toll on both sides of the Line of Control is said to be over 1 lakh. We are looking at a major disaster in 2006 and a number of minor crisis such as that which hit Mumbai during the monsoons in 2005. Having a functional disaster management agency should be the key priority for our internal governance management at the national and the state level. In the long term, very basic measures and standards such as building and construction norms, ensuring natural infra structure such as mangrove forests along the coast are not destroyed would have to be undertaken by legislative, proactive and actionable measures by the government as well as the community. Let us see why we have come to such a fatalistic conclusion in the succeeding paragraphs.

Why Disasters are Imminent in 2006?

The World Disaster Report 2005 released by the International Red Cross has brought out that in 2004 there were 360 natural disasters up from 239 in 1995. The number of people killed from 1995-2004 increased from 6,34,418 in the previous decade to 901, 177.[24] Long term trend indicators as portended by a study undertaken in the United States bring out that there is disaster in the making in the time frame of 2300. Thus as one of the author's of the Paper has brought out, "the question is no longer whether we will need to address the problem, but when we will need to address the problem." The reasons for the same are not far to seek, population growth, people living in high rises, a 60 percent increase from 1981 to 2000 and also population concentrated in high risk areas suspect to floods, cyclones, tsunamis and hurricanes. Despite population growth and risks associated with possible disasters people tend to settle in the areas of their birth or livelihood though it may not necessarily be the safest. Thus coast lines are increasingly over populated while the pressure on land in thickly populated countries as Bangladesh is so great that population density near the coast continues to rise despite vulnerability of people to natural disasters. The area of concern is what Bryan Walls has called as the seismic gap or the close difference between the rich and poor cities abilities to withstand an earth quake. For instance, in 1989, in San Francisco, a 7.1 magnitude earth quake killed 63 people while in 2003 a 6.5 magnitude earthquake has destroyed 80 % of the city of Bam in Iran killing 26,000.[25] The Kashmir earthquake of 8 October 2005 was of 7.6 magnitude and it has killed almost 100000 people on both sides of the line of control in Kashmir.

There is thus a need to take immediate measures to control environment degradation that is underway today. In the year 2006, let us gear up our disaster management authority which has been recently set up to face the challenges of the myriad quakes and other types of natural disaster we will be faced with.

Climate Change, Environmental Degradation and Disasters

Climate change is another phenomenon which will result in disasters. Some of the long term ruinous consequences of climate change will be as follows:-

(a) The Arctic tundra, an important ecosystem is likely to vanish as climate zones will shift hundreds of miles north.

(b) Alaska will lose its evergreen boreal forests and become a largely temperate state. In that case temperate states of the tropics as India could possibly become hot houses.

(c) The area locked beneath ice will diminish from 13.3 percent of the planet's total land area to 4.8 percent. This is already evident with the retreat of glaciers in the Himalayas.

(d) Conditions that nurture temperate and tropical forests could expand so that these could grow to nearly 65 per cent land surface instead of 44 percent as at present.

(e) Marine life will also be greatly affected as the pH of oceans will fall because of build up of carbonic acid from dissolving carbon dioxide and eroding coral reefs and the shells of plankton.[26]

"India is clearly one of the countries which is vulnerable to climate change impact in a very significant way" Dr Pradipto Ghosh, Secretary in the Ministry of Environment and Forests has said recently. The impact can manifest in many ways as outlined by Ghosh, apocalyptic due accelerated glacial melt, increased frequency of extreme weather events, changes in long term precipitation patterns, a rise in sea level and increased spread of water borne diseases as malaria and dengue.[27] Indian record in control of environmental problems through climate change has been cited as good, with our emission levels per capita of greenhouse gases being 25 % of the global average and less than one twentieth of the US per capita emission. The government has put in place policies for shift of energy use from coal to natural gas, promotion of renewable energy resources and adoption of efficient technologies in the industrial sector are some of the control measures. Officials at Tata Energy Research Institute or TERI feel that pervasion of awareness and measures for implementation across the board to the common man who can reduce his energy consumption will have to be achieved to ensure significant results in the future.[28]

Mr R K Pachauri, Director TERI and Chairman of the Intergovernmental Panel of Climate Change has brought out that scientific evidence on climate change due to man's own creations is overwhelming and generally accepted. He also states that its control is not excessively expensive as is thought to be, thus concentration of CO_2 stabilized at 450 ppm by 2050 would cost around 4 % of total GDP of the World and thus the level of prosperity would be delayed by only a year or more. The positive effects would be felt in human health, availability of water, swamping of coastal areas and biodiversity around the World.[29] Developing countries as India will be particularly affected as these do not have their systems in place to face the hazards and vagaries of environmental threats resulting in disasters as was seen during the floods in Mumbai or the earthquake in Kashmir most recently. Implementation of long term disaster management measures with a disaster mitigation agency which can effectively provide relief across the country is thus essential.

Disaster Proofing the Nation

In the immediate term, the functioning of the Disaster Management Authority and the Crisis Management Group have to be activated through a number of proactive measures. This should not be a problem with the Bill having been introduced in the Indian Parliament recently. In addition to the central authority, at the state level disaster management authorities have to be activated and a legislation introduced at the earliest. Presently only states which have been victims of recent disasters have undertaken measures in this regard while others continue to languish or cynically speaking await for a disaster to shake them from their somnolence. On the other hand the response of existing agencies and organizations has to be prompt and effective and not like the inaction displayed by the United States administration in the New Orleans disaster during 2005, when even the President George W Bush has been castigated for lethargy.

Closing the seismic gap is the long term answer to reducing casualties. Very little money is reportedly spend for this purpose, only 10 percent as per a Tearfund estimate. Simple measures as building raised platforms to escape high waters in Bangladesh have achieved excellent results.[30] Disaster proof standards have been promulgated by various bodies such as the builders and construction firms but are routinely violated with the connivance of these regulators. This practice is causing very heavy loss of life as the very shelters which are meant to protect become a death trap. There is a need to sensitize our monitoring agencies to carry out their role of being watch dogs of construction activities both public and private in the country with a view to ensure that these are disaster proof. Legislative measures in the form of a notification of a National Disaster Management Authority with the Prime Minister as its chairman is essential. This has to be followed up by having provisions in our plans made by the Planning Commission for long-term rehabilitation, reconstruction and providing multi-hazard proof permanent houses. Tsunami Early Warning System in the Indian Ocean is another necessity and collaboration with other Indian Ocean states could be undertaken by the Department of Ocean Development to have a joint approach for overlapping surveillance and analysis of threats.[31] Cooperation with benign states as Japan on disaster management is called for which would ensure an integrated approach in making resources as well as technology available for disasters.[32]

The warnings are ominous. Let us not delay the inevitable and adopt the standards as that in San Francisco in 1989 as brought out and avoid precious loss of lives in our country in 2006.

References

1. Marwah, Ved. "Absentee landlords". The Hindustan Times. 2 December 2005. Lucknow. p. 6.
2. Ghosh,Avijit. "The New DNA of Riots" The Times of India. 7 December 2005. Lucknow. p. 5.
3. Ghosh,Avijit. "The New DNA of Riots" The Times of India. 7 December 2005. Lucknow. p. 5.
4. George, K Varghese. Et Al. "You want". Sunday Indian Express. 11 December 2005. Lucknow. p. 1,2.
5. Deshpande, Rajeev. Sunday Times of India. 27 November 2005. Lucknow. p. 7.
6. Zakaria, Fareed. "Europe Needs A New Identity". Newsweek. 21 November 2005. p. 15.
7. Zakaria, Fareed. "Europe Needs A New Identity". Newsweek. 21 November 2005. p. 15.
8. Economic Times Report. "Centre, West Bengal". The Economic Times. 7 December 2005. New Delhi. p. 3.
9. Tewary, Amaranth. "174 Companies to ensure fair polls in Bihar". The Pioneer. 19 September 2005. Lucknow. p. 5.
10. Mishra, Neeraj. "Without Fear or Favour". India Today. 19 December 2005. New Delhi. pp. - 22
11. Dalmia, Archna. "The Only Way". The Sunday Pioneer. 4 December 2005. Lucknow. p. 4.
12. Mitta, Manoj. "Centre drops" The Times of India. 29 November 2005. Lucknow. p. 7.
13. Narendra, Anil. "Mere good intentions". The Sunday Pioneer. 4 December 2005. Lucknow. p. 4.
14. Mander, Harsh. "When the Law Runs Riot.". The Times of India. 15 December 2005. Lucknow. p. 7.
15. Mander, Harsh. "When the Law Runs Riot.". The Times of India. 15 December 2005. Lucknow. p. 7.
16. Mander, Harsh. "When the Law Runs Riot.". The Times of India. 15 December 2005. Lucknow. p. 7.
17. Mander, Harsh. "When the Law Runs Riot.". The Times of India. 15 December 2005. Lucknow. p. 7.
18. Ribeiro, Julio. "How to Reform the Police" The Times of India. 14 October 2005. Lucknow. p. 7.

19. Shukla, Nityanand. "Police modernisation" The Pioneer. 7 November 2005. Lucknow. p. 5.
20. Menon, Amarnath k. "Uniform Demand" India today 17 October 2005. pp. 26-27
21. Singh, Sanjay. "Arms and the City". Express Newsline. The Indian Express. 17 December 2005. Lucknow. p. 1.
22. PTI Report. The Indian Express. 2 December 2005. Lucknow. p. 6.
23. Downloaded from ndtv.com on 13 December 2005.
24. Walsh Bryan. "Why More People are dying?" Time 24 October 2005. p. 22.
25. Walsh Bryan. "Why More People are dying?" Time 24 October 2005. p. 22.
26. Revking, Andrew C. "New climate" The Indian Express. 2 November 2005. Lucknow. p. 11.
27. Nevatia, Shreevatsa. "A Recipe for Disaster". Sunday Hindustan Times. 4 December 2005. Lucknow. p. 9.
28. Nevatia, Shreevatsa. "A Recipe for Disaster". Sunday Hindustan Times. 4 December 2005. Lucknow. p. 9
29. Pachauri, R K. "Can global warming" The Economic Times. 5 December 2005. New Delhi. p. 12.
30. Walsh Bryan. "Why More People are dying?" Time 24 October 2005. p. 22.
31. Downloaded from ndtv.com on 13 December 2005.
32. Pioneer Report. The Pioneer. 15 December 2005. Lucknow. p. 2.

13
A Terror Decade

"One day when the Americans have gone, we will need to fight another war, against these jihadis. They wont leave quietly".

Al Tamimi, a suicide coordinator in Iraq.

India is in the throes of a terror decade. Taking the past decade from 1994 to June 2005, terrorist strikes are said to have killed 19,662 civilians as compared to 7320 armed personnel. In the North East states during the same period, 7140 civilians lost lives to violence as opposed to 1958 security personnel and 4835 terrorists.[1] International Islamic Front (IIF) led by Osama Bin Laden, has been providing volunteers of Pakistani origin for suicide terror all over the World. The Lashkar-e-Taiyyaba is a part of the IIF. All these are ominous signs for the year ahead. As per noted political analyst and commentator, Mr Arun Shourie, who having brought out that 64,000 persons were killed in the country in the last 20 years identified three principal threats to the country as Islamic fundamentalism, Left Wing Extremism and Ethnic fundamentalism.[2] The terror industry World over is said to be worth $ 1.5 trillion. It also services other industries like heroin running, human trafficking, black financiers and arms smuggling. Strategic intelligence is the most essential aspect of counter terror operations and the most important part of intelligence collection. Terrorism will not fade away it will continue and can only be kept under check as the cycle of state and fundamental terror will continue.[3] Thus it is better to be prepared for the worst case scenario than found repenting with the blood of many of our own citizens on our hands due to negligence or worse still indifference of the ostrich in the year ahead. Nothing signifies this better than the terror strike at the Indian Institute of Science in Bangalore on 28 December 2005 when intelligence inputs on the likelihood of such an attack went unheeded. However time is not lost let us renew our resolve our fight this poisonous venom before its permeation in the nations systems.

How Terrorists Strike ?

Terrorists will continue to strike in India at will, choosing targets which are well exposed and which will give them maximum propaganda value to draw in more and more people towards their cause in a seemingly successful story of bringing about transformation in society, both political and social. A major terrorist strike such as the 29 October 2005 serial blasts in Delhi which killed more than 70 people and injured 200 plus will have some or all of the characteristics as given below from conception to launch:

- Overall control will be by the lead members of the group which in this case the Lashkar-e-Taiba or LeT's Abu Alqama and Abu Huzefa. Alqama is said to operate from Pakistan and is reportedly responsible for operations in the Valley, while Huzefa is the in charge of terrorist operations in Srinagar. These names are not actual but are merely, "kunaits" or posts assigned to these individuals who's actual names may be different.

- The module led by Tariq Ahmed Dar was selected as the main operative. He worked as a sales representative with the multi national firm Johnson and Johnson and hence was well familiar with the layout of cities as Delhi.

- Dar carried out a reconnaissance of Delhi in the first week of October to select the sites.

- The explosives were prepared and brought to the three sites in bags which were left in the bus in one case, in a shop in another and a cycle rickshaw in the third case.

- The escape route was also well planned as the group retreated to Srinagar quickly. While Dar has been apprehended, others are still at large.

- The give away occurred as Dar on reaching Srinagar boasted of his success to his leaders on telephone, which was tapped by the police who were able to apprehend him.

- Lashkar operatives were the main suspect due to

the type of devices used employing RDX with timers.[4]

Thus we can safely presume that terrorists will continue to strike at soft and vulnerable targets in the year ahead. They may even attempt attacks on high security areas as was carried out at Ayodhya in 2005, where they took advantage of the complacency that generally sets in the security set up at such locations over a period.

How are suicide missions organized by terrorists is an enigma which is wracking the nerves of security specialists and perhaps victims relatives as well. "My job is to know how I can get a bomber to the best spot for an attack, at a time when he is sure to inflict the most damage" says a suicide attack coordinator in Iraq, aliased as Abu Qaqa al Tamimi who is reported to have coordinated 30 suicide bombings since September 2004 for the hard core jihadi group led by Abu Mousab al Zarqawi as covered in a Time report.[5] The first task is to gather intelligence of the target, the police, their check points and so on. Then is setting up the bomber in a safe house providing him all requirements especially, religious books as the suicide bomber has to be motivated through religious fervour of the right kind. Stimulus has to be for a millenarian cause and not nationalism and other worldly issues as no one dies for a nation, they would rather live in it. While the target is continuously tracked the bomb belt is prepared. The bomber is then familiarized with the area by pre launch reconnaissance. In the case of killing of Kashmiri minister, Lone in November 2005, the suicide attackers had carried reconnaissance of the high security zone, Gupkar colony in Srinagar specially housing state government ministers as Lone.

Terrorist Ideologies – Expanded Goals

Ideology and terrorism are an entrenched myth which are difficult to overcome, says an Economist quote. The Islamic terror led by the Lashkar-e-Taiyba and the Jaish-e-Mohammad in India is now not limited to seeking independence of Kashmir, but also has a larger goal of Nizam-e-Mustafa or Islamic rule in India on similar lines as the Al Qaeda pan Islamic vision for the rest of the World.[6]

This has established a powerful link of ideology between these terrorists waging war against India and the Al Qaeda causing alarms in the Indian intelligence community. This has very serious consequences for India as would entail mobilization of individuals from a large base of Muslim population of over 13% of India's 100 Crore plus for the jehad cause. When linked with the predominantly Muslim nations on India's western and eastern borders, Pakistan and Bangladesh, it portends a torrid terrorism battle ahead for the nation in 2006 and beyond.

In combating the fundamentalist the perils of an anti Islamic ideology has to be avoided as to view every Muslim as an enemy of the state is grossly unfair to the 99.99 percent of the totally secular Muslim population of our country, who have assimilated its varied culture as well as adjusted to the multi religious and ethnic society.[7] Thus Pan Islamic ideology has to be defeated by playing the soft Islam card entailed in the Shia and sufi culture rather than the Sunni wahhabi mores. Hindu fundamentalism too cannot be an anti dote to Muslim extremism, a fact which is not understood by the masses who seek comfort in the hype and hoopla created by fanatic bantering of leaders with a skewed ideological leaning, seeking power rather than solutions to the crisis of radicalism affecting religions all over the World. Thus the ideological, political, social and economic ostracization of fundamentalists of all hues is essential, while at the same time fostering secularism and sanity.

The World needs to understand that terrorism is a tactic and not a strategy for achieving transformation. Terrorists get a daily dose of adrenalin as one or other of their ilk strikes at helpless targets across the World in the hope that this attack would bring the victims to their knees and their rulers to a compromise. However the impact of such dastardly acts is only temporary at best a few days to weeks particularly when in the 21st Century India, terrorist acts have limited or no communal impact in fanning riots as happened in 1984, the Gujrat riots not with standing. While it is little solace for the victim and his family, terrorism ultimately will not win in a modern world.

Terrorism The Trends

Organic growth of terrorist violence is the result of easy availability of rapid, automatic, hand held weapons as the Kalashnikovs also called as AK 47/56 depending on the version being used by the terrorists, explosive devices which are electrically and electronically triggered, thereby not requiring the direct presence of the perpetrators of violence close to the scene. Communications provides the terrorist the ability to network, to serially attack his targets for greater psychological effect and create a feeling of being all pervasive while the security agencies are shown to be extremely vulnerable and effete.[8]

Political growth of terrorist violence is promoted by the duality of interpretation of terrorism as being good when conducted by ideologues miscued as freedom fighters or bad when conducted without any ideology. However the point is very clearly differentiated by strong words by noted strategic analyst K Subrahmanyam who says, "Those who refuse to distinguish between the violence used in genuine freedom struggles and in terrorism against innocent civilians are closer to war criminals than freedom fighters"[9] In India the tolerance of corruption and criminalization of politics which are the matrix of terror continues unabated thus demonstrating lack of political will to root out terrorism.[10] Political sagacity has been abandoned to short time political expediency due to which the country continues to suffer the travails of terrorist violence.

Terrorism – Technology

Terrorists though smaller in number have established a technology edge by being one step ahead of the security forces in Jammu and Kashmir. Terrorists inducted two digit IED remotes, security forces upgraded to two digit by which time terrorists had graduated to three digit. Now the stand off is at four digit activators and jammers. Availability of Thuraya satellite phones with terrorists in Jammu and Kashmir is well known. It enables them to converse without jamming and taping, have global cellular capabilities and can send and receive messages. Along with cellular phones, the Thuraya is giving a nightmare to the security forces.

Lap tops and cyber cafes are also used for passing messages. A terrorist or a mole enters a cyber café in Kashmir and drafts a cryptic message which is read by the person for whom it is intended to who then deletes the message without sending it. Simple cryptography is used by terrorists with code changing every 15 days.[11]

Gun Running and Licencing

Gun running supports terrorists on ground through regular supply of weapons for protection as well as conduct of reprehensible raids. Terrorists employ ingenuous means to acquire weapons. A massive gun running and licensing racket is on through the route of transfer of licences of people whose weapons and licenses were seized during insurgency in Nagaland. In Surat alone, 2200 licences are reported to be procured from Nagaland though the authority of the Deputy Commissioner to issue all India permits had been withdrawn in mid 1990's. Some of the licences were not even signed by the Deputy Commissioners but on their behalf denoting involvement of lower staff with pecuniary benefits.[12] There is a need for centralizing powers of issue of licences at a much higher level than the Deputy Commissioners. May be only the Commissioners could undertake this role though it would be cumbersome but would add to effectiveness of security as the approachability and political culpability of Commissioners would hopefully be lesser than that of the Deputy Commissioners.

Terrorist Tactics in Chechnya

150 – 200 militants attacked a police and military station in Kabardino-Balkaria near Chechnya on 13 October 2005. Reports indicate that militants operated in ten mobile groups targeting five to six strategic points to include the regional airport. The attack on the police, army and Federal Security Service (FSB) was said to be the first major operation after Abdul-Khalid Sadulayev took over leadership of the Chechen separatists in March 2000. This attack was reminiscent of the operation in June 2004 when pro Chechen rebels have said to have attacked police buildings in Nazran, and effectively took control of the Ingushetia

region, near Kabardino-Balkaria for several hours. About 60 people were killed in the attack.[13] Similar operations by Indian Naxalites were reported in Bihar and Jharkhand during the year which is an alarming trend and needs to be checked at the earliest.

Funding Terrorism

Cheque book jihad is the term used by the Economist to those who support jihad by funding it and there are many funding sources for the Islamic jihad particularly rich Saudi Sunnis.[14] One way to avert this threat is to put a block on cheque book jihad. The Delhi blasts of 29 October 2005 are said to have been funded by Sheikh Abdul Aziz, a business tycoon who has been funding Lashkar-e-Taiyaba (LeT). LeT now uses hawala route or personal accounts for funding terrorism after 9/11. The money flows in from Saudi Arabia, Libya, Sudan, Afghanistan and other Muslim countries. It is reported that for the Delhi serial blasts Saudi riyals worth Rs 7 lakhs was brought in the country.[15] Other sources have attributed the source of funds to Abdul Bari and Abdul Karim both long term operatives of the Lashkar.[16]

The Naxalites are dependent on fund raising through extortion. Thus these select the period of November to March when government contracts are in full swing to, "tax" the contractors while from March to April they are known to collect money from tendu leaf and forest contractors in Uttar Pradesh. In the North Eastern states, National Highways on which all supplies are inducted in the region and through which forest and other produce is transshipped are a major source of income through, "road tax" levied on each truck running in thousands of rupees. Thus all business transactions in the North East are carried out with a fixed percentage of, "militancy surcharges" by each contractor which varies based on the level of intensity. In Kashmir at times it was as high as 200 percent but given the need of the hour, the security forces or the general public had no option but to give in to the unjustified demands, while the terrorist organizations could get away with threats.

TERRORISM THE SOLUTIONS

Terror Black List

US, India, Malaysia, Canada, UK and Australia have banned the LTTE. LTTE runs a wide network of propaganda activities across at least 54 countries and gets donations from a number of countries as the UK, US, Switzerland, Canada, Australia and Scandinavia where a large community of Tamil expatriates reside.[17] Hizbul Mujaheedin has been recently banned by European Union. India is playing for the ban of other outfits as Harkat-ul-Jehadi-i-Islami or HUJI, a trouble maker in Bangladesh, Jammat ul Mujahideen, Khalistan Liberation Force and LTTE. All these boast of several offices in Europe. A black listing in European Union would imply freezing funds across 35 member states.

Terror black listing ensures that these outfits cannot garner funds and support terrorism overtly, through their over ground worker network spread across the globe. The kinship of organizations as the LTTE is providential and extends across many states. Remittances in foreign currency have greater value in developing countries. The wider the ban in terms of national and geographic spread of an organization the greater would be its impact. There is however a need to lobby for such bans with Western nations with a liberal strain who still face the dilemma of the terrorist as a freedom fighter. Comprehensive details have to be provided with facts and figures to convince leaders of such countries that the ban is justified. In the Indian functional hierarchy the details are normally compiled by the Home Ministry and the actual ban is taken up by the Ministry of External Affairs. Does the Ministry of External Affairs carry out any compilation of lists of foreign nationals who are over ground sympathizers of such organizations in foreign countries? Should it do so? Will it affect the credibility of the Indian government abroad are questions which we need to ask ourselves while continually striving to ensure that all antagonist organizations are placed on the terror ban list.

Terrorism - Hostage Policy

A position paper prepared by the Cabinet Committee on Security highlights that the government will not concede to any demands of individuals or groups holding its citizens as hostage. No ransom will be paid or conceded for release of prisoners.[18] This will provide some essential guide lines to the Crisis Management Group handling any hostage crisis which has to consider a number of factors such as the intelligence, terrain, rapport with local government, ground situation, language, contacts with the terrorist organizations and so on.

The dichotomy of acceptance of demands versus rejection poses a great dilemma for the government in power. If it does not concede then the possibility of hostages being killed is very live as it happened in the case of the five foreigners executed in Kashmir in 1995, Dirk Hasert, Paul Wells, Keith Mangan, Donald Hutchings and Hans Christian Ostro by Al Faran when negotiations continued for long but could not be concluded successfully. The extreme position adopted by the government then of rejecting demand for rewards for information provided on the hostages does not appear justified.[19] On the other hand the release of three top militants, the Jaish-e-Mohammad leader, Maulana Masood Azhar, Syed Sheikh alleged killer of Daniel Pearl and Ahmed Zargar after hijacking of the IC 814 in December 1999 to Kandahar or the release of five militants on kidnapping of Rubaiya Sayeed in December 1989 denote abject surrender of the government to the minions of hardened terror mongers. Release of three Indian truck drivers in Iraq after successful negotiations in September 2004 had raised hopes of a similar achievement on capture of M R Kutty in Afghanistan allegedly by the Taliban. However lack of contact with the kidnappers led sadly to killing of Kutty, the first victim of India's attempt at the great game in Afghanistan.

While the nuances of a hostage policy can be evolved after debate, it is essential to understand the need for the same for it provides firm guidelines to crisis managers while handling the most delicate phase of kidnapping, negotiating with the purpose of ensuring safety of the hostages, what ever their political significance and in an empowered state as India, a trio of drivers from the remote parts of Himachal Pradesh seem as empowered as Rubaiyya Sayeed in the 21st Century. It also indicates to the hostage takers the likely rewards or other wise of such tactics and it is felt that this itself reduces the possibility of a kidnap as if the kidnappers kill the victim, it is a lose-lose situation for all concerned and is particularly sad for the victims family.

The hostage policy needs to have enough flexibility for scope of negotiations and giving marginal concessions to the hostage takers in terms of monetary gains. In a democracy any policy which is publicized also ensures public support. This was most evident when public opinion build up for release of terrorists in the IC 814 case where in a supposedly hard line National Democratic Alliance government, under the Bhartiya Janata Party acquiesced to the demands of the terrorists. The IC 814 hijack case also highlights the need for a well stated policy lack of which had led to total inaction by India's leading anti hijack agencies who kept waiting for orders and coordinating instructions on Delhi airport and did not even consider the easiest of counters as blocking the Raja Sansi airport in Amritsar and not allowing the aircraft out of the country. Once the aircraft left Indian air space the battle for the hostages was perhaps already lost.

The airlines pilots and staff will also have firm point of reference on what line to take once such a policy is well publicized thereby supporting the tactical measures taught to all air crew on such incidents. The policy will not only have to be implemented but also supported by procedures on the ground. Some country's are known to have a policy which talks of no negotiations with any kidnappers. A firm hostage policy with sufficient flexibility appears to be the practical answer.

Overcoming the threat of strikes from the air is another essential measure which would avoid a 9/11 type of terror strike, the capability for which is not difficult to attain given the permissive security environment in the country. Physical and organizational measures are easier to implement and need to be undertaken at the earliest.

There is a basic need to integrate air force and civil air traffic controllers. India's air surveillance and interceptor assets have weakened due to ageing. Thus large space is devoid of active air surveillance. Communication links are poor. There is also a need to induct a number of modern air surveillance radars and integrate the existing radar assets, both air force and civil. Air force interceptors need to operate from a large number of air bases. Better navigational and airfield recovery aids to facilitate all weather operations is also called for. Real time monitoring and tighter control by the air force and civil aviation is also essential. Daily air traffic is over 2500 flights every day in India. With 10,000 flights over France, French interceptors scramble day in and night to shadow civil aircraft with suspicious behavior.[20] Are such exercises carried out in India? We have no indications.

But with new policies proposed the Indian Air Force will monitor all international flights besides civil agencies. Thus if any flight goes off course or if its transponder is switched off in the event of hijacking, fighter aircraft from the nearest IAF base will be scrambled to encircle the aircraft and force it to land. Orders for shooting down the aircraft would be given only by the Prime Minister and in his absence by the Defence minister and home minister in that order.[21]

On the ground in the United States extensive scanning of passengers is carried out to ensure that no weapons or explosives are sneaked on aircraft. We are yet to graduate to the stage when all personnel regardless of their status are willing to subject themselves to such checks. Leaders need to set example by implementation rather than exemption. Unless such a culture pervades the country, it is difficult to envisage a safe air journey environment in the country.

There are sufficient laws in the country to deal with a variety of crimes including financial terrorism and now even information warfare, the need is to ensure that our enforcement and judicial processes make these laws effective by implementation rather than mere statutes. Peripheral debates as the relevance of POTA should not allow the main issues to be sidetracked as per Pratap Bhanu Mehta, Director of Centre for Policy Research as this is just to appease our senses that we are a tough people who make tough laws. Effective law enforcement as per Mehta requires a far more sustained effort than mere enacting of laws.[22]

Determining the Capability of Militant Groups

Does the terrorist organizations have a well laid out chain of leadership, are the leadership networked or follow a bureaucratic chain? Do they have a logistics organization which is self sustaining or are cells dependent on arranging for their own supplies? For example the LTTE has a logistics organization which functions like that of an army . Do they have a sustainable financial network? Do they have significant political support? Does the political organization have an organized military wing or the militant organization politically supported and is it named as such? For instance the Karbis and Dimasa became potent threats when they formed United Peoples Democratic Solidarity (UPDS) and Dima Halim Daogah (DHD) as militant groups representing the Karbis and Dimasa respectively. Do they have a communications network which is self sustaining? Does it have an international network and presence? These are some of the issues which determine the effectiveness of militant organizations which will facilitate intelligence operatives in determining the dimension of the threat.

US Policy Shift Achieving Success in Iraq

To date US has 2108 casualties and 15804 wounded (Newsweek 5 December 2005). Public opinion is what is driving America to change its strategy in Iraq. US strategists have also recognized, as many other states, unfortunately only after two years that the main cause of Iraqi resistance is the presence of US troops on home soil.[23] After almost two years of staying in the barracks and armed camps, the US military has finally got going in Iraq as per noted political analyst Fareed Zakaria and started, "clear, hold and build" operations in the words of Condolezza Rice. Thus it is now securing the lives of people and population the prime task of any counter insurgent force. The prime sign of this change is clearance of the airport road, all of eight kms. About 70 Iraqi Special Police are said to have held this road backed by two Iraqi Army platoons. Iraqi forces were thus used effectively to secure this road the death run for American forces for last two years. These have also been holding out successfully in Mosul and Najaf and will facilitate gradually withdrawal of American forces from Iraq. For this Zakaria recommends that the key is not exit but implementation of a clear cut strategy.[24] Zakaria feels that the next step would be to protect infra structure, power plants and refineries which can produce electricity and gas. The strategy for reconstruction should thus be put in place.

Homogenising the Shia – Sunni divide is another task which is important. Sunni leaders are being bought off with incentives, tribe by tribe and village by village as per a Newsweek report by Khalilzad and Gen George Casey.[25] Move in, clear a area, place Iraqi troops on ground and move further is the strategy adopted by the Americans recently and more and more responsibility will be placed with Iraqi troops. It goes to the credit of the US administration and particularly of government strategists as Kahlilzad that they are recommending a stay in Iraq for any withdrawal at this critical stage spells civil war which ironically will increase the threat to the US as Iraq will fall in the grips of Al Qaeda type of terrorist forces facilitating launching operations on Europe as well as the United States. Khalilzad has used his Afghanistan experience effectively and is building up provincial reconstruction teams of a mix of civil and military personnel of about 70 – 100 to build the infra structure in Iraq.[26]

Counter Terror Intelligence and Network

Intelligence about terrorist strikes will never be complete as the exact target is not predictable by intelligence agencies which focus on only generalized inputs. Specific inputs are possible by the police at the local level, the Station House officers, thana in charges and so on who having received sweeping inputs can then carry out extra surveillance and vigilance, specific to identifying individuals with suspicious motives and routine in their respective areas. It is this field which needs to be really addressed if we want to avoid any more Delhi or Mumbai serial blasts in the year ahead. Similarly in the Jehanabad Jail Break in Bihar, the Naxalites are reported to have mustered strength against the targets two to three days in advance, which if the local police were vigilant or had not been subverted could have easily undertaken precautionary measures to preempt the attack. The Thana ICs thus will have to do a much better job than what he is doing today. For that the corruption in the police system will have to be checked as the, ubiquitous, "hafta" system mars the force at all levels. This is where the strategic or policy level reforms should come about. If the appointment system is not dependent on bribes, the SHOs need not resort to haftas and can then focus on the all important challenge of gathering intelligence and information of their beats in a comprehensive manner, thereby supplementing the effective strategic intelligence on terrorist operations being obtained today.

For ordinary citizens travel advisories as that routinely issued by the US government need consideration. The US government had issued travel advisory to its citizens traveling to New Delhi to stay low and avoid crowded places after the Delhi blasts in October 2005 even though these did not in any way denote a larger threat.[27] This is routine procedure for all Western Governments which warn the people through their embassies as well as in general travel advisory notes thereby ensuring citizen safety.

Information warfare and influencing public policy in the wake of an incident assumes significance. This is suggested by placing dossiers immediately after the strikes in the mail boxes of influential leaders and lobbyists the World over and particularly the USA.[28]

Growing network of anti terror nations was evident during the conference on Global Impact of Terrorism held at the World famous, Institute for Counter Terrorism of Herzliya, Israel (ICT) in September 2005. Motto of the ICT is "It takes a network to beat a network". An effective anti terror network is emerging and threat to India from terrorism has been discussed in World forums as per noted counter terrorism expert, B Raman. UN Security Council Resolution No 1373 against international terrorism unanimously passed immediately after 9/11 had laid emphasis on networking. This is also the theme of the publication of International Terrorism Watch Programme (ITWP) and Observer Research Foundation (ORF) wherein a large number of papers were presented by experts from India, Malaysia, Thailand, Singapore, Indonesia, the Philippines, Australia, the US and Turkey.

Role of moderate leaders of the Muslim community in countering activities of terrorist organizations is also highlighted. Maritime terrorism is an important aspect frequently neglected and would impact both on energy security as well as trade and commerce between nations. Forthcoming programmes on terrorism of ORF, "International terrorism in Central Asia and its likely implications for South Asia", Future Terrorism :Likely scenarios and capabilities required and Maritime terrorism and its threat on India's trade and energy security thus are seen to contribute to the knowledge in the country on this essential facet.[29]

Tactical Measures

For defence against Indigenous Explosive Devices (IEDs), jamming is said to be the best security. Jammer range and the ability to jam a large number of frequencies will decide effectiveness of the technique. All vehicles should be equipped with such jammers. It is said that President Musharraf was saved by the jammers during the strike on his vehicle.[30]

Control on guns, explosives and detonators is another measure which will go a long way to reduce its availability to the terrorists. While guns are seemingly under control, the arms licensing system is very porous and politically sensitive, explosives and detonators are available off the shelf. These need to be regulated more stringently to reduce availability to the miscreants. Effective surveillance of funding and transfer as is evident from the case of the Delhi serial blasts master mind, Tariq Ahmad Dar's case who had been transferring Rs 2.3 million wired from United Arab Emirates to HDFC bank's Srinagar branch demonstrates its need. However surveillance was left midway due to priority of other targets.[31] The individual was known to be staying in a palatial house in Srinagar.

The most interesting development which may possibly come about in 2006 is the use of helicopter borne missiles as the Delilah 2 which is a 400 pound, precision strike missile with a range of 230 miles and accuracy of 300 feet is slated to be mounted on Mi 17 and Mi 24 helicopters for low intensity operations in Kashmir as per a Defense News report.[32]

A final word is that the Frankenstein always rises as the Taliban and Osama Bin Laden propped up by the Americans to fight the Soviets in Afghanistan had to be tackled by the Americans themselves a few decades later. The lesson in Punjab is also clear as Bhindranwale is alleged to have been raised by one of our prominent political parties which had to fight him and his ilk from 1984 to 1994, a decade long of strife. Thus the lesson is never raise Frankenstein's as they would strike back at you. The quote at the beginning of this chapter should make this clear. Instead democratic institutions in the country need to be more responsive to the timely needs and aspirations of the people so that they do not have to resort to violence to get their voice heard.[33]

References

1. South Asia Terrorism Portal quoted in the Times of India 6 November 2005. Lucknow. p. 10.
2. Shourie, Arun. "Will the Iron Fence Save A Tree Hollowed by Termites." Rupa, New Delhi. 2005. p. 13.
3. Sood, Vikram. "Human Wrongs". The Hindustan Times. 23 November 2005. Lucknow. p. 6.
4. Times of India Report. Times of India 14 November 2005. Bangalore. p. 1.

5. Ghosh, Aparisim. "Professor of Death" Time 24 October 2005. p. 30-33.
6. Times of India Report. Times of India 14 November 2005. Bangalore. p. 8.
7. Also See the chapter on Islam which clearly brings out that Islam is a peace seeking religion.
8. Subrahmanyam, K. Economic Times Debate. The Economic Times. 8 November 2005. New Delhi. p. 15.
9. Subrahmanyam, K. Economic Times Debate. The Economic Times. 8 November 2005. New Delhi. p. 15.
10. Subrahmanyam, K. Economic Times Debate. The Economic Times. 8 November 2005. New Delhi. p. 15.
11. Soondas, Anand. "Terroists—" Times of India. 24 November 2005. New Delhi. p. 11.
12. John, Paul. "Wanted in Surat—" Times of India. 24 November 2005. New Delhi. p. 7.
13. Lowe, Chirstian. "Gunmen strike—" Indian Express. 14 October 2005. Lucknow. p. 7.
14. The Economist Report. The Economist. 26 November 2005. p. 29.
15. Times of India Report. Times of India 14 November 2005. Bangalore. p. 8.
16. Swami, Praveen. The Hindu. 16 November 2005. Hyderabad. p. 12.
17. Jain, Bharti. "India—". The Economic Times. Lucknow. 5 December 2005. p 2.
18. Economic Times Report. "India still—". The Economic Times. 25 November 2005. New Delhi. p. 2.
19. Economic Times Report. "India still—". The Economic Times. 25 November 2005. New Delhi. p. 2.
20. Krishnaswamy, S Air Chief marshal. Indian Express. 23 September 2005. Lucknow. p. 8.
21. Hindustan Times Report. "Garuda for Hijacks—" 09 October 2005. Lucknow. p. 15.
22. Mehta, Pratap Bhanu. "Moral Vertigo—" The Indian Express. 4 November 2005. New Delhi. p. ??.
23. Newsweek Report. 5 December 2005. p. 14.
24. Zakaria, Fareed. "Panic is—". Newsweek. 5 December 2005. p. 11.
25. Newsweek Report. 5 December 2005. p. 14.
26. Newsweek Report. 5 December 2005. p. 14.
27. Gopinath, Vrinda. "Blasts—" The Indian Express. 2 November 2005. Lucknow. p. 5.
28. Roy, Ranjan. "Where's the Battle Cry" The Times of India. 05 November 2005. Lucknow. p. 10.
29. Raman, B. "Network to beat a network". The Pioneer. 12 October 2005. Lucknow. p. 7.

30. Singh, Jatinder, "A global threat—" The Indian Express. 4 October 2005. Lucknow. p. 8.

31. Swami, Praveen. "Surveallance—" The Hindu. 16 November 2005. Hyderabad. p. 12.

32. Raghuvanshi, Vivek. "India mulls—". Defense News. 6 December 2005. p. 21.

33. Haksar, Nandita. Economic Times Debate. The Economic Times. 8 November 2005. New Delhi. p. 15.

14

Nuclear Picture – Development of Nuclear Resources

"India and Russia are successfully cooperating in nuclear energy sector ...We see India taking all the necessary steps to build its relations with the international community including NSG (Nuclear Suppliers Group) members. India has separated its civilian and military facilities. It has the necessary legislation in place. It is actively cooperating with NSG. We see India as a strategic partner."

Vladimir Putin 6 December 2005

"We see energy security as an area of tremendous potential. We feel that there is a vast potential for the expansion of cooperation in this area, given India's growing energy requirements and the importance of nuclear energy as a clean and viable alternative energy source."

Manmohan Singh

The World is nuclear safe in 2006, at least from threats emerging from states possessing nuclear weapons. The large inventory of over 20,000 warheads with Russia and the United States of America is capped and sealed and will not find any use in the year ahead. The same cannot be said about WMD (Weapons of Mass Destruction) threats from non state actors, the Al Qaeda's and Jemmah Islamiah's of the World. The threat from these organizations using chemical and biological weapons if not nuclear is omni present, though its exactitudes are difficult to estimate. The continuous need for vigilance and monitoring of all agencies involved in clandestine proliferation as the A Q Khan network of Pakistan is called for. This cannot be left to non proliferation nations and lobbies as the USA alone but there is a need for active monitoring by state and non state agencies in our country as well.

Of critical concern is the acquisition of a weapon of mass destruction, be it nuclear, biological and chemical by a terror network as the Al Qaeda and its use. This is an issue which has received limited attention both at home and abroad and the details are yet unclear. However statistically and other wise the possibility of a holocaust needs to be taken seriously. Control of clandestine nuclear trafficking by countries as Pakistan, now being projected as a private venture by the ubiquitous A Q Khan, though evidence suggests otherwise and nations as North Korea needs far greater attention of legislators from the USA than perhaps separation of the civilian and nuclear facilities of benign nuclear powers as India, who have abdicated the right for first use of nuclear weapons. India too needs to develop its nuclear intelligence capability considerably to check the growth of networks as that sponsored by Pakistan for it will be the worst affected along with the USA from acquisition of nuclear weapons by a terror network.

Rest of the year 2006 is likely to be taken up by international nuclear politics. Iran will be the main agenda for non proliferation while India will be engaged for implementation of the Indo – US Accord July 2005. India's prime interest lies in availing for itself nuclear technologies for growth of the power sector. Thus nuclear energy assumes considerable significance. India has set an ambitious target for growth of nuclear energy of 40,000 MW in the next 10 years. India's reactors are essentially uranium based, while it does not have supplies of the same. Conversion to thorium based reactors will provide us great benefits as India has adequate quantities of Thorium.[1] There are likely to be beneficial developments in the Indian nuclear energy sector. The over three and half decade old isolation of India in the nuclear field has been broken with the US - India understanding on civilian nuclear exchange and India will form part of Nuclear Suppliers Group shortly. The triggers for further development would be approval of the Indo-US Accord by the U S Congress with the confidence that India will separate its civilian and military nuclear facilities. The political hiccups at home will not prove a dampener for the developments abroad, the UPA government will have to sell the nuclear story as a need to make up the energy deficit in the country along with India's admission into the Nuclear Suppliers Group which is likely, making it for the first time a member of the elite club. The diversification which is being achieved in our nuclear supplies taking on board offers by Russia as is evident from the quotes above can provide an added dimension of reassurance.

In all probability India will provide to the International Atomic Energy Agency or IAEA the plan for separation of its civilian facilities and negotiate the safeguards to be placed on these. This will facilitate the US administration in overcoming congressional and non proliferation lobby resistance to placing India beyond sanctions and provide us the necessary wherewithal for furthering our nuclear energy programme. This ipso facto places us amongst the nuclear weapons powers, a first for a non signatory of the Nuclear Non Proliferation Treaty. Not a small diplomatic and nuclear achievement for a country regarded on the fringes of World polity just a few years back.

The issues for 2006 include, developing the capability to monitor clandestine WMD capabilities in nations and non state actors in the close vicinity particularly in antagonist states and organizations. It is India which should have blown the whistle in the case of Pakistan sponsored A Q Khan network but lacking adequate surveillance mechanism in place the proliferation went unnoticed with possibly grave consequences in the future, supporting the nuclear non proliferation efforts of the World community in general, acquiring the wherewithal for enhancing nuclear power generation capability, development of the command and control and other support network for operationalising the country's nuclear capability and continued development of nuclear weapons in quantity as well as quality. In the national sphere, the creation of a Strategic Forces Command is likely to come about in 2006 which would be a great achievement streamlining the employment of the country's nuclear arsenal and fleshing out the deterrence capability.

What are the issues involved and how will they pan out is being discussed here after.

India's Nuclear Capability - A Guestimate

Of the Indian reactors, two are said to be designed to produce weapons grade fuel, the Cirrus which produced the plutonium for Pokharan I in 1974 and Dhruva which produced fuel for Pokharan II in 1998. Dhruva was designed to produce 8 bombs a year but is reported to have suffered some setbacks, the capabilities of Cirrus are not available. Analysts as Swaminathan S Ankelsaria Aiyar believe that these two reactors are enough to produce 100 bombs which are enough as a deterrent.[2] Other estimates say that India has only about 75 bombs which are inadequate to counter China's possibly 300 plus. Some forecasts have claimed that India will have 300 to 400 nuclear or thermo nuclear weapons over the next five to seven years.[3] India's nuclear facilities for civilian use include that at Narora, Indore, Kaiga, Kakrapar, Tarapur, Trombay, Hyderabad, Mysore, Chennai, Kalapakkam and Koondankulam while those for military use include the one at Trombay, Kalapakkam, the Rare materials project at Mysore and test facilities in Pokharan, Rajasthan.[4]

Indian nuclear parleys are essentially based on this factor of achieving deterrence parity with China and a dissuasive parity with Pakistan. So far the possibility of a terror group attaining nuclear capability has not been factored in the discussion, while there is limited deliberation of how this capability is to be delivered, the command and control facilities, decision making loop and post strike management issues. A purely quantitative, "number of bombs" based capability is grievously lop sided. A public debate on developing full spectrum nuclear capability without focusing on weapon capability is thus called for in the year ahead.

Nuclear Policy of Nations – Preemptive use Possible

As per the website Acronym, five states, the "P-5", are defined as nuclear weapon states under the Nuclear Non-Proliferation Treaty (NPT): Britain, China, France, US and Russia. At least three more are de facto nuclear weapon possessors (the D-3): India, Pakistan and Israel. These eight have the most advanced missile programmes and in some cases may have biological and/or chemical weapons or programmes Several other states are viewed of proliferation concern or have programmes which have been exposed and are now being addressed and dismantled. These include: Iraq, Iran, North Korea (DPRK), Libya and Syria.[5]

A review of the nuclear policy by various states of interest to us would be important. The nuclear policy of the United States is designed to provide, "a range of options to pose a credible deterrent to adversaries whose values and calculations of risk and loss of lives may be very different and more difficult to discern than past adversaries.", as per Donald Rumsfield's statement in 2002. NATO nations reserve the right to use nuclear weapons against non nuclear weapon states in the event of an attack on them, their dependent territories, their armed forces, or other troops, their allies or on a state towards which they have a security commitment. The Russian federation too has abandoned the no first use policy.

Lt Gen Khalid Kidwai of the National Command Authority of Pakistan's Strategic Planning Division asserted that nuclear weapons were solely aimed at India. He stated that Pak will use these weapons if India conquers a large part of Pakistan's territory or destroys a large part of its land and air forces or economically strangulates it or pushes it to political destabilization.

China has a strong bilateral relationship with Pakistan to include the following issues –

(a) Nuclear and missile assistance to Pakistan.

(b) Deployment of nuclear weapons and missiles in Tibet and Xinjiang.

(c) Friendship treaty with Pakistan.

China has offered to sign agreements on no first use of nuclear weapons with other five NPT recognized nuclear weapons states. It has signed such an agreement with Russia as also a non targeting agreement with Clinton administration immediately after the 1998 Indian nuclear tests. China states that the no first use pledge is only for those countries which have signed the NPT or are members of regional nuclear weapons free zones.

India's nuclear doctrine decrees that the country should maintain a minimum deterrent and ensure that this remains credible at all times. Survivability of assets is very essential for this purpose. This has also been outlined in the doctrine. Initially drafted by the National Democratic Alliance government in 1998, it has been accepted by the present United Progressive Alliance government giving it greater sanctity.[6]

Nuclear Command and Control – India

India has established the Nuclear Command Authority in 2003 which comprised of the prime minister, the defence minister and the external affairs minister. It is slated to receive a phillip in the coming year with the creation of a Strategic Forces command which will control the strategic assets of the country. It will have two National Command Centres, and eight regional command centres.[7] The large number of agencies involved in such a command and control establishment has rendered it difficult to be created in the past. However budgetary allocations are expected to be made in 2006 to accelerate the process.

Indo-US Nuclear Agreement

China has reportedly 300 to 400 nuclear weapons to India's 75 as per reports. It is this disparity in nuclear capability which is preventing India from a moratorium on nuclear weapons. US strategic scholars have claimed that the Indo US July compact deal was made to cut China to size and balance the power relations in Asia. In this context, US also intends that India be made a major power in the years ahead. There is a need for the US Congress to amend the laws before the deal can be completed and will entail lifting restrictions on supply of reactors and fuel to India while India agrees to a series of obligations to overcome fears of proliferation. India has agreed to separate the military and civilian programmes and place the latter under the

International Atomic Energy Agency (IAEA) inspection. US is likely to face problems as it is against stated American policy from cooperating with a state that has nuclear weapons but is not a signatory of the Non Proliferation Treaty and may put the international non proliferation system to risk.[8]

US Congressman Dan Burton called for a complete separation of civilian and military components of India's nuclear programme for its approval by US Congress.[9]

The Joint Nuclear Working Group between India and the USA comprises of the Foreign Secretary of India, Mr Shyam Saran and US under secretary, Mr Nicholas Burns. A meeting was held on 21 – 22 December 2005.[10] The non proliferation lobby in the US bid for safeguards for six nuclear fuel fabrication plants, two breeder reactors, four reprocessing plants, four enrichment facilities, nine research reactors and nine heavy water production plants.[11] The five facilities in Trombay used for production of fissile material for possible military use are likely to be out of the ambit.

US apprehensions are essentially focused on two facilities, the Cirrus reactor in Trombay and the uranium enrichment plant at Rattanhalli, Mysore generally known as the Rare Metals Plant or RMP. This plant is said to have a large number of centrifuges capable of producing several kilograms of highly enriched uranium each year, the exact details of which are obviously not in the public domain.

The issue of separation of civilian and military facilities is a vexing one as it involves the maximalist position of United States hawks who want a total separation of Indian civilian and military facilities to cap its capability to produce nuclear weapons and Indian nuclear hawks who want to retain their independence to produce as many nuclear weapons as required. Cost of separation is a critical issue which can be managed with some help from other agencies hence is a mere pressure tactic used in the negotiation paradigm. Separating of the civilian and nuclear facilities is a foregone conclusion at this stage, it is now up to the Government how to manage the political fall out.

Pakistan's Bid for Entry into Nuclear Suppliers Group

The agreement between the United States and India on 18 July 2005, has had a spill over effect with India been offered civil nuclear supplies by a number of nations including United Kingdom, Canada and France. This perhaps prompted Pakistan's Atomic Energy Commission (PAEC) Chairman Pervez Butt to ask President Pervez Musharraf to seek a nuclear deal from the US and the West to meet the country's 8800 MW electricity needs over the next 25 years. Pakistan has overcome its diffidence borne out of the involvement of nuclear scientist, A Q Khan in nuclear proliferation and stepped up its campaign to secure advanced nuclear technology. Pakistan's demand is for 13 nuclear power plants against India's 6 as a substitute to oil and global warming and agreed to active supervision by the International Atomic Energy Agency (IAEA). It is reportedly not hesitant in playing the terrorism card, of , "no stability" if India continued to be favoured vis a vis Pakistan.[12]

Iranian Proliferation – International and Domestic Policies

The key issue in Iranian nuclear proliferation is the inability of the IAEA to certify that Iran does not have any clandestine sites, equipment, material and so on due to the link of A Q Khan of Pakistan with the country from 1987 to 2003. Iran is thus claimed to have carried out clandestine proliferation for 18 years. The China – Pakistan – A Q Khan proliferation links have been reportedly concealed by the pro China lobby.[13] North Korea has willingly acceded to come to the negotiating table on the nuclear non proliferation issue highlighting the success of negotiations. Basic issues involve security guarantees, economic aid, proliferation resistant light water reactors in exchange for it sticking to the Nuclear Non proliferation Treaty. Analysts believe that this will also facilitate a treaty with Iran which is far more engaged than North Korea with the World and is also less towards the path of nuclearisation.[14]

Iran's nuclearisation has generated fears of an Islamic nuclear triad of Pakistan, Iran and possibly Saudi Arabia. Nuclear weapons acquisition by Shia Iran can unleash Sunni Arab backlash particularly from Saudi Arabia. Iran-Iraq Shia nexus could be a destabilizing factor in the Middle East with large number of Sunni Arab states. It may also invite Israeli counter vailing response.[15] This is a marginal issue which India is playing up to assuage the hawks in the US administration and cannot be harped upon as that of abandoning autonomy in policy in any way.

The impasse on the Iran nuclear issue is likely to have blown over with no reference of Iran's proliferation being made to the UN Security Council in the near future and Iran given additional time to consider other proposals by the IAEA board. The proposal to centralize enrichment for countries which did not have the full fuel cycle in facilities under international supervision was likely to be accepted by Iran. Though Iran has the facility to convert uranium into gas, its enrichment to the levels permissible for peaceful uses will be done in Russia under international supervision. Since financial control will be with Iran this will be a financial bonanza for Russia. This is also likely to reduce costs of inspections for all countries if such common facilities are established. The question of sovereignty of nations and right to develop atomic energy for peaceful purposes also appears to have been affected. India has gained as its vote in September 2005 against Iran has resulted it being considered an important player in the international nuclear energy scene.[16] India has all along been claiming that the decision on Iran has been taken not due to but inspite of US pressure which had made the decision all the more difficult as it would be seen to be currying favour to the US especially after the relative, "threat" by US top democrat in the House International Relations Committee that India could not expect Congress to support a deal extending US civilian nuclear cooperation if India totally disregards US interest on the Iran resolution.[17] India's vote against Iran at the IAEA meeting in Vienna in September 2005 was stoutly defended in all forums by the Government and even justified by linking with nuclear proliferators as Pakistan's A Q Khan with Iran's nuclear capability development. The US President had also called up Indian Prime Minister Manmohan Singh on US - India understanding on supply of nuclear technology, this further bolstered the Indian resolve to stick to its stand against Iran in November 2005 meeting.[18] In the political space however this repeated US injunctions are being seen as kowtowing to the Americans rather than following an independent foreign policy initiative based on national interest. Information management in such a situation assumes great significance.

Technologies for Nuclear Energy Harnessing

Indian Nuclear Society or INS is a non governmental professional body promoting nuclear science in the country. India is following the three stage programme of nuclear energy uranium-plutonium route towards thorium utilization, relying on reprocessed fuel. Nuclear fuel cycle is said to be desired as a closed one, thus providing for continuous use of reprocessed nuclear fuel. India has taken up the proposal for participation in two futuristic atomic energy programmes which are multi lateral. International Thermonuclear Experimental Reactor Project (ITERP) is a programme conceived by the United States, Russia, China, Japan, Korea and the European Union to build a reactor with hot fusion. India has been granted admission in this exclusive club. The Large Hardon Collider project is being built by the European organization for Nuclear Research or CERN. ITER is to provide unlimited, clean and cheap energy wherein one kg of fusion fuel would be able to produce the same amount of energy as 10 million kg of fossil fuels. The reactor is expected to be build by 2016.[19] The admission of India into this exclusive club can be said to be a feather in the cap after the recent shift in US policy of not linking India's non signatory status of the nuclear Non Proliferation Treaty with assistance in the civilian nuclear energy sector. The European Union and significantly other major states as China, Japan and Russia also seem to have taken such a stand. The success of ITER is not guaranteed, yet as a positive in international policy this move should be welcomed by India. During the South East Asian leaders summit in December, 2005, the Prime Minister thanked China and Japan for support on India's entry into the ITER for development of thermal energy.[20]

Bhabha Atomic Research Centre has the country's most advanced computing systems, such as the Teraflop class 512 node Anupam supercomputer, High resolution tiled display cluster and many powerful computing clusters integrated seamlessly using ultra fast network technology via a computer grid.[21] This places it in one of the leading nuclear research establishments.

Nuclear Trade

An MI 5 document of the British Intelligence Agency entitled, "Companies and Organizations of Proliferation Concern" compiled to prevent British companies from inadvertently exporting sensitive goods or expertise to organizations covertly involved in weapons of mass destruction programmes has revealed that 95 Pakistani organizations and government bodies including the Pakistan high commission in London as having assisted the country's nuclear programme. UAE has been reported as the most important of the fronts which may have been used and 24 private firms have been identified as having acquired WMD technologies for Iran, Pakistan and India. 11 Israeli organizations and 73 Indian bodies are also said to have been involved. Some 114 organizations including chemical and pharmaceutical companies and university medical schools have been identified as having acquired nuclear, chemical, biological and missile technology. Nuclear ambitions of Egypt and Syria are also included in the report. A private company in Egypt identified as having procured technology for use in a nuclear weapons programme while Syrian atomic energy commission also faced similar charges. This report has been seen by the British Newspaper, "The Guardian" and was compiled two years ago in 2003.[22]

Indo Russian Nuclear Cooperation

Indian Atomic Energy Commission Chairman, Anil Kakodkar and head of Russia's Federal Atomic Energy

Agency, Sergei Kiriyenko held separate talks in the background of the visit by the Prime Minister to Russia in the first week of December 2005. Putin had already promised India all the help with the assistance of Nuclear Supplier Group.[23]

Russia will take over as the Chairman of the NSG in July 2006, hence its cooperation will assist India in gaining support in this controlling body. The US is also committed to full cooperation in the civil nuclear field in the light of the 18 July 2005 agreement, with Russian support India's quest for harnessing civilian nuclear facilities for its energy requirements will be further strengthened. India can take advantage of the likely competition between various nations of the NSG to supply nuclear technology to hungry states as India and hence the growing interests in both the United States and Russia the main players in this field. Russia in particular is basing its international and economic relations on the three corner stones of nuclear, military and space technology and hardware sales.

All this augurs well for the growth of Indian nuclear energy sector. Major gains are expected to accrue, after the US government is able to overcome apprehensions of its legislators and the powerful non proliferation lobby. The inevitability of India as a nuclear weapon state has now been accepted by the World at large. Time is now ripe to harvest the goodwill by optimizing our nuclear energy generation capability with the aid of the Nuclear Suppliers Group.

References

1. Patnaik, Nageshwar. "India ready—". The Economic Times. 28 December 2005. New Delhi. p. 2.
2. Aiyar, SSA. "One hundred bombs will do". The Economic Times. 7 December 2005. New Delhi. p. 16.
3. Raghuvanshi, Vivek. "India, Russia—". Defense News. 1 November 2005. p. 9.
4. Rajaghatta, Chidanand. "US think-tank—". The Times of India. 21 December 2005. Lucknow. p. 1.
5. Downloaded from Acronym Institute website. Acronym.org.uk on 23 December 2005

6. Raghuvanshi, Vivek. "India, To—". Defense News. 1 November 2005. p. 9.
7. Raghuvanshi, Vivek. "India, To—". Defense News. 1 November 2005. p. 9.
8. Economic Times Report. "Nuke Deal—" Economic Times. 10 November 2005. New Delhi p. 2.
9. Economic Times Report. 29 November 2005. New Delhi. p. 2.
10. Economic Times Report. The Economic Times. 16 December 2005. New Delhi. p. 3.
11. Rajaghatta, Chidanand. "US think-tank—". The Times of India. 21 December 2005. Lucknow. p. 1.
12. Times of India Report. Times of India. 5 October 2005. Lucknow. p. 10.
13. Subrahmanyam, K. "The Case against Iran." The Times of India. 21 November 2005. Lucknow. p. 5.
14. Times Editorial. The Times of India. 21 September 2005. Lucknow. p. 12.
15. Subhrahmanyam. K. "If Iran Went Nuclear—" Indian Express. 05 October 2005. Lucknow. p. 8.
16. Sreenivasan, T P. "Iran Cloud Blows Over". The Times of India. 2 December 2005. Lucknow. p. 9.
17. Associated Press Report. Indian Express. 01 October 2005. Lucknow. p. 7.
18. Roy,Bhaskar. "India—" The Times of India. 1 October 2005. Lucknow. p. 1.
19. Reuters Report. Sunday Hindustan Times. 4 December 2005. Lucknow. p. 17.
20. Pioneer Report. The Pioneer. 15 December 2005. Lucknow. p. 2.
21. The Hindu Report. The Hindu. 16 November 2005. Hyderabad. p. 12.
22. Hindustan Times. "India, Pak—" The Hindustan Times. 9 October 2005. Lucknow. p. 16.
23. Samanta, Pranab Dhal. "We will boost—". The Indian Express. 7 December 2005. p. 1,2.

15

The Nation Arms Itself – Arms Acquisitions In Progress

"There is no such thing as an inevitable war. If war comes, it will be from the failure of human wisdom".

Bonar Law

Acquisition of arms and war like stores and equipment is based on a country's strategic needs. India's strategic requirements have been dictated by the recent threats emerging from its neighbourhood, a nuclear China and Pakistan with both country's having credible nuclear capability. While budgetary constraints ruled India's arms acquisition process till the Kargil Operations in 1999, post Operation Vijay, India has undertaken realistic spends on capital procurements in defence. However the process continues to be marred by allegations of kick backs which are politically sensitive and lack of a sound long term procurement policy. While the latter has been resolved to some extent by adoption of the Defence Procurement Policy 2005, fears of corruption has at times put the entire process of acquisition in reverse gear.

India's policy on arms development is indigenization of maximum components if not the main systems. However developing state of the art weapons and equipment is a complex process which requires considerable investment in research and development and manufacturing infra structure which being monolithic in nature is cost prohibitive. Indian defence industry is essentially in the public sector which creates insufficiencies as well as hurdles for development restricted by labour laws and regulations which inhibit hiring best talent due to salary restrictions. There are a number of areas where India has a leverage if it can collaborate with other nations and industries such as aerospace where Indian capabilities are said to be of a high quality. Lockheed Martin,

Boeing, General Dynamics are global leaders in the aerospace industry which can provide considerable enhancements to the Indian industry in a shared effort.[1] A shift in outlook is also evident with the recent statement by Dr R Chidambaram, Scientific Adviser to the Government on India's procurement policy, "India wants intellectual collaboration on equal partnership, not on a donor recipient basis".[2] India's Defence Procurement Policy also stipulates that all foreign vendors should buy related equipment or ancillaries from the country up to 30 percent. This is not only designed to built up capabilities at home but also ensure that security of spares is maintained in case of likely sanctions. This can also boost our defence production base.

The story of indigenous production however does not generate confidence of excellence in products manufactured in the country. A recent Comptroller and Auditor General Report on quality assurance cover provided by the Directorate General of Quality Assurance which examined the period from 1999 to 2004 with the audit carried out between June 2004 and March 2005 states that had the Indian Army gone to war during Operation Parakram, it would have done so with defective tanks and personal arms as INSAS rifles. The details of the report indicate that Tank T 72 quoted as Tank X had multiple defects in reliability trials conducted in 1998-99 to include gear system, laser range finder and gun stabilizer system. Tanks inducted between October 2001 and January 2003 and 2003-04 were also found to be defective. INSAS rifles again referred to as Rifle X also had quality problems with 62 types of defects reported and many thousands returned for repair. In addition ammunition of several types valued up to Rs. 888 Crore was held in unserviceable condition.[3] Thus reliance on foreign supplies is likely to continue for a long time to come.

The biggest setback of the year 2005 for the Armed Forces was the destruction caused by the Tsunami in December 2004 in the Andaman and Nicobar Island, the home of the Andaman and Nicobar Command, the first joint command of the Indian Armed Forces. Maximum damage was suffered by the air force base which was completely wiped out in the Car Nicobar islands. Rebuilding of the base is on and substantial progress is reported to have been made. For effective consolidation of aerial and space assets an Aerospace Command is likely to come up in Trivendrum given the large number of space agencies located there. Examination of the concept by the Government including organization of space organizations of other nations is in progress.[4]

India's arms acquisition over the next few years includes a wide variety of weapon systems. There is a doctrinal shift from platform centric to network centric warfare, however this has not translated on ground in the acquisition priorities so far. The focus is now on critical mobility assets and precision guided munitions. Some major arms acquisitions in terms of budgetary allotments and enhancement of capabilities during the next decade include :-

(a) 66 Hawk jet trainers – Rs. 12,000 Crores

(b) Aircraft Carrier Gorshkov – Rs. 12,000 Crores.

(c) Phalcon AEW from Isreal – Rs. 10,000 Crores.[5]

An event of critical concern for Indian defense watchers was the test of Babur missile by Pakistan in August 2005. This Cruise missile is said to have a range of 500 kms, can strike deep with its terrain hugging features and would have limited answers in the Indian air defence arsenal. Pakistan's claim of being able to field this system in a couple of years has also been viewed with concern in India and efforts are on to discover the source of this sudden augmentation of Pakistan's missile manufacturing capacity with a quantum leap in technology. Some major developments in the defence acquisition field in the country are as per succeeding paragraphs.

Defence Procurement Procedure 2005 (Capital Procurements)

In June 2005, the Indian defence ministry announced a new policy for Defence Procurement Procedure 2005 (Capital Procurements) aimed at, "expeditious procurement of the approved requirements of the Armed Forces in terms of capabilities sought and time frame prescribed by optimally utilising the allocated budgetary resources. While achieving the same, it will demonstrate the highest degree of probity and public accountability, transparency in operations, free competition and impartiality. In addition, the goal of achieving self-reliance in defence equipment will be kept in mind."[6] The main issue was that of offsets which would imply that foreign companies will have to outsource approximately 30 percent of the components from Indian industry though defence industry sources felt that further clarifications on this vital issue are required. Other important provisions include open tendering instead of limited tendering prevalent presently and strategic and political considerations over riding lowest bid criteria.[7] The last will provide considerable leverages to the government of the day to offer considerations which could lead to allegations of subjective selection. Active involvement of private firms in the defence procurement process is another facet which is under consideration by the Indian government. Wide spread consultations have been held with the private firms under the Confederation of Indian Industries, a representative body of manufacturers and the Ministry of Defence. The off set clause being introduced will favour Indian industry but its lack of production capability and defence related manufacturing norms will prevent it from benefiting immediately from this consent by the government which had reserved the defence sector for public firms in the past.

Indo – Russian Arms Cooperation

India and Russia have had a symbiotic relationship on arms supply and cooperation. India has sourced its arms exclusively from Russia or the erstwhile Soviet Union in the 1970's and 1980's however the collapse of the Soviet Union saw Indian armed forces denied of spares and accessories due to disintegration of the mechanism for manufacture and supply of these to client states. As India turned to other countries for upgrades as well as supply of spares, this naturally irked the Russian government, particularly when some of these states were erstwhile Soviet satellites with which Russia did not enjoy favorable relationship. India had been negotiating with Cenrex, a

Polish company for upgrading 60 Pechora air defence systems until 2015 which were unutilized due to lack of parts and was also negotiating with Israel for upgrading the Tu 142 Maritime Surveillance aircraft.[8] Thus Russia has been insisting on an Intellectual Property Rights agreement and is not willing to part with technology and arms without the same. It must thus be noted that this is not just a technology transfer but also a political issue of Russia wanting to exercise influence on the arms industry of the erstwhile Soviet bloc. While such an accord is becoming a standard international norm, India has adequate scope for getting a best bargain by playing up the political aspects of the issue.

A meeting of Indo Russian Inter Governmental Commission (IRIGC) on military technical cooperation was held in Moscow on 15 November 2005, attended by the Defence Ministers of both nations, Pranab Mukherjeee and Sergei Ivanov. $9 billion defence deals are in the Indo-Russian pipe line, while a 10 year programme till 2010 includes more than 200 projects worth $ 20 billion. Intellectual Property Rights agreement to protect defence secrets was finalized and signed during the Indian Prime Minister's visit to Russia on 6 December and will remove the last hurdle to transfer of advanced defence technologies to India by Russia. This will give a fillip to joint research and development projects with Russia particularly for development of a fifth generation fighter and multi purpose transport aircraft.

Indian delegation pressed for steady supply of air craft spares and assistance in replacing high accident prone technologies of the Russian fleet. Proposal for joint manufacturing of a medium aircraft for cargo and transportation role to replace the 100 strong ageing fleet of the IAF is also under consideration. Production capability of BrahMos cruise missile which should be produced at 400 missiles per year was also discussed.[9] 70 percent of India's military hardware comes from Russia and official sources have put spend on Russian weapons since 1960 at $ 40 billion. Initially these were made against deferred rupee payments which were beneficial to India followed by licensing and manufacturing them. Russian apprehensions on duplicating technology in the indigenous markets and passing it to companies abroad has been overcome by signing the Intellectual Property Rights agreement with the country.[10]

Russia has also formed a company, Rosoboronservice India Ltd (RIL) which will cater exclusively for Indian defence spare parts and service needs. RIL is expected to have a warehouse in Mumbai stocking spare parts to avoid awaiting these from original manufacturers, specialists available on call, train Indian officers in maintenance and coordinate all activities with the Russian manufacturers and Indian users.[11] This is a measure which was perhaps long over due and thus will overcome one of the long standing demands of the Indian Armed Forces for direct contact with Russian vendors for improved serviceability and maintenance. This will also ensure that the cooperation on arms acquisition and development with Russia will be strengthened in the years ahead by jointly designing, producing, developing and selling defence goods such as the BrahMos supersonic cruise missile.[12] The proposals in the pipeline include Russian Tu 22 Backfire Bombers which could be used for maritime surveillance as well as bomber role, two to four Il 30 maritime patrol aircraft, SMERCH multi barrel rocket launchers, leasing of a nuclear submarine apart from upgrades and spare parts.[13] These acquisitions have to be made after ensuring that the Russian defence manufacturing infra structure has restructured to ensure continuity and assurance of supplies and spares.

IBSA – Dynamics of a New Cooperation Agreement

An India - Brazil – South Africa (IBSA) cooperation is the latest partnership between three nations in three different continents for a collaborative venture in the lucrative South American defence market. Indian presence in the Latin America Aero and Defence 05 International in April was marked by the public sector enterprise, Bharat Heavy Earth Movers. However the main initiator of this process is the South African arms firm, Denel which demonstrated interests in missiles, turrets for combat vehicles and ammunition and has been cooperating with Brazilian arms industry for a long time now.[14] As defence research and development and production becomes increasingly cost prohibitive, the need for cooperative ventures between various interested nations is accepted. India could benefit considerably from such a venture with Brazil and South Africa despite the controversy surrounding charges of kick offs by Denel in the Anti Material Rifles case in India.

French Scorpene Deal

Indian submarine requirement by 2015 is said to be 20 submarines while present holding is 14-16 submarines. This includes six platforms of Western origin and six of Russian origin. The Scorpene induction includes two submarines purchased from France and four to be build at the Mazagon docks in Mumbai. This would take at least four to six years by which time four ageing submarines of the Navy would have been phased out. The 30 years submarine building plan approved by the Indian government commencing in 2005 to 2035 includes the following -

(a) 24 diesel powered submarines.

(b) As Scorpene will be inducted 8-10 old platforms will be deinducted.

(c) Phasing out of submarines may necessitate operational improvisation by the Navy as there would be certain periods of minimal availability.

The first Scorpene will be inducted after seven years and one submarine each will be inducted in yearly intervals. Indigenous content will gradually rise to 60 %. Scorpene is a diesel powered conventional submarine incorporating advanced stealth characteristics making detection difficult. It has Advanced Early Warning system and integrated information technology with a high level of automation, enhanced endurance and anti ship missiles. Italy, Malaysia and Chile are already using the submarine.[15] Scorpene is powered by diesel engines and is a state of the art platform firing Exocet anti ship missiles upto a range of 200 kms with IT based weaponry and EW platform. The Exocet SM39 missiles which is a variant of the stand off fire and forget stealth missile is launched from a self propelled container thereby ensuring that the location of the submarine is not revealed.

The deal was signed after four years of intense negotiations after initial short listing in the early 1990's. France agreed to overlook the delay clause costing India Rs 5 Crore per day and also agreed to the integrity clause. This clause is mandatory for deals over Rs 300 Crores. The Scorpene deal of $2.30 billion was signed in first week of October in New Delhi after this was announced during visit of Indian Prime Minister to France in September.

Allegations of bribery were made by an executive of Thales, a French armament firm sub contractor in the Scorpene deal worth Euro 600 million for his company devising key sub systems like integrated combat systems including underwater sensors, communications and optronics and electronic warfare equipment. Michel Jesserand alleged that the company had, "slush funds to bribe corrupt officials" through a secret internal system of 2 percent commission of annual sales.[17] But these allegations were brushed aside as it had taken four years for the agreement to fructify with Navy insisting on probity and transparency. Indigenization will be the key element in the Scorpene programme.

Indian Air Force – A Precision Strike Force by 2015

The Indian Air Force has plans for converting into a precision strike force with dependence on smart ammunition including laser guided bombs, beyond the visual range missiles and integral aircraft and airborne radars. The 29 Squadrons of the IAF fielding a wide variety of aircraft ranging from Mirage 2000H, MiG 29, Su 30MK1 and Jaguars are also slated to acquire all weather capability, navigational attack systems, self protection suites, air launched decoys and electronic warfare suites. Smart sensors will also be introduced to include intelligence suites, reconnaissance suites, electro-optical pay loads and forward looking infra red systems.[18]

Indian Air Force (IAF) Fighter Aircraft Acquisition

IAF has 26 types of aircraft from Russia, UK, France and Brazil.[19] It has an acquisition plan of 126 multi role fighter aircraft worth Rs 10,000 Crores. The requirement was identified in 2001. The first phase of the acquisition process, request for information is over. Request for proposals have been sent to manufacturers of four aircraft by end of 2005 to include F 16, F 18, (both USA), Grippen (Sweden), Mirage (France) and Mig 29 (Russia). The request for proposals were issued in first week of December and were being received by top executives, Boeing's Chris Chadwick and Managing director of Lockheed Martin Global Inc, Royce L Caplinger.[20]

It will take five years for fructification of contracts. The negotiations will include transfer of technology with 30 % offset, weapons integration to life cycle costs and uninterrupted supply of spares. 15-20 aircraft will be bought off the shelf, balance will be manufactured under licence. Lockheed Martin manufacturing F 16 and F 18 aircraft has given detailed presentation in last two months. FA/18 being naval carrier borne aircraft, its information provided was said to be unsolicited. The competition is said to be between F 16 and Mirage 2000V. The contract is likely to be $ 6.5 billion twice the Scorpene deal. [21] In addition the IAF is also scouting for 80 helicopters, 20 medium lift aircraft, 19 Low level transportable radars and more mid air refueling aircraft after having acquired 6 IL 78. Recent reports indicate that the quantity of aircraft purchased is also likely to be increased to 200 with more than one supplier coming into the fray with a total value of $ 8.5 billion. This will enable smooth replacements after phasing out 60 of the 140 Jaguars held by the IAF over the next five years.[22] The two supplier policy will speed up the acquisition process, however details of the same are yet to be publicly revealed.

India proposes to buy 16 MIG 29 aircraft from Russia, the deal was finalized during the visit of the Prime Minister Mr Manmohan Singh to Russia on 7 to 8 December 2005.[23] A joint statement during the visit brought out cooperation between the two states on energy, security, trade, high technology, defence and nuclear fields. India's key areas of concern with Russia remain availability of spares for the large quantum of Russian equipment fielded by the Armed forces, civil nuclear technology development and increase in trade. Russia will be amenable to defence deals as that is the driver of Russian economy today which is beset by problems of recession due to loss of production and oligarchic management by the satraps who having dismantled the Soviet system are now out to loot it.

MIG 25 the super spy plane in the IAF inventory is slated to be phased out in Mid 2006. Equipped with powerful cameras and sensors, it can fly at speeds three times that of sound, climb upto heights in excess of 70,000 feet in the stratosphere. The MIG 25 was extensively used in the Kargil conflict in 1999 and also during Operation Parakram 2001.[24] UAVs and Satellite Imagery have made these aircraft obsolete to an extent, however these are still useful for strategic reconnaissance. Spares are a major problem as per Air Marshal A K Singh, C in C Western Air Command.

Fifth Generation Fighters

India's quest for a fifth generation fighter will see it being invited for the first flight of the F 35 Joint Strike Fighter at Fort Worth Texas in 2006. F 35 is a joint Anglo-US project for a fifth generation aircraft for all three services, cheap to procure and maintain with possibility of multiple roles. Partner countries include Italy, Netherlands, Turkey, Canada, Australia, Denmark and Norway who will induct the fighter over the next 15 years. Sale could also be to non partner countries as India which is likely to be on commercial motives. Air Chief Marshal S P Tyagi took flight in a US Navy F/A 18 Super Hornet at Paris Air Show 2005. Air Chief Marshal S Krishnaswamy had flown an Israeli F 16 Falcon in October 2004. Indian teams have witnessed Patriot 3 in action at White Sands New Mexico. India's interest in P8 A Boeing maritime mutli role jet was received favourably by Office of Defence cooperation, USA. Super Hornet and Falcon are said to be formal contenders for commercial purchase by India.[25]

Close on the heels of development of the BrahMos cruise missiles, India and Russia are slated to go in for a strategic partnership to develop a fifth generation fighter with Russian companies Sukhoi and Mig prepared to push for the large fighter requirement from the country. The recent agreement on intellectual property rights between India and Russia which caters for notification of any transfer in technology to a third country has enhanced assurance levels to the Russians who may be amenable for joint collaboration.

India's large requirement of fighter aircraft has placed it in a favourable bargaining position in acquisition of this strategic asset for the country. It should be able to leverage this advantage to get the best aircraft technically as well as the best bargain including indigenization of the production line. Large defence hardware conglomerates in the United States and Europe are openly vying for contracts from the Indian defence industry. India should carefully weigh its options based on long term interests and not fall in the spares trap as it had in the case of the Migs in the past decade or so. Transparency in the acquisition process will add to value and should be encouraged from the very outset to avoid falling in the Bofors blind spot. A realistic appraisal of requirement is essential given our present as well as future necessities.

Kaveri – Light Combat Aircraft Engine

The Defence Research and Development Organisation's efforts to develop the Kaveri engine for the Light Combat Aircraft (LCA) has suffered another set back in terms of time and the DRDO is now looking for partners for developing the same. The DRDO has already begun negotiations with a number of engine manufacturers as Snecma, Rolls Royce, General Electric, CFM International, Pratt and Whitney, NPO Saturn and MMPP Salute for help in the project.[26] At the current rate of development, the first few LCAs are expected to be powered by the GE 404 engine which is now available after lifting sanctions by the USA. In case the Kaveri engine is not developed by 2007, the project is likely to be scrapped and a foreign engine provider will have to be contacted for provision. The negotiations with the engine provider could depend on the size of the contract. Presently only 40 LCAs are on order by the Indian Air Force demonstrating lack of interest, which is not good enough for gaining substantial discounts. All in all the project of the LCA is likely to be on a slow keel over the next few years.

AWACS – Embraer Deal Delayed

India is in the process of procuring AWACS which can fly for 6 to 10 hours and ceiling of 35,000 feet with a radar which could look for 2 square meter targets upto 300 kms distance. The aircraft is required to carry upto 3000 kgs with a primary and secondary radar mounted on the fuselage, this would be weighing 1000 kgs thus leaving 2000 kgs for crew and other support systems. The Brazilian Embraer 145 or EMB 145 which had been short listed after detailed interaction between Indian Defence Research and Development Organisation (DRDO) and Brazil's Embraer with construction of three EMB 145 aircraft costing $ 450 million had a set back with new guide lines which required more than one vendor.[27]

Hindustan Aeronautics Ltd (HAL) and Snecma Joint Venture

HAL and French company Snecma Moteurs is forming a 50:50 joint venture to produce Snecma engines on license by HAL at its Bangalore based facility. While Snecma has been active in the country's aircraft manufacturing industry for many years the joint venture will be on a profit sharing rather than a royalty basis. Snecma has been developing engines for the Advanced Light Helicopter, Intermediate jet trainer and Kaveri engine for the Light Combat Aircraft of the Indian Air Force. The partnership is set to grow in a period of four years and straddle the civil as well as military aviation sectors.[28]

Improving Aircraft Survivability

Since 2001, 21 MiG-21s of the IAF have crashed in the country. In a recent case a MiG-21 aircraft crashed near Assam's Tezpur airbase, with pilot Squadron Leader S Bansal ejecting safely. The crashed MiG-21 was reported to be Type 77, a version on the way out. [29] This was the ninth crash reported in 2005. There have reportedly been over 600 crashes in the IAF since 1970-71 with 175 pilots and several civilians killed.[30]

An IAF Canberra crashed on 19 December 2005, near Agra killing two pilots. The aircraft was on a routine flying mission. An engine or component failure is said to be the initial reason put forth by IAF authorities. These aircraft originally inducted as bombers and used extensively in bombing missions in the 1971 Bangladesh operations are now used for photo reconnaissance. The Canberra, five of which are with the Lynx Squadron in Agra has been in service for the past 50 years or so with its golden jubilee of induction planned in 2006-07.

The two crashes during 2005 at the Aircraft and Systems Testing Establishment (ASTE). Bangalore of a Mig 21 and a Kiran Mark 1 trainer is an indicator of lack of adequate measures for ensuring safety in our flying establishments.[31] The ASTE is the premier flying institution which along with the Test Pilot School is expected to set standards of safety as well as safe flying. Perhaps the culture of bravado of flying in age old coffins needs to be overcome.

The continuance of phased aircraft in service even with upgrades needs debate.[32] Why should the IAF continue to fly such an aged fleet which is difficult to maintain and causes loss of trained and valuable man power is mystifying. It may be better to train pilots on the aircraft available in air worthy conditions rather than forcing them to fly in age old coffins. Another aspect of concern is the availability of precision reconnaissance manned aircraft with the IAF with the deinduction of the MiG 25 Foxbats planned in the near future and the ageing fleet of Canberras, the IAF seems to be veering towards a purely UAV based reconnaissance capability which may be lopsided.

Measures to enhance pilot training and cockpit survival in modern fighter conditions are however being taken continuously. Exposure to dynamic G or Gravitational forces is one of the hazards faced by modern jet fighter pilots during combat maneouvres in a supersonic fighter jet due to decrease of blood pressure in the head. This can cause loss of vision, grey outs, black outs or in extreme cases, G LOC or G induced loss of consciousness. Institute of Aerospace Medicine, Bangalore has decided to install state of the art, advanced human centrifuge from Austria which will be fully operational by 2008. This will enable advanced G tolerance training for pilots presently being carried out on 1965 vintage human centrifuges. G Force training will enable pilots to tackle sustained high G forces and G onset conditions, comparable to most advanced jet fighters while being trained on ground. This will facilitate pilots in handling G forces while flying new superiority fighters as the Sukhoi 30 MKIs. In addition a disorientation simulator has also been installed at the Institute of Aerospace Medicine, Bangalore and two more are likely to be installed at the Hindon air base and the Air Force Academy. This will enable pilots to take corrective actions when faced with spatial disorientation and improve situational awareness.[33] Such simulators are the need of the hour and investments will be fully recovered by limiting the loss of life.

Nuclear Defence Research and Development

Concerted efforts have been undertaken by Indian Defence Research and Development Organisation (DRDO) to enhance protection from NBC attacks after Pakistan's nuclear fangs were exposed in 1998. The focus is essentially on three facets :–

(a) Training and equipping troops to face NBC strike.

(b) Equipping a specialized force to react promptly to an NBC attack.

(c) Manufacturing NBC protection equipment such as respirators, clothing, shelters, detection and decontamination systems and NBC troop carriers.

Development of protective integrated field shelters which can shield 30 persons for 96 hours from toxic vapours and nuclear radiation has been undertaken. It also includes a monitoring system, power source, water supply, sewage disposal, communication equipment and decontamination system. A prototype decontamination vehicle has also been developed to decontaminate vehicles, aircraft, personnel, ships and equipment. A number of DRDO labs have been engaged in this all important field to include –

(a) Defence Materials and Stores Research and Development Establishment – Developing clothing and decontamination suits that will shield against chemicals and bio agents.

(b) Defence Research and Development Establishment, (DRDE), Gwalior – Studying toxicology, biochemical pharmacology and developing antibodies against bacterial and viral agents.

(c) Defence Bio Engineering and Electro Medical Laboratory – Developed respirator face piece which provides for protection against toxic gases, vapour, smoke, radioactive dust and bacteria.

(d) Private firms such as Shrivatsa International Ltd, Kanpur collaborating on developing NBC clothing and flame retardant material. Trioka Pharmaceuticals, Ahmedabad has collaborated with DRDE on developing first aid kits containing anti dotes and anti bodies for deadly bio chemical agents.

DRDO has already developed and introduced in service the following NBC protection equipment :–

(a) 3 layered permeable NBC protection suit.

(b) NBC respiratory mask, integrated hood mask.

(c) Decontamination suit.

(d) Integrated field shelter.

(e) Residual vapor detection kit to detect deadly chemical agents in the air.

(f) Water poison detection kit.

(g) Nerve agent detector.

(h) Nuclear radiation detection systems.[34]

Some other Key Procurements under Process

155 Artillery Guns

The Indian artillery is slated to acquire 1600, 155 mm guns in the next 15 years. This will thus be the standard artillery weapon with upgraded range of 65 kms. In the wake of controversy over payment of bribes by Denel's, fresh tenders have been proposed for acquisition of upgraded 155 artillery guns. No trials will be held for previously short listed candidates. Trials are only proposed for new entrants. The selection process would take 2-3 years and Soltem, Israel,

SWS, Sweden are in the race along with Denel. Allegations of Denel being the single vendor in the acquisition process of the guns in 2001, have led to rebidding which would delay equipping the artillery regiments. It is stated that while Denel had given a price of $5.5 million per gun an earlier bid by Russia's Rosoboronexport in 2004 had made a bid at $ 2.2 million per piece.[35]

Controversy in defence deals has been the bane of the defence procurement process in India. Large sums involved leads to various contentious payments allegedly by vested interests. Politicization of procurement and transfer of power in the country between two opposing parties in the past one and a half decades and playing up of fratricidal tendencies between political opponents by arms procurement agencies has led to complications which are difficult to resolve. Investigations in such cases linking a number of Indian and foreign agencies including arms suppliers, manufacturers and banks are complicated and long drawn out thus procurements are invariably delayed. This process has to be made increasingly transparent with public auction followed by price negotiations with the short listed firms being a simple yet accountable procedure which can be introduced.

Nishant Unmanned Aerial Vehicle (UAV)

The Nishant UAV has been a pioneering effort by the DRDO in meeting the requirements of the Indian Army for electronic intelligence and electro-optical reconnaissance. The Nishant is a 360 kg vehicle with a payload of 45 kgs, altitude ceiling of 12,000 feet, endurance of four and half hours and range of 100 kms. It has the capability of sending instantaneous data and can carry out target acquisition and tracking. The Indian Army has reportedly ordered 12 Nishant UAVs from the Aeronautical Development Agency (ADE) Bangalore at a cost of $ 3.5 million as opposed to $ 7.5 million for the Israeli Heron. Four Nishant UAV systems and ground support equipment is likely to be delivered by end of 2006. The Army already has about 150 UAVs from the Isreali stable to include Searcher 1, 2 and Heron. Israel is likely to continue as the preferred source of supply for the Indian Army in the future.[36]

Air Defence Artillery

Indian Air Defence Artillery which has been an off shoot the Indian Artillery has recently christened itself as Army Air Defence or AAD. Such cosmetic changes may not help the arm of considerable significance on the modern battlefield as it is still holding antiquated Russian made equipment as the Kvadrat mobile SAM, the Osaka SAM, Strela 1, Pechora, Igla, Schilka and Tangushka self propelled systems and the age old L 70 guns.[37] While its efforts to acquire 1100 Igla missiles from Russia along with 120 digitized launchers, 12 mobile testing stations and unit trainers, three room trainers and 120 heavy motor vehicles at a cost of $ 200 million were stalled in November 2005 as India refused to pay the technology fees for the upgraded missile. The upgraded Igla is reported to have a 2 kg warhead, with a range of 5200 m and a ceiling of 3500 metres with improved guidance and electronic security.[38]

Akash

Akash dubbed as the poor man's Patriot ground to air defence missile has been cleared for export by the Indian government. Each missile costs $ 260,000 with the entire system priced at $ 20 million. It is claimed to be effective against a variety of targets such as low flying missiles, UAVs and helicopters and will replace the currently held Kvadrat system. The missile is 650 kgs and with a pay load of 50 kgs attains a range of 25 kms and speed of 3.5 Mach, with a precision homing system. A battery will have three tracked vehicles, with four missiles each and linked to the Rajendra Phased Array radar system. The Defence Research and Development Laboratory (DRDL), Hyderabad has confirmed orders for 1350 missiles from the Army and is expecting approximately 3000 missiles order from the Indian Air Force and Army over the next 20 years. With the capability to provide air defence to large sized areas as airfields and large installations, the Akash would prove extremely versatile.[39]

Akash was test fired thrice within 17 minutes from integrated test range, Chandipur on Sea, near Balasore on 3 October 2005. A second test was held at Chandipore on the Sea aiming at a moving target from a missile launcher on 3

December 2005.[40] Akash has had several delays due to guidance and propulsion problems. Full scale user trials are proposed in 2006.[41]

Anti Material Rifle (AMR) Procurement Controversy – Denel

Allegations of payment of bribes in sale of Anti Material Rifles by Denel, the South African arms supplier entailed $ 4.54 million being paid to British Firm Varas Associates as reported by the South African paper, Cape Argus.[42] Subsequent follow up by the Indian government has led to three letters rogatory (LR) by Central Bureau of Investigation to UK, Isle of Man and South Africa seeking specific information on the anti material rifles contract with Denel's to the Central government for approval for routing through diplomatic channels. The LR to South Africa is said to be to verify a newspaper report that claimed that the government owned company bribed Indian defence ministry officials to get the contract. The LR also wants to enquire why Varas Associates was employed by Denel when written assurance was given that no middlemen will be employed. 12.75 % commission is alleged to have been paid to Varas, a shell company based in the Isle of Man. LR for London is to find out who are the owners of Varas, their bank details and other information. Contracts under the scanner include, 100 AMRs, 98,000 rounds deal signed in July 1999 and same number of AMRs with one lakh ammunition on deal signed on two occasions on 20 March 2002 and 27 March 2002. Final two contracts signed on 7 March 2005 by UPA were for the supply of 400 AMRs and transfer of technology to the Ordnance Factory Board. Interpol has also been approached with various queries. CBI has consistently failed in seeking information on LRs in the case of HDW submarine deal as also Airbus deal due to lack of cooperation by the concerned nations and reservations have been expressed by the Delhi High Court on Swedish documents procured by it in the Bofors deal.[43]

Infantry Upgrades

The Indian infantry is to receive a major upgrade boost once the plan submitted by the Army to the Ministry of Defence is accepted. It involves a massive induction of a wide variety of weapon systems to include surveillance and target acquisition system, the Kornet E missile, 84 mm Rocket Launchers and carbines. With a focus on improving the capability of the soldier in the low intensity conflict battle in Kashmir and other Indian states where the Army is deployed, it entails induction of hand held thermal imaging system, rifle mounted optical sights, under barrel grenade launchers, global positioning systems and light weight navigation and binocular aids. The powerful surveillance suite is multi system, to include the battlefield surveillance radar, unattended ground sensors, hand held thermal imagers and night vision systems.[44]

In the long term, the Indian Infantry is looking for a Land Warrior or Future Integrated Soldier Technology concept for the prospective infantry soldier. As a start, induction of 5.56 mm rifles, helmet mounted sights, radio and data link sets, light weight individual load carrying packs and other sustenance equipment is being sought for the infantry.[45] All this is proposed to be linked in a soldier suit providing integrated fighting capability. It may have to be compatible for both roles, conventional and low intensity in Indian terrain and weather conditions which are widely varied from Kashmir to the North East.

Mechanised Forces Upgrades

The mechanized forces upgrades include providing 1200 T 72 tanks with stand alone thermal imaging system with 900 of these with thermal imaging fire control system. While 2000 BMP 2 mechanised infantry combat vehicles will also be provided with thermal imaging system. 9000 Konkurs M missiles are also being contracted for the Mechanised forces from Bharat Dynamics in the next decade or so considerably enhancing the anti tank punch.[46]

Special Forces

A concept paper has been prepared on creating a Special Forces Command by Army Training Command (ARTRAC) responsible for framing policies and doctrines of the army. Special Forces would be provided with separate assets including air support. Commando units of all three services include five battalions, one Garuda of Air Force, Marine Commandoes (MARCOS). Garuda forces have responsibility of guarding air assets including fighter jets, vital installations, sensitive airfields and communication networks. MARCOS were battle tested with elite commandoes during IPKF operations and J and K. Special forces are also likely to be issued with high voltage assault rifles, night vision devices, sniper rifles, combat parachutes which are under procurement. The proposal to convert all para trooper battalions into special forces has also been under consideration for some time now.[47]

Cabinet Committee on Security has cleared the employment of Garuda force for the Indian Air Force for anti hijacking operations besides its original purpose of air and sea rescue operations. The IAF is also acquiring armoured personnel carriers for equipping Garuda which will be bullet proof. Garuda Training Centre is in Hindon where 500 personnel are being trained.[48]

Indian Navy - Forward Ahoy To The Future

Geography should denote that India is essentially a maritime nation. Ashok K Mehta a noted defence analyst reflecting on Navy Day 4 December 2005 has very succinctly brought out the significance of the Navy in the present day context and laments its neglect over the years. Mehta's arguments are convincing. India has a 7516 km long coast line, 1197 islands on both the sea boards, 2.01 million sq km of Exclusive Economic Zone which is likely to increase to almost three million sq kms after the delineation of the continental shelf. It has maritime interests in Antarctica and has established a research station there in 1989. There are 200 major and minor ports on India's coast line. 90 percent of India's trade by volume worth $137 billion and 77 per cent of trade by value is seaborne. Indian shipping has registered 584 merchant ships making it in the 20 largest maritime nations of the world. 68 percent of India's oil production comes from offshore resources and off shore discoveries on the East Coast. Cost of the off shore infra structure is estimated to be Rs 175,000 Crore. 70 percent of India's crude is imported all of it comes by sea. India is expected to be the single largest importer of oil by 2050 and oil consumption is expected to rise to 150 million tons by 2020. In terms of international shipping, 60,000 ships transit through the Indian Ocean every year carrying goods estimated to be over $1800 billion. Of $ 200 billion worth of oil coming through the Strait of Hormuz annually, $ 60 billion passes through the Straits of Malacca, approximately 11 million barrels of oil move through the Malacca every day.[49] However being a continental state, inasmuch as it has adequate land mass for development of its population and potential as well as conflictual interests on the sub continental terra firma, the sea has been neglected over the years. The last known sea farer adventurist was the Maratha warrior, Kanohji Angre.

The Indian Navy is taking up the mantle of a sea faring nation afresh and thus a review of India's sea power capability is essential. A Navy is said to have multiple roles, military, diplomatic, constabulary and benign. The strategies for achieving national aims and interests exercised by the Navy are sea control, sea denial, support of the exclusive economic zones, economic and energy security of the country and low intensity maritime operations. During active operations a Navy also has to carry out operations in support of the land battle. Its diplomatic roles are said to be showing the flag, disaster relief, force projection and deterrence. The constabulary role consists of anti poaching, anti smuggling and anti piracy. Benign tasks include aid to civil authority during natural calamities as the tsunami operations carried out with mobilization of 32 ships, 8 aircraft, 21 helicopters and 6000 personnel in the largest peace time mission undertaken by the Indian Navy.[50]

In 1947 the Indian Navy had 33 ships, two frigates, four sloops, one corvette and other small yards and craft. The present force levels include 65 vessels, 16 submarines, 13 frigates, eight destroyers, one aircraft carrier and other smaller ships, 46 aircraft and nearly 150 helicopters with over 100,000 personnel. Manpower wise its size is one tenths of the Army. Compared to modern armed forces the Indian Navy is lopsided in terms of manpower proportion. For instance the US Navy has a strength of 375, 521 active duty personnel approximately three fourths of the US Army's 500, 203.[51]

While this is also due to the global interests of the USA, the present manpower state of the Indian Navy certainly needs to be enhanced.

Present off carrier capability of the Indian Navy includes INS Viraat which operates with 18 Sea Harrier jump jet fighters inducted in 1983 and the only fighters capable of operating thereof. These are from White Tigers squadron at Goa and also the Harpoon squadron which operates from Mumbai. One Sea Harrier jet crashed on 5 December 2005, Lt Cdt HPS Pannu died in the crash during the take off run. This was the third Sea Harrier to crash in the past 12 months. Concern is being expressed as the Sea Harriers are considered too old to fly in a safe mode. 17 of the 24 fighters procured in 1983 are still surviving. A Rs. 476 Crore upgradation programme has been announced for the Sea Harriers to be undertaken by Hindustan Aeronautics Ltd which has been approved by the Cabinet Committee on Security in early 2005. This includes integration of the Isreali Elta EL/M-2032 multi mode fire control radar and Derby beyond visual range air to air missiles for the fighters. This may not be fully cost viable as the aircraft is due to be phased out within a decade to be replaced by MIG 29Ks on the Vikramaditya or Gorshkov in 2008.[52]

There is thus a need for development of the Indian Navy in a holistic manner which has been undertaken recently with a well thought out modernization plan. The ship acquisition plan envisages a strategic indigenization process to maintain operational force levels and is scheduled to design and manufacture 36 ships in the next few years including an aircraft carrier, Scorpene submarines, patrol craft, missile carrying destroyers as well as frigates.[53] This will entail a planned ship manufacturing effort undertaken for the first time in the history of the country over the ages. Perhaps only Kanhoji Angre had such a fleet expansion plan though the scope and magnitude of his Navy essentially a coastal one cannot be compared to what the Indian Navy will be a couple of decades hence. The indigenous process will be supplemented by acquisition of Russian made stealth frigates of the Krivck class. These are replacement acquisitions to make up for platforms which are being phased out or decommissioned in the years ahead. The Russian aircraft carrier retrofitted as per Indian requirements will be named as Vikramaditya and inducted in 2008. Price negotiations were on for three submarine deep sea rescue vehicles which presently India has an agreement with the USA.

The sum total of naval acquisition is impressive. By 2010 the Navy will field the Vikramaditya or Gorshkov with 30 aircraft costing Rs 10,000 Crore. By 2011 it would have in ducted the Air defence ship capable of flying LCA and costing Rs 5000 Crore. It would have 18 submarine accretions upto 2030 including the six Scorpenes and two nuclear submarines to be leased from Russia. Russian help is also anticipated in the Advanced Technology Vessel the country's indigenous nuclear submarine production programme.[54] Two P3C Orions on lease from the US Navy will provide it the much needed airborne early warning capability. However the Navy Chief was quoted to be bidding for three P3C Orions either acquired or on lease.[55] Training facilities with the new naval academy in Ezhimala and naval base at Karwar by 2010 will provide the necessary developed manpower edge to a modern Navy.[56]

The Indian Navy's plans to acquire additional Barak ship defence missile systems to beef up the existing seven systems and arm the three frigates; Sahyadri, Satpura and Shivalik fell victim to the new policy of multiple vendor acquisition. Thus the widened missile systems visage would now include apart from Barak, the Crotale NG, MBDAs Astor and Rosoboronoexport's Shtil. The Barak is said to be a supersonic, low altitude, stealthy missile with a 10 km range, 22 kg blast-fragmentation warhead installed on the INS Viraat. Each system comprises of eight missiles and costs approximately $ 40 million.[57]

The Navy has also set up a Directorate of Indigenization. Through a focused indigenization plan three ships are likely to be produced annually every year in Indian shipyards. 19 ships are already on order in various Indian shipyards and 74 ships planned to be built by the end of the 11th Plan with 85 percent of the components being Indian.

Indian Navy in 2005

In 2005, the Indian Navy had undertaken extensive sea faring operations and was reportedly deployed in Male, Indonesia and Sri Lanka for tsunami relief operations. The Navy also handed over the INS Tarmugli a fast attack craft to Seychelles. This craft can detect, locate and destroy fast moving surface craft essentially to deploy quick reaction teams of the navy. April 2005 also saw commencement of construction of the Air Defence Ship with an envisaged target of completion by 2012. The Air Defence Ship is a $ 1 billion, 37,500 tonne carrier which will carry 18 combat aircraft including Sea Harriers and Mig 29 K fighters, Advanced Light Helicopters and Ka 31 Helicopters.[58] This along with the Vikramaditya will enable the Indian Navy to have a separate air defence ship for each of its Western and Eastern coast.

INS Beas built by Garden Reach Shipbuilders and Engineers (GRSE), Kolkata was commissioned into the Indian Navy on 11 July 2005. This Guided Missile frigate is what in today's terms called as the fully loaded platform with Barak anti missile system, 04 quad packs of the Uran Surface to Surface missiles, 01 medium range 76 mm Super Rapid Gun Mount, 04 Close Range 30 mm AK 630 Guns, 02 Triple tube torpedo launchers, sonar and the sophisticated Ellora Electronic Warfare suite.

In September over 6500 US Navy personnel from the Carrier Strike Group 11 engaged in air, surface, sub surface operations and professional military exchanges with their Indian counterparts in India's South Western waters. Malabar is considered the key to US Pacific Fleet anti submarine warfare training cycle. This was topped by an Indo- Russian joint exercise INDRA 05 at Vishakhapatnam in October 2005 with air and anti submarine defence, search and destruction of submarines. 22 – 24 November 2005 saw the Indian Navy and French Navy's joint exercises, the seventh in the series since 2001 with deployment of a large number of ships from both sides.[59]

The Indian Navy through a focused programme on indigenisaiton of ships will perhaps have an Indian built force by the year 2020, the most indigenized of all the three services.

It is also building its maritime capability through active engagement with Western as well as Russian Navies. Geographically and territorially it has to expand its sphere as most of the exercises are being carried out in brown waters off coasts. Gradually the blue water capability will have to be build up to enable domination of the Arabian Sea, the Bengal Sea and then the Indian Ocean. Will the great powers, especially the US allow the Indian Navy to emerge as a power of influence in the Indian Ocean is an issue which needs consideration? Another facet is the wholly indigenized perspective of the Navy, will it enable it to achieve the goals? The advantage however is that the Navy has finally emerged from its cocoon and the nation is looking forward to a new sea faring epoch, after the Kanohji Angre era a few centuries ago.

Navy War Room Leak – Information Security

In July 2005 a security breach was revealed in the Naval War Room wherein K Shankaran and his associate Kulbhushan retired Naval officers were obtaining commercial information from Naval HQs under dubious names. The commercial firm had contacted three officers DNO Capt Kashyap Kumar, Commanders V Rana and VK Jha in the Naval War Room to procure sensitive information on procurement. However no operational data was reported to have been stolen.[60] Involvement of Captain Kashyap Kumar, Director Naval Operations, Commander V Rana, who headed the Ocean Management Department and Commander V K Jha in charge of war room security was evident. Recipients of the leaked information were Lt K Sankaran, Head of Shanks Ocean Engineering engaged in outsourcing contracts for the Indian Navy and Commander KK Sharma. There had been problems in off shore patrol craft reportedly being procured from the company floated by these personnel and hence the firm had been black listed in 1996. The computers in the War Room being used for presentations were the source of leak as presentations were not deleted from these and were downloaded on pen drives.

The Board of Inquiry led by Rear Admiral Ganesh Mahadevan clearly established that leakage of information of commercial nature has taken place to unauthorized personnel. Board was entrusted with responsibility to ascertain information leakage source, lacunae in the existing system and recommend remedial measures. Information parted consisted that on patrol boats, diving support craft, electronic chart displays, breathing air compressors and other such equipment. Inquiry was instituted on 22 July and submitted report on 14 September to the Naval HQs. No compromise related to operational matters was confirmed.[61]

This is perhaps one of the many information leakage through computers discovered of late in which even the Defence Headquarters has been involved. While a number of data security measures have been recommended such as –

(a) Blanking out USB ports which can be used for transportable data devices as pen drives.

(b) Blocking access to war room computers.

(c) Serving officers to steer clear of retired personnel operating commercial firms.[62]

No level of security however would be enough where personnel compromise themselves as in this case where consumerism and easy money seems to have enticed the officers.

References

1. Prasannan, R. "Fighter Race". The Week. 18 December 2005. p. 40.
2. Prasannan, R. "Fighter Race". The Week. 18 December 2005. p. 40.
3. Patranobis, Sutirtho. "To war with bad tanks, guns". The Hindustan Times. 23 December 2005. Lucknow. p. 1.
4. The Pioneer Report. 7 October 2005. Lucknow. p. 3.
5. The Pioneer Report. The Pioneer. 1=28 September 2005. Lucknow. p. 2.
6. Downloaded. mod.nic.in, on 30 December 2005
7. Raghuvanshi, Vivek. "New Policy—". Defense News. 20 June 2005. p. 19.
8. Raghuvanshi, Vivek. "India OKs—". Defense News. 9 May 2005. p. 22.
9. The Hindu Report. The Hindu. 16 November. Hyderabad. p. 12.

10. Guha, Kunal. "Brothers in arms." The Economic Times. New Delhi. 2 December 2005. p. 21

11. Raghuvanshi, Vivek. "Russian Firm—". Defense News. 26 September 2005. p. 14.

12. Shaumian, Tatiana. "Man's visit—". The Sunday Pioneer. 11 December 2005. Lucknow. p. 11.

13. Raghuvanshi, Vivek. "India OKs—". Defense News. 9 May 2005. p. 22.

14. Chuter, Andrew. "Denel—". Defense News. 2 May 2005. p. 26.

15. Pioneer Report. 7 October 2005. Lucknow. p. 3.

16. Defense News Report. Defense News. 17 October 2005. p. 26.

17. Times of India Report. "On the eve—" Times of India. 4 October 2005. Lucknow, p. 8.

18. Raghuvanshi, Vivek. "India mulls—". Defense News. 6 December 2005. p. 21.

19. The Pioneer Report. 7 October 2005. Lucknow. p. 3.

20. Aroor, Shiv. "IAF—" The Indian Express. 28 November 2005. Lucknow. p. 5.

21. Pandit, Rajat. "Aircraft—" Times of India. 7 October 2005. Lucknow. p. 10.

22. Raghuvanshi, Vivek. "India Boosts.—" Defense News. 21 November 2005. p. 34.

23. Hindustan Report. The Hindustan. 8 December 2005. Lucknow. p. 14.

24. Pandit, Rajat. "IAF Foxbats—" The Times of India. 8 November 2005. Lucknow. p. 6.

25. Aroor, Shiv. "India—" Indian Express. 28 September 2005. Lucknow. p. 5.

26. Raghuvanshi, Vivek. "India seeks—". Defense News. 25 July 2005. p. 38.

27. Raghuvanshi, Vivek. "Embraer—". Defense News. 27 June 2005. p. 23.

28. Raghuvanshi, Vivek. "HAL-Snecma—". Defense News. 11 July 2005. p. 14.

29. Downloaded from ndtv.com on 13 December 2005.

30. Times of India Report. "Pilot—". The Times of India. 20 December 2005. Lucknow. p. 8.

31. Indian Express Report. "IAF". The Indian Express. 28 December 2005. Lucknow. p. 2.

32. Indian Express Report. "Two IAF—". The Indian Express. 20 December 2005. Lucknow. p. 5.

33. Pandit, Rajat. "IAF pilots—" Times of India. 12 October 2005. Lucknow. p. 8.

34. Times of India Report. Times of India. 05 November 2005. Lucknow. p. 10.
35. Raghuvanshi, Vivek. "Denel Is—". Defense News. 2 May 2005. p. 28.
36. Raghuvanshi, Vivek. "India Orders—". Defense News. 6 December 2005. p. 22.
37. Raghuvanshi, Vivek. "Russia Denies—". Defense News. 28 November 2005. p. 15.
38. Raghuvanshi, Vivek. "Russia Denies—". Defense News. 28 November 2005. p. 15.
39. Raghuvanshi, Vivek. "Akash Seeks—". Defense News. 7 February 2005. p. 21.
40. Express News Service. Sunday Indian Express. 4 December 2005. Lucknow. p. 4.
41. Times of India Report. 4 October 2005. Lucknow. p. 9.
42. Raghuvanshi, Vivek. "Denel Is—". Defense News. 2 May 2005. p. 28.
43. Economic Times Report. "CBI—" Economic Times. 17 October 2005. New Delhi. p. 2.
44. Raghuvanshi, Vivek. "Indian Army—". Defense News. 15 August 2005. p. 14.
45. Raghuvanshi, Vivek. "India seeks—". Defense News. 31 October 2005. p. 26.
46. Raghuvanshi, Vivek. "Indian Army—". Defense News. 15 August 2005. p. 14.
47. Pioneer Report. "Army to—" The Pioneer. 4 October 2005. Lucknow. p. 3.
48. Hindustan Times Report. "Garuda for Hijacks" 09 October 2005. Lucknow. p. 15.
49. Mehta, Ashoka K. "Navy : Full Steam on Course". The Pioneer. 30 November 2005. Lucknow. p. 6.
50. Mehta, Ashoka K. "Navy: Full Steam on Course". The Pioneer. 30 November 2005. Lucknow. p. 6.
51. Downloaded from the internet.dod.gov on 10 December 2005.
52. Unnithan, Sandeep. "Harrier Hassles". India today, 19 December 2005. New Delhi. p. 54.
53. Pioneer News Service. "Navy for sea—". The Pioneer. 3 December 2005. Lucknow. p. 2.
54. Mehta, Ashoka K. "Navy:Full Steam on Course". The Pioneer. 30 November 2005. Lucknow. p. 6.
55. Pioneer News Service. "Navy for sea—". The Pioneer. 3 December 2005. Lucknow. p. 2.
56. Mehta, Ashoka K. "Navy:Full Steam on Course". The Pioneer. 30 November 2005. Lucknow. p. 6.

57. Raghuvanshi, Vivek. "India to hold—". Defense News. 18 July 2005. p. 14.

58. Raghuvanshi, Vivek. "India Begins—". Defense News. 18 April 2005. p. 22.

59. Bhat, Anil. "Calendar year of Indian Navy". The Pioneer. 8 December 2005. Lucknow. p. 7.

60. Aroor, Shiv. "War Room leak : Navy has evidence". Indian Express. 27 September 2005. p. 5.

61. The Pioneer Report. 30 September 2005. Lucknow. p. 5.

62. Unnithan, Sandeep. "Leaking Ship" India Today. 17 October 2005. p. 48-49.

Index

D

Q

R

V

W

Y